UNIX® Desktop Guide to the Korn Shell

UNIX® Desktop Guide
to the Korn Shell

John Valley

HAYDEN BOOKS

A Division of Macmillan Computer Publishing
11711 North College, Carmel, Indiana 46032 USA

Trademark Acknowledgments

Publisher, Programming Books
Richard K. Swadley

Acquisitions Manager
Joseph B. Wikert

Managing Editor
Neweleen Trebnik

Acquisitions Editor
Linda Sanning

Development Editor
Ella M. Davis

Technical Editor
Peter Holsberg

Senior Editor
Rebecca Whitney

Production Editor
Andy Saff

Copy Editors
Kezia Endsley
Anne Clarke

Editorial Assistants
Molly Carmody
Rosemarie Graham
San Dee Phillips

Cover Designer
Tim Amrhein

Cover Illustrator
Polly McNeal

Book Designer
Michele Laseau

Indexer
Susan VandeWalle

Production
Brad Chinn
Brook Farling
Denny Hager
Audra Hershman
Phil Kitchel
Laurie Lee
Tad Ringo
Sarah Rogers
Linda Seifert
Bruce Steed
Suzanne Tully

Composed in ITC Garamond and MCP Digital by Macmillan Computer Publishing

Printed in the United States of America

Dedication

This book is dedicated to my parents, Jay and Dorothy Valley, who taught me a love of knowledge, an affection for books, and a deep and unshakable conviction in my ability to achieve any goal I set for myself. You are the best of parents, and I love you both very much.

Overview

Contents

Acknowledgments

This, one of the first parts of the book, is the last to be written but the most enjoyable to write. The people who have helped in the writing of this book deserve my thanks and appreciation, and should share a little in the glory that comes with authorship.

My first thanks must go to Fred Marks of U.H. Corporation in Dallas, Texas, who provided me a complete copy of UHC UNIX System V Release 4 for this project. I had seen a brief review of UHC UNIX before I received the package and had noted several difficulties the reviewers encountered during product installation. Happily, I report no such difficulties and can find nothing in their product to criticize. UHC UNIX proved to perform excellently and was a reliable and accurate implementation of System V Release 4. You can reach Fred's company at:

UHC
3600 South Gessner, Suite 110
Houston, Texas 77063
(713) 782-2700

I also would like to give words of thanks to Gateway 2000 Corporation, whose 486/33 system met my very limited budget requirements and far exceeded my expectations of the hardware quality and performance. The system, equipped with 200M of disk and 8M of high-speed memory, costs less than half its nearest competitor, yet executes the heavy load of System V Release 4 and the ridiculously burdensome demands of a graphical user interface, and does so with lightning-quick response. If not for Gateway, I would have done the book without a reference system.

Linda Sanning, the developmental editor for this book at Macmillan, who is no longer with the company, deserves my gratitude for her endless encouragement and guidance of my writing career. This book was her idea. She convinced me to take the project when I had other goals and suggested the overall approach to the subject. I'll miss her cheery voice, and wish her the best in her future career.

Ella Davis took Linda's duties and, even as I write, she, Kezia Endsley, and Andy Saff are bringing this book through the final stages of publishing.

I can only guess at the amount of work this entails, especially for Andy Saff. My thanks to all for a difficult and demanding job well done.

Of course, everyone makes mistakes, and I must apologize to you, the reader, for each and every one of them. This book is meant to inform, and I have tried to make it do so. We all owe a debt of gratitude to the technical editor who reviewed its pages for technical accuracy. Thanks, Pete Holsberg. Pete is one of those rare birds who widely proclaims his ignorance of UNIX as he repeatedly demonstrates his broad knowledge. This is the second of my books you've waded through; haven't you had enough yet?

I also owe special words of thanks to my wonderful wife, Terri, who tolerates my book writing yet resents it for stealing so many of our hours that otherwise would have been spent together. I never did send her the flowers Linda Sanning suggested, but she surely deserves them.

My biggest thanks must go to you, the reader, who is the ultimate purpose for the book's existence. Thanks for buying the book and for your interest in UNIX, my favorite operating system. I had you in mind as I wrote it, and I hope you find it instructive.

John Valley

Introduction

UNIX is essentially a simple environment designed from the outset to be easy and fun to use. Its complexity (and it is indeed a complex system) arises from the great number of its parts and the relationships between them, and not from any single part. This characteristic allows beginners to work effectively with UNIX, yet provides an ever-present challenge to the growing skills of the experienced user.

Not everyone likes UNIX. Certainly UNIX features a huge array of commands, many with names that are difficult to remember, and some with functions that are hard to understand. UNIX command options are a cryptic code that defies the capabilities of human memory. The list of complaints people have about UNIX seems endless.

As one who spent the first 15 years of my career working with other systems, and who disliked UNIX the first time I saw it, I think I understand why so many people dislike UNIX. The reason is that UNIX must be *studied* and *learned*. Those who are too impatient, those who expect the software to do the teaching, those who eternally expect the system to treat them as beginners, will find UNIX unsympathetic.

UNIX is designed to treat its users with respect; to give people short cuts, alternatives, control over their environment, flexibility, power, scope, and depth. These things cannot be captured on a menu screen. Above all, UNIX is efficient and effective for those who know how to use it. In other words, there is a pay-off if you spend the weeks or months needed to become fluent with UNIX: for the rest of your career with UNIX, its features and flexibility will save you incredible amounts of time and effort, and make your job easier.

The UNIX shells are sophisticated tools with many features and capabilities. Remember, you don't need to know everything about the shell to use it. The best teacher is experience, and the best way to learn is to try new things.

Until you know your way around the shell, check the book frequently for new ways to simplify your work. You must try to grow and expand your body of knowledge—otherwise, your skill level will stagnate. The reward for your efforts will be increased productivity and fluency, and a growing feeling that you and UNIX are partners in the job of computing.

The Korn and Bourne Shells

The Bourne shell is the standard command interpreter for UNIX. Built by Stephen Bourne at AT&T Bell Laboratories many years ago, the shell still is the only one that is universally available on all UNIX systems. The Korn shell is by comparison a recent introduction, but it is quickly replacing the Bourne shell as the shell of choice because of its compatibility with the Bourne shell and its many advanced features.

This book is a tutorial and a reference for both the Bourne and Korn shells.

For the beginning or intermediate user, the nearly 300 pages of tutorial text provide a comprehensive explanation of all the features of the Bourne and Korn shells. The implementation and features of the AT&T System V versions are used as the standard for describing the Bourne and Korn shells. Unfortunately, there are so many versions of UNIX and of the shells (even the Korn shell) that it is not possible to describe them all in one book.

For the experienced user, each major section of the book includes a technical summary of the syntax and usage of the features discussed in that section, and the book concludes with a comprehensive reference section.

How This Book Is Organized

Most sections of the book begin with a box that provides a complete and technically precise summary of the material presented in that section. If you're already familiar with the topic of the section, and only need a reminder of the technical details, you'll find those details quickly summarized in the box.

Part I, "Using the UNIX Shell", is oriented toward the new UNIX user. It explains the basics of the UNIX environment and teaches you how to use the shell at the keyboard. This section emphasizes end-user features of the shell and avoids programming issues. If you do not intend to write shell scripts, the information in Part I will focus on just those features of the shell that you need to know.

> **Organization of this Desktop Guide**
>
> Part I   Overview of fundamental UNIX concepts and shell
>   features for use at the keyboard
>
> Part II   Programming facilities of the shell
>
> Part III Quick reference

Part II, "Shell Programming", explains the programming features of the shell and shows how to create working applications using both the Bourne and Korn shells. Part II is intended for advanced users who want to write shell scripts for their own and others' use.

Part III, "Quick Reference", contains four appendixes, A through D. Each appendix provides a brief summary of shell syntax and built-in commands. Because some versions of UNIX now omit the on-line manual pages, Part III also contains a summary of the command syntax for most UNIX commands, with brief explanations of the meaning of each command option.

Special Notations

This book describes two shells: the Bourne shell and the Korn shell. The material is intermixed because the two shells are very similar and share many features. However, they are *different programs*, and you cannot use features unique to either shell when you are running the other shell.

Information applicable only to the Korn shell is indicated by the presence of the *ksh only* icon to the left of the paragraph. This information describes features which are not available when using the Bourne shell. Text that is not so marked is applicable to both shells.

Information that is primarily of use to shell programmers is marked by the *shell programming* icon. If you do not intend to use the programming features of the shell, you can skip over the passage with no loss of continuity. Because Part II is concerned specifically with the programming features of the shell, this icon is not used in Part II.

Conventions

This book uses a number of stylistic conventions to help you wade through the thicket of technical explanations. Conventions are absolutely necessary when discussing UNIX, where command names that look like ordinary words abound (for example, read or if). If you take a minute to read these notes, you will be rewarded with a better understanding of what you read.

- Command names and options are shown in monospace type:

  "The -i option of the typeset command ..."

- The variable parts of a command's syntax are named in *monospace italics* in the command description and in the explanatory text that follows it:

  cat -v *filename*

  "For *filename* specify the file name or path of the file to be printed."

- Optional parts of a command are enclosed in brackets:

  cd [*dirname*]

- Italics are also used to highlight technical terms, and sometimes for emphasis.

- Names of predefined shell variables and parameters are shown in UPPERCASE MONOSPACE type:

  "The PATH environment variable specifies the directories to be searched for a command."

- Command output and examples are shown in monospace. In examples, the portion that you type is shown in **monospace bold**:

  ```
  $ echo Hello
  Hello
  $
  ```

- The notation ^x indicates a control character that you enter by pressing the control key and the x key at the same time:

  "Enter ^d when you have finished typing your input."

Terminal Keys

Most computer books can refer to keyboard keys by their real names so that if the book mentions the Enter key you can look down at your keyboard and find a key labeled Enter. This is true because most software in the world today is written for and will work on only one manufacturer's hardware (sad though this fact may be).

The situation is quite different with UNIX. UNIX in general, and the UNIX described in this book in particular, is expressly and purposely designed to run on a vast array of widely disparate computer systems. Usually this portability is an advantage. However, it also implies that no author of UNIX books can know how the keys are labeled on your terminal.

As a result, UNIX users have evolved a body of terminology to refer to terminal keys, which often bear strikingly little relationship to any real keyboard. This way, nobody's products receive undue preference.

Table 1 introduces the most commonly used names for terminal keys. I will use these key names throughout the book since they are already familiar to UNIX people.

To some extent you can control which key on your keyboard is assigned to each of these functions. You do this by using the stty command, which you use to specify the code received from the keyboard that is to be recognized as one of these key names. For more information, refer to the description of the stty command in Appendix D of this book.

UNIX systems generally do not require and may not support the use of other keys such as program function keys, cursor movement keys, and the like, primarily because terminals (as opposed to PCs) cannot be relied on to be so equipped. If you have such keys you may be able to use them, but the study of terminal support is beyond the scope of this book. Consult the documentation for your particular hardware and software for more information.

Table 1. UNIX terminal key names.

Key Name	Function of the Key
^	Often called *control*, *ctrl*, *Ctrl*, or *CTRL*, this key, when pressed simultaneously with a letter key or [, generates an ASCII code in the range 0 to 37 octal.
EOF	The *EOF* key signals the end of input from the keyboard (analogous to the MS-DOS ^Z key). Usually assigned to ^d.
INTR	Also called *cancel* or *interrupt*, this key terminates the currently executing command. Usually assigned to ^c.
ERASE	Also called *backspace*, this key moves the cursor backward one character. This is the key that generates the stty erase code, usually ^h or ^? (ASCII DEL).
KILL	Discards everything you have previously typed on the current line. Usually assigned to ^u.
Return	Generates a newline code (^j). Signals that you have finished typing and now want the computer to observe and react to what you have typed.
space	The space bar. Generates the ASCII 20 code.
tab	Usually labeled *tab*, *Tab*, or *TAB*, generates the ASCII 09 code.

Part

Using the UNIX Shell

Introduction to UNIX

This chapter introduces the basic concepts needed to understand the rest of the book. These concepts are fundamental to the way UNIX operates, and therefore, to the way you must interact with UNIX. If you already have a working acquaintance with UNIX, you can skim this chapter, taking note only of those topics that are new to you.

If you are new to UNIX, you probably will find this chapter to be a little difficult. Even so, you should read the chapter in its entirety. Do not panic and stop if you fail to understand something: Later, when you have read more about the shell and tried a few terminal sessions, read this chapter again. You probably will discover you understand passages that previously made no sense to you.

The information presented in this chapter may seem rather vague and conceptual to you, but it is not. UNIX usually hides the inner complexities of computers from its users. There are many details that you never have to concern yourself with. UNIX deals with the details and oddities of hardware and multiuser software, and leaves a clean user interface on which to work.

You will gain more mastery of UNIX from this chapter than you realize. Similarly, if you gloss over this material, you might find later chapters to be confusing. When learning UNIX, you must begin with the basics.

What Is a Shell?

1

Essentially, a *shell* is a program that reads commands from an input source, converts the commands into an internal format, then executes the commands.

Every operating system must have a shell. MS-DOS calls its shell *COMMAND.COM*. Other operating systems use different terms. Whatever the shell is called, users write commands in a command language and submit those commands to the computer to describe the work they want the computer to do. The shell decodes each command and invokes the services of the operating system to accomplish the unit of work implied by the command.

UNIX provides not one shell, but several. Each of the shells supports a different command language. You can choose the shell you like to use because UNIX does not force you to use any particular shell.

Three shells are widely available: The *Bourne shell*, the *Korn shell*, and the *C shell*. This book describes the first two, which were both developed for the System V variant of UNIX. (*UNIX* and *System V* are trademarks of AT&T. UNIX was originally developed by Ken Thompson and others at AT&T Bell Laboratories, and many people think of System V as the "official" version of UNIX. Others take offense to this view.) The C shell is commonly used with the BSD variant of UNIX. (The Berkeley Software Distribution [BSD] is another version of UNIX originally developed by the University of California at Berkeley.) In AT&T's Release 4 of System V, all three shells are available to you because Release 4 merges the features of the System V, BSD, and XENIX versions of UNIX. (XENIX is an older version of UNIX offered for IBM PC computers.)

Basic Concepts

UNIX is founded on a few basic concepts. An understanding of these concepts is crucial to using the shell effectively. In this section, you look at how these concepts affect your interaction with UNIX.

Users

Although this chapter has implied it before, it is important to state explicitly that UNIX is a *multiuser* system. As the term suggests, UNIX allows more than one person to use the computer at a time. But beyond this, UNIX embodies a *user concept*.

User concept means UNIX includes the necessary facilities to identify users and to distinguish between them. UNIX also includes facilities to protect yourself, your programs and files, and information entered into the computer from disruption by others, and, if you wish, even from being viewed by others.

Logging In

To be able to protect one user from another, UNIX must first know who you are, as well who all the others are that may be using the system. To gain this knowledge, UNIX requires you to *log in* before you may use the computer.

When you first confront a terminal under the control of UNIX, you see an almost blank screen containing only the one word

```
login:
```

What UNIX wants you to do is to type your *login name*. If your login name is jjv, you simply type those three letters and press the return key. If you do this, the computer prompts you again, this time for your *password*. The display now looks like this:

```
login: jjv
password:
```

You must now type a secret word and press the return key. The purpose of the password is to prove to UNIX that you are who you say you are. If you keep your password secret, no one else can give both your login name and your password.

The combination of login name and password thus serves to uniquely and positively identify you as one of the system's authorized users. Having that information, the system can then allow you to access your own files while preventing others from accessing them.

You can not invent your own login name; you must request one from a special person called the *superuser* or *system administrator*. The superuser is simply that person who has the responsibility of managing the computer system. The superuser also has a number of special privileges, including the

1

ability to add new people to the list of authorized users. The superuser also assigns you a starter password. You must use that password the first time you log in. You can change your password anytime thereafter simply by executing the passwd command.

User-ID and Group-ID

You use your login name to identify yourself to the system. But once you have logged in, the system identifies you not by your name, but by your *user-ID* and *group-ID*.

When adding you to the system, the superuser assigns you a user-ID, which is a number from 1 to 65000. You do not have to know or remember what your user-ID is; UNIX remembers it for you. All you have to remember is your login name and password.

Your group-ID is another number, also in the range of 1 to 65000, that identifies the *group* to which you belong. A group is simply a particular combination of users. UNIX manages access to system resources based not only on your user-ID, but also on the group with which you are affiliated. The group concept provides a way to grant access to a group of several people without granting access to everyone else. You do not have to specify your group-ID when you log in. UNIX keeps a record of the group that you are associated with, and automatically determines your group-ID when you log in.

Occasionally you may have to be aware of your user-ID and group-ID numbers because the system internally uses these numbers to identify you. Some commands show your ID numbers. You rarely, if ever, are asked to enter your ID numbers.

You can find out your own user-ID and group-ID numbers by entering the id command:

```
$ id
uid=201(jjv) gid=4(user)
$
```

Here you see the standard UNIX abbreviations for user-ID (uid) and group-ID (gid). The user-ID shown is 201, which corresponds to the user name jjv. The group-ID shown is 4, which corresponds to the user group called user.

You can find out someone else's numbers by viewing the system's /etc /passwd file, which contains your complete identification (as well as everyone else's) in lines that look like this:

```
$ cat /etc/passwd
root:7HYz1a3Z09:0:0:0000-admin(root):/:/bin/sh
jjv:a3Bc1H9a4.:201:4:John Valley:/u/jjv:/bin/ksh
$
```

Each line contains seven fields of information separated by colons (:). They are, from left: your login name, your password (scrambled, of course), your user-ID, your group-ID, your full name, your home directory path name, and your login shell. In this example, the user-ID for login name `jjv` is `201`, and the group-ID is `4`.

The `/etc/passwd` file, of which the preceding code is a sample, is the same file that the system uses to check your name and password when you log in.

Protecting Your Files

Because UNIX knows who you are as well as the identity of everyone else who is logged in, UNIX can use that information to control access to resources.

The main class of resources you want to protect are your files. Everything else you do on-line is transitory, but files last from session to session and generally you do not want other people disturbing your files.

To prevent access to a file, you must set the access *permissions* (or *mode*) of the file the way you want them. Permissions are permanently associated with the file; only the file's *owner* can set a file's permissions. The owner of a file is simply the user who created the file.

To understand file permissions better, take a look at a sample output line from the `ls` command:

```
-rwxr-xr-x   1 jjv      user       21914 Apr  6 10:01 inb
```

This line describes the characteristics of a file named inb. The third column shows the owner of the file as `jjv`, and the fourth column shows the group as `user`.

The permissions are shown in the first field as `rwxr-xr-x`. The leading dash (-) is not part of the file's permissions.

The permissions are shown in three sets of three codes: `rwx`, `r-x`, and `r-x`, reading from the left.

The first group of three codes are the permissions that apply to the file's owner, in this case `jjv`. The `r` indicates you may *read* from the file; the `w` indicates you may *write* to the file; and the `x` indicates you may *execute* the file.

1

The second group of three codes (r-x) describes the access permitted to members of the file's group, in this case user. The same meanings apply as before; for this example, the codes mean any user in the group user may read (r) or execute (x) the file, but may not write to the file (there is a - in place of the w).

The third group of three codes describes the access permitted to any other user. They indicate that users other than the file's owner and members of the file's group may read or execute the file, but may not write to it.

You can display a file's access permissions with the ls command. You can change a file's owner with the chown command, change the file's group with the chgrp command, and change the permission flags with the chmod command.

Advanced File Protection Systems

The file owner, group, and permission codes provide sufficient security for most purposes. However, for secure installations such as military systems, this protection system is inadequate. For example, suppose Bill wants to let only Sally and no one else read one of his files. The only way Bill can accomplish this task with the standard UNIX file permissions is to establish a group containing only Bill and Sally. This action cannot be done without assistance from the superuser, and, although Bill and Sally can switch from one group to another using the newgrp command, this would not be a very flexible system. Various standards organizations are currently working on ways to extend the capabilities of the UNIX file protection system. You can expect more complications in this area in the future.

Learning about Users

A multiuser system would not be complete without ways for you to get information about other users. There are four specific commands that accomplish this task:

- The who command lists the other users who are currently logged into the system.

- The id command tells you what your current user-ID and group-ID are. You might have to use the id command if you log onto an unattended system, or if you have used the su command to switch your login to another name.

- The ps command lists all the commands the system is currently executing, and tells you who issued each command.

- The /etc/passwd file lists all the users known to the system, whether or not they are logged in, and the /etc/group file lists all the valid group names.

Files

So far this chapter has mentioned files in a general way without explaining in detail what UNIX means by the word *file*. One of the reasons for deferring the subject so long is that the UNIX concept of *file* is quite simple.

In general, UNIX files fall into two main categories: *data* files, which you can read and write however you want; and *system* files, which have a prescribed format and a special meaning to the UNIX operating system. In this section, you will look at data files. System file formats are discussed in later sections of ***.

A file is simply a series of *bytes*. Computer technologists use the term *byte* for a cell of memory that can hold one character of data. The capacity of the computer's memory, for example, is expressed as a number of bytes. The word *computer* requires eight bytes of data when stored in memory or on disk. The bytes of a file are arranged sequentially in their natural order, and UNIX does not insert any extra control information in the file.

Figure 1.1 is a (realistic) illustration of a UNIX file. The first byte of the file contains the letter *T*, the second byte contains the letter *b*, and so on. By convention, the byte positions of the file are numbered relative to *zero*. Using this convention, byte 145 in the file contains the letter *p*. The last byte in the file is at byte position 317; the file is, therefore, 318 bytes long.

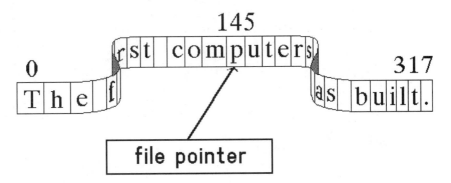

Figure 1.1. Illustration of a UNIX file.

1

When processing a file, UNIX keeps track of its current position in the file by using a *file pointer*. The pointer simply identifies the position of the next byte in the file to be read. The file pointer keeps track of where you are in the file. Programs are allowed to skip around inside a file and to read or write any number of bytes at a time.

Files have a number of attributes associated with them. This chapter has already discussed several, including the file's owner, group, and permissions. A file also has a *size*, meaning the number of bytes in the file; a *link count*, which tells you how many different names (aliases) there are for the file; and a *timestamp*, which tells you when the file was previously changed.

Some other operating systems organize the data in a file into a series of *records*; UNIX does not. The closest UNIX comes to the concept of records is *lines*. Many UNIX commands consider files to be a series of lines separated by end-of-line marker characters (usually the ASCII LF character—commonly called the *newline* character), and if you hand a file to one of these commands, it tries to interpret the file as a series of lines.

UNIX does not, however, require a file to contain even one newline character. A 10,000 byte file can consist of one line. UNIX does not impose any restrictions on the length of a line, in part because UNIX does not require files to be formatted as a series of lines. Program files, for example, are stored in a binary format, and, although such files may accidentally contain one or more newline characters, program files contain no lines as such.

On the other hand, because UNIX imposes no restrictions on the content or structure of a file, the programmer can structure information in a file into fixed-size records. You may develop quite sophisticated file structures, because UNIX views a file as a byte array and is insensitive to how you arrange the bytes in a file.

The negative side of this is that UNIX offers no built-in file-management systems. Although you can develop any file structure you like, you also must develop a file-management system if you want to use anything other than line-oriented text files in your application. Because UNIX is not a new operating system, you might rightly expect there are numerous packages available, ranging from the free to the expensive, to provide you with anything from simple keyed files to sophisticated database systems.

File Descriptors

A file is a collection of information stored somewhere outside the computer's main memory—on a hard disk or a magnetic tape, for example. Obviously, you cannot write information onto a disk by hand, or read it from a disk by sight; you must use a program to read and write files. The program you choose determines what is done with the information. For example, if your program merely copies information from one place to another, you might use the program to display a file by copying it from the disk where it resides to your terminal where you can see it.

The UNIX operating system does not allow other programs to read or write directly to files. (*Other* is used because the UNIX operating system is, itself, a program.) To ensure all input (reading) and output (writing) is performed properly, and to relieve information-processing programs of the burden of operating complex devices such as disk drives, UNIX performs all input and output in response to program requests. This imposes a measure of order and reliability on the behavior of the system as a whole.

To gain access to a file, either to read or write it, a program must first *open* the file. The program must say which file it wants to access, and whether the program reads the file or writes to the file. In response, the operating system confirms the file exists (or can be created, as the case may be), and the program has the necessary permissions to access the file. If everything is in order, the operating system sets up an *access path* for transferring the information between the program and the file. If an error is discovered (for example, a file to be opened does not exist, or there is no space on the disk to hold a new output file), the operating system denies the request; the request *fails*, and no access path is established.

To the program, the access path looks like a number, typically in the range 0 to 59 on System V Release 4 Systems, although this maximum number can change depending on the UNIX system and even on installation. As part of the routine of opening a file, the operating system assigns the number and tells the program which number represents the file. Henceforth, the program must supply this path number whenever the program wants to read or write the file. In UNIX, this path number is called a *file descriptor*.

To the operating system, the access path looks like a collection of tables and buffers. (A *buffer* is an area of computer memory used to hold information while it is being read from or written to an external device.) When the program supplies a file descriptor number with a read or write request, the operating system uses that number to direct the information flow to or from the right place.

You should be concerned with file descriptor numbers when you write shell commands, because it is your job as a user not only to tell the shell which program to run, but also to tell the program which files to use. Sometimes you do this by giving the command a *file name* (see the next section, "File Names") and leaving it up to the program to establish the necessary access path. But you also can open a file with the shell and specify which file descriptor to assign to the open file.

1

This latter technique is called *Input/Output redirection*. Input/Output redirection is basic to using the shell and to using UNIX. Chapter 3, "Simple Commands," includes a full discussion of the shell facilities for I/O redirection.

At this point, it may be difficult to understand when you would use Input/Output redirection, and how file descriptors work in practice. That understanding comes with studying the text and examples in Chapter 3, so you should defer your questions until then and reread this section after working through the material in Chapter 3.

File Names

Every file must have a name. You use the name to tell UNIX which file or files you want to process. Most UNIX commands allow you to specify the names of the files that the command is to operate on. For example, you can tell the sort command to operate on a file called names, as in the following example:

```
$ sort names
```

This command produces a sorted listing of the contents of the names file.

Not surprisingly, UNIX imposes some restrictions on the names you can choose for a file. The restrictions are few and easy to remember:

File Name Rules

- A file name usually must have between 1 and 14 characters on System V Release 4.

- A file name may not contain either the ASCII NULL character or the slash character (/).

Besides these hard-and-fast rules, you also should try to avoid building file names that contain nondisplayable characters or characters having special meaning to the shell. It is best to restrict file names to the upper- and lowercase letters, the ten digits 0 through 9, the dot (.), the underscore (_), and the dash (-). Other characters can create confusion when you try to use them in commands. Also, you should avoid beginning file names with a - (dash) because many commands can erroneously construe such a file name as a program option.

Here are some examples of good and bad file names:

Table 1.1. Examples of good and bad file names.

Good File Name	Bad File Name	Problem with Bad File Name
main.c	MainProgramFile.c	Too long
listing-1	-listing1	Starts with -
output.file	output file	Contains a blank
PayrollSummary	$pay	Contains $

Directories

Although UNIX supports only one kind of *data* file—namely a series of bytes on which applications may impose any desired structure—UNIX reserves a number of special-purpose file types for its own use.

One such special file is the *directory*. A directory is a kind of file that contains other files in it. A directory is like a manila folder in which you have stored several documents. The folder corresponds to the directory file, and the documents correspond to your data files.

UNIX also allows a directory to contain a directory. To continue the analogy with office filing systems, a high-level directory is similar to a file drawer that stores several manila folders, each of which contains several documents. This nesting of directories within directories can continue to a great depth.

A directory might contain only directories or only files, but UNIX does not impose such a restriction. A directory may contain a mixture of files and subdirectories. (A subdirectory is not a special kind of directory; the term *subdirectory* merely stresses the subordination of one directory to another.)

UNIX requires that the name of every file (including directory files) be unique in the containing directory. However, files in different directories may have the same name. When you store thousands of files on a UNIX system, you can select the name of a file without worrying about conflicts with the names of files in other directories.

The ability to use the same name for files in different directories does present a naming problem, though. How can you clearly specify which of two such files you mean? This brings you squarely to the concept of the *path name*.

Path Names

Directories have names like regular files. To refer to a file contained in a directory, you must tell UNIX the name of both the file and the directory. Such a compound name is called a *path name*. Use the slash character, / (not the backslash character, \), to separate directory and file names when you write a path name. Table 1.2 shows some examples of path names.

Table 1.2. Interpretation of path names.

Path Name	Meaning
xyz	The file xyz
memo/xyz	The file xyz in directory memo
jjv/memo/xyz	The file xyz in directory memo in directory jjv

Every file must be contained in a directory. Every directory also must be contained in some other directory. Obviously, however, this process cannot go on forever. There is a top directory (called the *root* directory) that is not contained in anything else. It is called the root directory because it is like the bottom of a tree that forks into more and more branches as it grows upward. Figure 1.2 illustrates a directory tree.

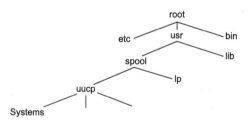

Figure 1.2. A directory tree.

In the figure, the root directory is represented by a path name of /. The full path name of the file Systems shown in figure 1.2 is therefore /usr/spool /uucp/Systems. Notice that it would be wrong to write root/usr/spool/uucp /Systems because the top directory does not have a name. Similarly the path name //usr/spool/uucp/Systems, although allowed, is not exactly correct either, because one leading / is enough to indicate that the path name starts at the root directory.

A path name beginning with "/" is called an absolute path (or sometimes a full path) because it completely specifies the location of a file by beginning at the root directory and naming all the intervening directories to reach the file.

To prove / is the path name of a directory, enter the following command:

```
$ ls -l /
```

The output resembles the listing of any directory's contents; it lists the files and directories contained in the root directory.

As far as UNIX is concerned, the root directory is special only in that it has no parent. "Parent Directory" is a term often used by UNIX users to refer to the directory that contains a given directory by drawing an analogy between a directory tree and a family tree. (Technically, the parent of the root directory is itself. The top directory of every file system points to itself as its parent.) But in practice, the system's root directory is special because it contains critical resources, such as all the UNIX command programs. To protect these resources, the root directory and many of the directories and files in the root directory are writable only by the superuser. Be aware that this protection, although normal and advisable, is nonetheless optional.

The Current Directory

It is impossible to avoid working with directories in the UNIX environment. Even if you never create any directories yourself, the system as a whole contains many directories, some of which you inevitably must deal with. Your own *home directory* is certainly not the least of these.

As an authorized system user, one directory is set aside for your exclusive use. This directory is called your home directory. It belongs to you; you are its *owner*. You may store files in it, or partition it into an arbitrarily complex tree of subdirectories.

In addition to your home directory, you also must be conscious of your *working directory* (also called the *current directory* or sometimes *current working directory*).

Your working directory is the directory that is searched when you use a path name without a leading /. That is, you can refer to any file in your working directory by giving just its file name. For example, the file name xyz could refer to the file /bin/xyz or to /usr/xyz, depending on whether /bin or /usr is your working directory. The idea of a working directory is important for this reason. Without the concept of a working directory, you would always have to type the full path name of every file—a tedious and error-prone situation at best.

When you log in, your working directory is always set to your home directory. To change your working directory to anywhere else, you must execute the cd command.

There are two handy special directory names you can always refer to, no matter what your current directory is. One of these is . (dot), which is an alternate name for your current directory. The other is .. (dot dot), which refers to the parent of the current directory.

The path name ./xyz has an identical meaning to the unadorned path name xyz; both refer to the file xyz in the current directory. If your current directory is /u/jjv, for example, then the path name ./xyz is equivalent to the absolute path name /u/jjv/xyz.

The path name ../xyz, however, means something quite different. Look at Figure 1.3. Assuming your current directory is /u/jjv/mail, then the path name ../bin is equivalent to the absolute path name /u/jjv/bin. Remember, the special notation .. is equivalent to the parent of the current directory; in the example, that is the directory /u/jjv, so writing ../bin is equivalent to writing /u/jjv/bin.

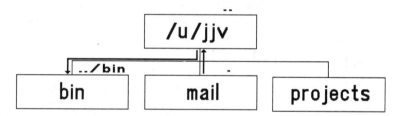

Figure 1.3. Interpretation of the path name ../bin from /u/jjv/mail.

Identifying Directories

From the previous discussion, it is obvious there is a significant difference between regular files and directory files. You cannot tell whether a file is a regular file or a directory file simply by looking at its name (the same naming rules apply to both regular files and directory files), nor by looking at its path name (a path name three levels deep can be a regular file such as /usr/bin /lint, but a path name four levels deep, such as /usr/spool/uucppublic /receive, can be a directory).

One way to identify a file as a directory file is to display its description with the long option of the ls command:

```
$ ls -l
```

In the listing produced by the command, the first character of each line shows the type of the file. A regular file is marked with -. A directory file is marked with d. Look at the following example:

```
drwxr-xr-x   2 jjv      user       1024 Jan  2  1990 .
drwxr-xr-x   5 root     sys        5120 Sep 15  1989 ..
drwxr-xr-x   2 jjv      user       1024 Feb 15 14:21 bin
-rw-r--r--   1 jjv      user        512 Mar  1 09:41 mbox
```

This listing shows that the current directory contains one subdirectory (bin) and one regular file (mbox). It also contains the two reserved directories . and ...

Tapes, Printers, Disks, and Other Devices

Besides directories, UNIX also uses two other kinds of special files: The *character-special* file and the *block-special* file. These are not files in the normal sense; they are actually symbolic names for devices.

UNIX uses the term *device* for any peripheral hardware attached to the computer. There are many different kinds of peripherals; common examples are disk drives, tape drives, printers, and terminals.

In general, you cannot write output directly to a peripheral device; such privileges usually are reserved for system utility programs and for the superuser.

You always can read and write to your terminal, however. To find out the path name of the special file for your terminal, invoke the tty command:

```
$ tty
/dev/tty0
$_
```

In this sample dialog, the output from tty is the path name /dev/tty0. This is the path name of your terminal. You can use the ls command to display information about the path name, as for any other file:

```
$ ls -l /dev/tty0
crw--w--w-   1 jjv      root        7,2 Feb 19 12:35 /dev/tty0
$
```

What you discover from the output of ls is rather surprising: The permissions are such that others may write to your terminal as well as yourself.

The rules for reading and writing to special files (that is, devices) can be quite complicated and do not have to follow the conventions for reading and writing to regular disk files. This difference is because physical devices, by their nature, often have restricted or specialized capabilities. For example, it is nonsense to imagine reading from a printer.

Once again, the ls command can identify special files. The following output line from ls shows what a description of a character-special (type c) and a block-special (type b) file look like:

```
brwxrwx--- 1  root    sys   2,  0  Mar 31  1989  /dev/dsk/0s0
crwx-w--w- 1  bill    user  0,  4  Feb 12  15:04 /dev/tty021
```

The first line describes /dev/dsk/0s0, which is an entire disk drive. It is a block-special file, indicated by the b as the first character of the line. Block-special files usually are mass-storage devices, such as disk drives and tape drives.

The second line describes the special file for a hypothetical user's terminal. The file is marked as a character-special file, which is usually a serial device such as a terminal or printer. The device is owned by bill, who may both read and write it; other users may write only to the terminal, perhaps to send Bill a message.

For the most part, there is little to say about special files in this book. Utility programs can assist with access to some kinds of devices. For example, you should never send output directly to a printer; instead, you should send output for printing to the lp command, which schedules your printing to occur between the printing of other users' output.

At this stage, it only is necessary for you to realize that not all path names refer to disk files; some refer to devices. Because devices have path names like disk files, you can use devices as the input or output to a command, just as you might use a disk file. There are situations where this flexibility is useful.

Commands and Programs

Most of this book discusses using the shell to execute commands. Yet people often speak of using computers to run programs. What is a *command*, what is a *program*, and what is the difference between them?

The difference is primarily one of viewpoint. In UNIX, you execute a program simply by typing the program's name. When you enter the wxyz command, the system responds by executing the program named wxyz. So, the term *command* refers to the line of text you enter, and the term *program* refers to the stored set of instructions used to perform the action of the command.

The term *command* often is used interchangeably with *program* because a command cannot be executed without a corresponding program that instructs the computer what to do, and a program normally can be invoked only by entering its name as a command.

For example, consider the ls command. You can use the ls command to list the files you have stored in the computer. The ls command has a syntax that allows you to specify a number of options and operands to modify its behavior.

Sometimes you might enter the ls command as follows:

```
$ ls -l
```

This command produces a listing of file names on your terminal. If you enter the command

```
$ ls -l /bin
```

you receive a listing that describes the ls command itself. Buried somewhere in the listing is a line that looks something like this:

```
...
drwxr-xr-x   1 bin      bin        14682 Jan  2 1987 ls
...
```

The precise meaning of this output is irrelevant, beyond the fact that ls outputs a list of files, and here it has output a listing of itself. Clearly, then, ls must not only be a command but also a file. And so it is. This particular file in the /bin directory is executable. (Notice the three xs in the permissions.) If you enter the name ls, the system reads the contents of the ls file into memory and begins executing it as a program.

Thus, the difference between the terms *command* and *program* is small indeed. This book uses the term *command* to refer to an abstract facility consisting of a syntax and an operation description, and reserves the term *program* to refer to the concrete set of instructions, stored on disk or in memory, that implement the command.

Processes

Some operating systems are capable of performing only one task at a time. Others can perform multiple tasks at once. UNIX is an example of the latter. A typical kind of task consists of executing a program in response to a user's request. The UNIX operating system calls each task being executed a *process*.

1

You can now look at commands in another light. Earlier, you viewed commands as programs. Now you can view commands as processes. Why the different terminology?

Suppose two different users, Bill and Sally, both try to execute the ls command. They both enter the same command, and the same program is executed for both users. But there are two different executions of the program: One execution displays Bill's files, the other displays Sally's files. The two executions differ because, although they use the same program, they operate on different data. UNIX actually creates two distinct processes to execute the ls command, even though both processes are running the same program.

Most computers can perform only one instruction at a time, so how do operating systems such as UNIX execute multiple processes simultaneously? By switching rapidly between the active processes, UNIX gives the appearance of simultaneous execution. This switching usually occurs so fast you never notice it, and you have the impression that you have the computer all to yourself.

The ability to switch rapidly between processes means you do not have to wait for the computer to finish one command before it can begin another. It would be awkward indeed if Bill had to wait until Sally's command finished before he could enter his command.

UNIX allows one user to execute a command at the same time that you are executing a command. Although the process takes longer to execute when overlapped in this manner, most users rarely notice the increased execution time.

When you stop and think about it, most of your time in front of the computer is spent interpreting the display, deciding what to do next, and entering the next command. The time the computer spends executing commands is a small fraction of each person's time in front of the terminal. UNIX capitalizes on this fact: During the time you spend thinking—and during the delay between each character you type—UNIX is executing other users' commands.

But UNIX does more. Not only can UNIX execute several users' programs at once, it also can execute several programs at the same time for you. After all, if a system can overlap the execution of several programs at once, there is no reason to limit that capability to one program per user, and UNIX does not enforce such a limitation. There are a number of ways you can get UNIX to run two or more programs at once for you. Some of those are discussed in this book.

To summarize, a *process* is one execution of a program. UNIX can support the simultaneous execution of several processes at once. Some of the processes may have been created by other computer users, but it also is true that more than one of the active processes may have been created by you.

UNIX keeps track of each active process by assigning it a number, called the *process-ID (PID)*. You sometimes have to know the process-ID of a process, for example, to forcibly terminate (*cancel*) its execution. To discover the list of processes you are currently executing, enter the ps command:

```
$ ps
   PID TTY      TIME COMMAND
    53 cons1    0:06 ksh
    69 cons1    0:00 ps
    70 cons1    0:00 cat
$
```

This particular output shows that you are currently executing three processes. Process 53 is executing the ksh program (probably your login shell), process 69 is executing the ps program itself, and process-ID 70 is executing the cat program.

When the shell waits for a process to complete its execution before prompting you for another command, that process is called a *foreground* process. When a process runs without terminal input and the shell proceeds without waiting for the process to complete, it is called a *background* process. In other words, the only difference between the two kinds of processes is the way the shell manages the execution.

Summary

In this chapter you have reviewed the basic concepts of the UNIX operating system by taking a quick look at such topics as processes, user identification and security, commands, shells, and the UNIX directorized file system. This review focused on breadth of coverage rather than depth. If you are new to UNIX, there is still much to learn. As you become familiar with UNIX, you should read a more detailed book, such as Kochan and Wood's *UNIX Shell Programming* (SAMS, 1990; ISBN 0-672-48448-X).

The most critical concepts in understanding the shell are those of *directory* and *process*. UNIX shells are primarily a vehicle for entering commands, and you cannot use UNIX commands without referring to directories and the files they contain. The shell does its work primarily by creating a process to execute a command. One of the most powerful features of the shell is its ability to create simultaneously executing processes.

1

You might feel uncertain about the meaning of directories, files, and processes until you log in and actually begin to use these things. Do not review this chapter too hard or too long without first logging in and trying some of the material in later chapters.

The remainder of this book digs into the details of the shell's operation. Because this book is part tutorial and part reference manual, the presentations may be too full of facts and short of explanations for your needs. If this is the case, do not lose heart. Pick up a copy of *UNIX Shell Programming* for a leisurely introduction to using the shell. Keep this desktop guide by your terminal and refer to it frequently to find quick answers to your specific questions. In no time at all, you will be using UNIX like a pro.

Basic Tools

he previous chapter described some of the basic concepts of the UNIX operating system. These concepts are facilities of just one part of UNIX, namely the *kernel*. The kernel is the main control program that manages the operation of the computer. The kernel offers many services, such as creating and scheduling processes, enforcing file access permissions, and using directories to find files.

UNIX also consists of many other service programs that assist users in performing their work. You cannot work effectively with UNIX unless you are aware of the facilities available to help you. This section is intended to highlight the services that you will most likely have to use on a frequent basis.

There is not enough space in this book to explain in detail how to use these tools. A number of other good books explain these tools in depth. I recommend the following:

- *The Waite Group's UNIX Primer Plus*, by Martin and Prata (SAMS, 1990; 0-672-22729-0), is a good introduction to UNIX, showing how to use the facilities just mentioned here. References to this book are called *Primer*.

- *UNIX Step-by-Step* by Ben Smith (SAMS, 1990; ISBN 0-672-48469-2) provides more detail than *Primer* but covers fewer subjects. I especially recommend this book for an introduction to the Vi and Emacs editors.

- *The Waite Group's UNIX System V Bible: Commands and Utilities* by Martin and Prata (SAMS, 1987; ISBN 0-672-22562-X) provides a thumbnail sketch of many System V commands, and therefore makes a good reference. The *Bible* provides information about more commands than either *Step-by-Step* or *Primer*.

2

The Shell

The shell is the one part of UNIX with which you will become most familiar. Indeed, for many people the shell is the essence of UNIX, because it is the one tool you use all the time.

Depending on your tastes and what is available on your system, you can choose one of three shells to use as your standard shell. You only have to inform your system administrator (superuser) which one you prefer to use.

All UNIX systems offer the Bourne shell, known by its command name, sh. This shell, named for its author Stephen Bourne, is described in full in this book.

Users of the BSD version of UNIX, XENIX, and some of the more modern implementations of System V, also have access to the C shell (csh). Written by Bill Joy (who also wrote Vi), the C shell offers a syntax that is closer to the C programming language and feels more natural to some programmers than the Bourne shell. The C shell is not covered in this book.

The Korn shell, ksh, named for its author David Korn, comes from the same AT&T Bell Labs as the original sh. The Korn shell supports all the Bourne shell syntax and offers many extensions that make it easier to use at the keyboard. This book also describes all the features of the Korn shell.

Whichever shell you prefer to use, you should always have a good working knowledge of the Bourne shell because the other shells are not available with every version of UNIX.

File Management

UNIX provides a set of commands for managing files. Table 2.1 contains a list of all the basic file-management commands. Each is discussed in detail in the following sections.

Table 2.1. File management commands.

Command	Function
cat	Display the contents of files
cp	Copy files
ln	Link to (add an alias for) a file or directory
ls	List (information about) files
mkdir	Make directories
mv	Move (rename) files and directories
rm	Remove (delete) files and directories
rmdir	Remove (delete) empty directories

The cat Command

The name of the cat command comes from the verb *cat*enate, meaning "to combine by joining end-to-end." The command takes one or more file names as its arguments. The command displays the files named in a continuous stream to the terminal (called *standard output*).

- To display the contents of a file: cat `file name`

- To combine several files into one: cat `file1 file2 >file3` (Rather than going to the terminal, the > symbol *redirects* the output into a file, named `file3`. Redirection is discussed in the next chapter.)

- To safely view a file that might contain nondisplayable characters: cat -v /etc/utmp

The ls Command

Use the ls command to display lists of files. The ls command lists information about the files, not their contents.

If you specify the -1 option, the ls command prints a full line for each file listed; this is called the long listing format. The information displayed is as follows:

Long Listing Format

```
$ ls -l fsck
drwxr-xr-x 2 root    bin     36748  Jan  2 14:41 fsck
```

Item	Meaning
drwxr-xr-x	File type and permissions flags
2	Number of links for this file
root	Name of file's owner
bin	Name of file's group
36748	Size of the file in bytes
Jan 2	Month and day the file was previously created or modified
14:41	24-hour time the file was previously created or modified
fsck	The name of the file

Normally, the ls command does not list files with names that start with . (dot). There are two ways to see such files:

- Use the -a option. This displays all the files in the directory.

- Use the command ls -d .* to show only files having dotted names. The -d option prevents the ls command from displaying the contents of the . and .. directories.

The -CF options together present an output format that is most helpful for general use, because it identifies directories and executable files and lists the files in a multicolumn format.

The cp **Command**

The cp command provides the basic file copy function for UNIX. Use it only when ln does not serve (see the following section on ln command). There are tricks to using cp, for example:

- To copy a single file to your current directory:

  ```
  cp /usr/fred/projects/main.c .
  ```

- To copy dissimilarly named files from one arbitrary directory to another arbitrary directory:

  ```
  cd /usr/fred/projects
  cp main.c sub.c pr.c /usr/jjv/src
  ```

- To copy a file from your current directory to another directory:

```
cp main.c /usr/fred/payroll
```

The ln Command

The ln command is similar to the cp command, but makes a *link* rather than physically copying the files. A link is nothing more than a directory entry, because the directory entry establishes a connection (a *link*) between the name by which you call the file and the location on disk where its data resides. The ln command, in other words, creates additional directory entries for a file. When more than one directory entry exists for a file, the file can be referenced by more than one path name.

It is more efficient to use ln rather than cp whenever possible because less disk space is needed to create a directory entry than to create a copy of the file. Because both the old and new directory entries point to the same file, a change to the file is seen by either of its names.

The first format of the ln command creates a new link named *newname* that refers to the same file as *oldname*. *Oldname* must name an existing file; *newname* must not exist. A file can have up to 1000 links; that is, it can be known by up to 1000 different names. Both *oldname* and *newname* can specify path names rather than simple file names. The result is that the new name for the file is created in a different directory.

The second format creates a link for each named file—*file1*, *file2*, and so on—in the directory *dir*. The new links have the same file names as the original names.

Command Syntax of cat

```
cat [ -suvte ] file ...
```

The following options can be used with the cat command:

-s *Silent*. Suppresses messages about files that cannot be found. Use this option when it's not certain that all the files you list exist, and you don't want error messages for the missing files.

-u *Unbuffered*. Causes the cat command to write its output character-by-character rather than a block at a time. Use this option to cause output to be written continuously rather than in large chunks. (Note: This option is new with System V Release 4.)

2

- v   *Visible.* Causes cat to print nongraphic characters in a visible format. Use this option when you want to view the contents of a file that might contain unprintable characters.

- t   *Tabs.* Causes cat to print tab characters as ^I and form feed characters as ^L. This option is valid only in combination with the -v option. Use this option when you want to visually check the input file for the presence of tab or form feed characters. (Note: this option is new with System V Release 4.)

- e   *End-of-line.* Causes cat to print the newline character as a dollar sign ($). Normal line breaks still occur. Use this option when you want to visually inspect the output of cat for white space at the end of lines. This option is valid only in combination with the -v option.

Command Syntax of ls

ls [-1abcdfgilmnopqrstuxCFLR] [*name* ...]

The following options can be used with the ls command:

- 1   List one file name per line. By default, ls prints a multicolumn listing of file names. (Note: this option is new with System V Release 4.)

- a   Print all file names, including those beginning with a dot (.).

- b   Show nonprintable characters in listed file names with octal notation (\nnn).

- c   Show the time when the file status was last changed rather than the time of last modification. A status change is any change to the file's permissions, owner-ID, group-ID, or timestamp.

- d   List directory entries rather than their contents. Use this option when you want to see information about a directory rather than the files it contains.

- f   Force a file to be treated as a directory even if it is not. The contents of the file are interpreted as directory entries. If the file is not a valid directory, the listed information might be meaningless.

- g   List the group of each file but not its owner. Use this option when you want to drop the owner name from output listings.

- i   List the i-node number of each file. The *i-node* number is a unique identifier for a file. It can be used to determine when two file names are aliases for the same file.

-1   Long listing format. Lists one file per line giving the file's type, access permissions, number of links, owner, group, size, date and time of last modification, and name.

-m   List file names in *stream* format; that is, as many names as possible are listed across the line, separated by commas.

-n   Print owner and group numbers rather than names. This option produces a slightly faster listing than -1 because the ls command does not have to look up owner and group numbers in system files to convert them to names.

-o   The same as -1 except that group names are omitted. The combination of the -g and -o options produces a long listing with neither the owner nor group names.

-p   Print a slash (/) after each directory name printed.

-q   Show nonprintable characters in file names as a question mark (?).

-r   List files in reverse order. By default, files are listed in ascending order by name. If one of the -c, -t, or -u options is specified, files are listed in ascending order by the selected date and time. In any case, the -r option reverses the order of the listing.

-s   Show file size in blocks.

-t   Sort the listing by date and time of last modification rather than by file name.

-u   Use the date and time of last access to each file for determining the order of files listed. When used in combination with the -1, -n, -g, or -o options, the -u option also causes the date and time of last access to be shown rather than the date and time of last modification.

-x   List file names in multicolumn format. Consecutive files are listed across the page rather than in vertical columns (see the -C option).

-C   List file names in multicolumn format. Consecutive files are listed down the page rather than across the page (see the -x option).

-F   Identify the type of each listed file by appending one of the following characters to the file name: / if the file is a directory; * if the file is executable; @ if the file is a symbolic link.

-L   Follow symbolic links. This option causes the ls command to show information about the file pointed to by the symbolic link rather than about the symbolic link itself. (A symbolic link is a short file that contains the path name of another file so that a reference to the symbolic link is equivalent to a reference to the file named in the link.) By default the ls command lists the symbolic link file itself. (Note: this option is new with System V Release 4.)

-R   Recursively list the contents of all directories. Without this option, the ls command lists only those files named on the command line. When specified, a directory listing is followed by a listing of the contents of the directory.

Command Syntax of cp

cp [-ipr] *file1* [*file2* ...] *target*

The following options can be used with the cp command:

-i   If the copy would overwrite an existing file, prompt whether the copy should be performed. (Note: this option is new with System V Release 4.)

-p   Set the date and time of last modification for the copied file to the same value as the original file. (Note: this option is new with System V Release 4.)

-r   Recursively copy all files in each named directory to the target directory. Note that *target* must be a directory name. (Note: this option is new with System V Release 4.)

Command Syntax of ln

ln [-fns] *oldname newname*
ln [-fns] *file1* [*file2* ...] *dirname*

The following options can be used with the ln command:

-f   *Force.* Suppresses any error message if the link cannot be created. The ln command attempts to create the link even if ownership or access permissions would appear to be violated.

-n   Do not overwrite an existing file. (Note: this option is new with System V Release 4.)

-s   Create a symbolic link. When this option is specified—as *file1*, *file2*, and so on—it can name directories as well as files. (Note: this option is new with System V Release 4.)

Command Syntax of mv

mv [-fi] *file1* [*file2* ...] *target*

The following options can be used with the mv command:

-f   *Force.* Suppresses any error message if the move cannot be performed. The mv command attempts to rename or copy each named file even when ownership or access permissions would appear to be violated.

-i   Prompt for permission to overwrite an existing file. (Note: this option is new with System V Release 4.)

2

Command Syntax of rm

rm [-fi] *file* ...
rm [-rfi] *dirname* ... [*file* ...]

The following options can be used with the rm command:

-f   *Force.* No error message will be generated even if a named file cannot be removed. The rm command will attempt to remove the file even if ownership or access permissions would appear to be violated.

-i   Prompt for permission to overwrite an existing file. (Note: this option is new with System V Release 4.)

-r   Recursively remove all files and the directory for each named *dirname*. Use this option when you want to remove the directory and its files and the rmdir command fails because the directory is not empty.

Command Syntax of mkdir

mkdir [-m *mode*] [-p] *dirname* ...

The following options can be used with the mkdir command:

-m   Create a directory with the access permissions specified by *mode*. Specify *mode* in the same format as the *mode* operand of the chmod command. (Note: this option is new with System V Release 4.)

-p   Create all missing directories in each *dirname* specified. Without the -p option, mkdir will create only a named directory if all higher-level directories exist. (Note: this option is new with System V Release 4.)

2

Command Syntax of `rmdir`

`rmdir [ -ps ] dirname ...`

The following options can be used with the `rmdir` command:

-p   Use the -p option to remove not only the named directory but also all parent directories of *dirname* that are empty after the removal of *dirname*. Use `rm` to delete occupied directories. (Note: this option is new with System V Release 4.)

-s   Suppress error messages about occupied directories created by the -p option. (Note: this option is new with System V Release 4.)

The first two command formats create "hard" links, which means the directory entry contains an actual pointer to the i-node of the file. Hard links cannot cross file systems.

When to Use `ln` Rather Than `cp`

Use `ln` rather than `cp` whenever:

• The new copy is in the same file system as the original file.

• You want any change to the original file to appear in the copied file as well.

Using `ln` whenever possible saves considerable disk space because `ln` only creates a new directory entry.

When the -s option is specified, the `ln` command creates a *symbolic* link. A symbolic link is an actual file rather than just a directory entry. The file created by the symbolic link contains the path name of *oldname*. When UNIX tries to open *newname*, it recognizes that *newname* is a symbolic link file and reads the path name stored in the symbolic link file. UNIX then restarts the open procedure with the new path name. Symbolic links are available in BSD UNIX and in System V Release 4.

The -s option allows you to create an alias for a directory, and is especially handy for that reason.

For example, by using symbolic links you can create an abbreviation for the directory where `uucp` stores your electronic mail, as follows:

```
ln -s /usr/spool/uucppublic/receive/jjv/seismo seismo
```

After executing this command, you can display the contents of your E-mail directory with the simple command ls seismo.

The mv Command

Use the mv command to rename a file or to move it to another directory.

The first form simply renames a file if both *oldname* and *newname* are file names in the same directory, as in the following examples:

```
mv a.out users
```

```
mv bin/a.out bin/users
```

If *oldname* and *newname* are in different directories, the *oldname* file is first copied to the new location, then removed from the old location. (If the copy step fails, the remove step is skipped.) For example, the following command moves a file from one directory to another:

```
$ mv src/headers/main.h tmp/new.h
```

Use the second form to move a group of files into a directory. This form also is useful when moving only one file. For example:

```
$ mv /usr/spool/uucppublic/receive/jjv/seismo/main.c .
```

moves the file main.c from the electronic mail directory into the current directory.

The mv command refuses to move a file if the move would replace a file that already exists *and* the user does not have write permission. The -f option forces mv to attempt the move anyway and to be quiet if the move is unsuccessful.

The rm Command

Use the rm (*remove*) command to decrement the number of links for each named file by one. If the number of links for a file becomes zero, the file is physically removed.

This strange phraseology is caused by the UNIX support of aliases for files, called *links*. A file can be known by more than one name, either in the same directory or in different directories (see the ln command). The rm command removes only the directory entry for each file name given. As long as the file continues to be referenced by other names, it continues to exist. Only when all names of a file have been removed is it actually deleted.

2

To tell whether an rm command will actually delete a file, use ls -l to display the link count for the file. If the link count is greater than one, rm only deletes one of the file's names. If the link count is one, both the file's name and the file itself are removed.

Normally, the rm command removes only files. You can specify the -r option to cause rm to recursively remove files from a named directory until the directory is empty, and then to remove the directory itself. For example, if /usr/spool/uucppublic is a directory, the command

```
$ rm -r /usr/spool/uucppublic
```

first removes all subdirectories and files in uucppublic, and then removes the uucppublic directory itself. Notice that the directory and its files are removed without user confirmation.

Use the -i option to cause rm to prompt you before removing files. You can use this option to selectively remove files from a directory, as in the following example:

```
$ rm -i *
bin is a directory
etc is a directory
mbox? y
junk? y
birthdays: n
tmp is a directory
```

In this example, rm refused to remove bin, etc, and tmp because these are directories. (You could have used the options -ir to remove directories as well as files.) The command prompted for each of the files: mbox, junk, and birthdays. The response of y caused the mbox and junk files to be removed, and the response n caused the birthdays file to be retained.

The -f option causes rm to attempt to remove a file even if the file is protected (by having another user's name as its owner, for example). When the -f option is specified, the rm command is silent about unsuccessful removes.

The mkdir Command

Use the mkdir command to create one or more new directories.

The command processes its arguments in a left-to-right order. This means you can create a new directory and add several subdirectories to the new directory all in one command, as in the following example:

```
$ mkdir memos memos/marge memos/mitch memos/myself
```

If you specify a simple file name, the command creates a new directory with that name in the current directory. If you specify a path name, the command creates a new directory with the ending file name in the given directory path. For example, the command:

```
$ mkdir src/fortran/headers
```

creates a directory named `headers` in `src/fortran`. If `src/fortran` does not already exist, or is not a directory, `mkdir` issues an error message to the file descriptor assigned to standard error, which, if not redirected, results in display of the message at your terminal.

The `mkdir` command creates only one directory for each argument; it does not create all the missing parts of a path. In the previous example, both `src` and `src/fortran` must exist. If only `src` exists, the `mkdir` command does not create `src/fortran` and fails when trying to create headers in the non-existent `src/fortran` directory.

The `rmdir` Command

Use `rmdir` to remove an empty directory. A directory is considered empty when it only contains the two entries . (dot) and .. (dot dot).

If a directory is not empty, you must first use `rm` to remove all files contained in the directory, and `rmdir` to remove any subdirectories in the directory. Or, you can use `rm  -r` to do it all for you.

Text Editing

You use text editors to modify the contents of line-formatted text files. UNIX provides a number of text editors. This section identifies the editors most commonly available.

The Ed Editor

The Ed editor is the oldest of all UNIX text editors and is available on all UNIX systems. Ed is called a *line editor*, meaning it operates strictly in teletype mode. Although most programmers consider it unpleasant to use, you should know something about Ed because it is always available and quick for small editing jobs.

The following is a sample terminal session with the Ed editor (line numbers have been added to facilitate discussion):

```
1    $ ed /etc/passwd
2    4125
3    /jjv
4    jjv:x:104:7:John Valley:/u/jjv:/bin/sh
5    s/sh$/ksh
6    jjv:x:104:7:John Valley:/u/jjv:/bin/ksh
7    $a
8    bill::137:4:Bill Smith:/u/bill:/bin/csh
9    .
10   w
11   4165
12   q
13   $
```

Table 2.2 explains this rather cryptic dialog.

Table 2.2. Explanation of the sample editing session with Ed.

Line	Action
1	Invoke the Ed editor on the /etc/passwd file
2	Ed reports the number of bytes in the file
3	Search for a line containing the string jjv
4	Ed prints the line it found
5	Change the string sh at the end of the line to ksh
6	Ed shows the line after the change
7	Add a newline at the end of the file
8	Text of the newline
9	Tell Ed to end the insertion of lines
10	Tell Ed to write back the changed file
11	Ed shows the number of bytes written
12	Tell Ed to quit
13	Prompt for the next command

You can find more information about the Ed editor in the book *UNIX System V Bible—Commands and Utilities* by Prata and Martin (Que; 1987; ISBN 0-672-22562-x).

The Vi Editor

The Vi editor was the first full-screen editor developed for UNIX. The Vi editor is an extended version of Ed that contains a visual mode; you can use Vi either as a line editor by entering the `ex` command, or as a full-screen editor by entering the `vi` command.

> **Note**: You can find an introduction to the Vi editor in the book *UNIX Step-by-Step* by Ben Smith (SAMS, 1990; ISBN 0-672-48469-2).

The Vi editor is called a *modal editor* because it has two modes: a *control mode*, in which the keyboard keys correspond to editor commands; and an *input mode*, where everything you type is entered as text into the file. Some programmers find it awkward to continually shift between command and input mode and find the editor commands cryptic and difficult to remember. Others find Vi fast and convenient to use.

When you approach Vi, you must do so with an open mind and a willingness to learn, as well as much patience. It can take several weeks to become proficient with it. Even if you do not like Vi, you should make an effort to become acquainted with it because it is the most widely available full-screen editor.

The Emacs Editor

The Emacs editor is newer than Vi. Its proponents think Emacs is both more powerful than Vi, and more intuitive. Emacs is not, however, as widely available as Vi, so even if it is your favorite editor, you should not depend on it completely.

> **Note:** You can find an introduction to the Emacs editor in the book *UNIX Step-by-Step* by Ben Smith (SAMS, 1990; ISBN 0-672-48469-2).

The Emacs editor has only one mode. You use control keys and escape key sequences to move your cursor around the screen and the file. To enter data, just type. The problem with Emacs, as with Vi, is that there are a great many control keys and escape sequences to remember, and it takes time to become proficient with it. However, if you are just beginning to learn UNIX, you might find you can survive with Emacs knowing only a small repertoire of commands. This helps you get some work done even if you have to look up almost everything in manuals.

Text Processing

UNIX provides many tools for processing *text*—that is, files consisting of readable characters divided into lines. UNIX text processing tools provide ways to modify files, to change the format of files, and to extract or process information stored in text files.

There is not enough room to describe these tools in detail. Table 2.3 describes the more useful text processing commands. When you have work that seems similar to the description of one of these commands, check your system documentation to see whether the command serves your purpose.

Print Spooling

Unless you have a UNIX system all to yourself or can reserve a printer for your own exclusive use, you must share the system's printers with other folks. UNIX includes a *print spooling* facility that lets users submit work for printing, and that sends submitted work to the printer one file at a time. The spooling facility owns the printer and uses it to print output that has been temporarily stored on disk.

When you want to send output to the printer, you must actually send it to the printer spooling facility. The spooling facility stores your output until the printer is idle, then prints your output.

One way to send output to a printer is to use the lp command to name the files you want printed. The following is an example of how you can use the lp command to obtain hard copy printout of all files in the current directory:

```
$ lp *
```

You might prefer to use pr to generate print files because the pr command automatically breaks the output at page boundaries, and titles and numbers each page; the lp command just prints the file as it appears, printing over the perforation between pages if necessary.

Table 2.3. Frequently used text processing commands.

Command	Use
awk	Write a report using a general file-processing language
cmp	Compare two files for equality
cut	Eliminate columns or fields from a file
diff	Display the differences between a pair of files
fgrep	Find all lines in a file containing any one of several words
grep	Find all lines in a file containing a string pattern
nroff	Generate a document for a line printer
paste	Convert two or more files into a single multicolumn file
pr	Print a formatted listing of a file Expand tab characters Convert a single-column to a multicolumn list
sed	Change all occurrences of a string to another string Delete all lines containing a specified string Select or list one or more lines or line ranges from a file Delete selected lines or line ranges from a file
sort	Sort a file by selected columns or fields
spell	Check a file for spelling errors
split	Split a file into m files of n lines each
tail	Display the last few lines of a file
troff	Generate a document for a photo typesetter
uniq	Find duplicated or unique lines in a file
wc	Count the number of words, lines, and characters in a group of files

In addition to the lp command you use to send output to the printer, there are two other commands you might find useful.

You can use the lpstat command to show which of your files have not yet been printed, or what printers are available, or the queue of work currently pending for a printer.

The cancel command discards a file that has been queued but for which printing has not yet started. Use the cancel command when you decide you do not want to print a file you previously have spooled with the lp command.

Electronic Mail

UNIX is especially good at exchanging messages between people. Using the correct facility, you can send messages to others, read messages others have sent to you, log into remote UNIX systems, and even circulate messages and files over long-distance networks of many computer systems.

The `mail` Command

The `mail` command is the basic method for exchanging mail. To send a message to someone else, simply type:

```
$ mail george
```

and then type your message. When you press ^d, your typed message is stored in the system for the user george to retrieve later. To read your own mail, just type:

```
$ mail
```

Each message is displayed individually. You then can save, keep, or delete each message after viewing it.

You also can use the `mail` command to send a message to a user on a remote system. Suppose you want to send a message to user bunny, and bunny is located on a remote system named zoo. Remote systems are those located in another room, town, or state. Suppose, also, you have previously prepared your message by using a text editor and you want the `mail` command to get the message from the file msg rather than from your keyboard. The following command does the job:

```
$ mail zoo!bunny < msg
```

What do you do if your system cannot reach the machine zoo directly from your own machine, but your system can reach zoo from another system, called psycho, which is reachable from your system? (Although these names are fictitious, administrators really do give their machines such crazy names.) Then use forwarding, as in the following example:

```
$ mail psycho!zoo!bunny
```

Even when mail is sent to you from remote locations, possibly even by complicated paths that use forwarding, you still read your own mail by entering the command `mail` with no arguments.

The `mailx` Command

The `mail` command is more than adequate for sending mail to other people, but it is a poor facility for reading mail.

The `mailx` command is an extended version of `mail` that provides you more flexibility for reading mail. You can, for example, review the list of messages waiting for you, select one you want to read, display the message by using a full-screen pager or your favorite editor, reply to the message after viewing it, and save the message in a special folder for later reference.

Note: See *UNIX System V Bible: Commands and Utilities* by Prata and Martin (SAMS, 1987; ISBN 0-672-22562-X) for more information on `mailx`.

Several options control the way the `mailx` command works. You can select the options you prefer to use and set them up in a file called `.mailrc`. You also should set the environment variables `VISUAL`, `EDITOR`, and `PAGER` to describe the commands you prefer to use for composing and displaying messages.

The `uucp` Command

Sometimes you want to transfer files between yourself and another user. You can use the `mail` command to send or receive a text file, but you definitely cannot use it to send binary files or a compressed version of a text file. To send binary files, you must use the `uucp` command.

The `uucp` command, named for the phrase *UNIX-to-UNIX copy*, has syntax much like the `cp` command:

Command Syntax of `uucp`

`uucp [ -r ] [ -c ] file1 [ file2 ... ] dir`

For `file1`, `file2`, and so on, specify the files to be sent. For `dir`, specify the directory on the receiving system where the files are to be stored.

Notice that you cannot transmit files to multiple receiving directories with a single `uucp` command. Each invocation of `uucp` transmits one or more files from the local or remote system to a single directory on the local or remote system.

The direction in which file transfer occurs is determined by the format of the *dir* path name. If it names a directory on the local system, then the files *file1*, *file2*, and so on are transferred to the local system. If *dir* names a directory on a remote system, then the files *file1*, *file2*, and so on are transferred to the remote system.

Each file name can specify a file on the local system or on any accessible remote system. To specify a file located on a remote system, you must identify the file by giving the remote system name followed by the path name of the file *on that system*. The general format of a file name (*file1*, *file2*, and so on) on the uucp command is

```
system![system!...]path
```

The *bang* character (!) must be used to separate system names from the final path name. If you give more than one system name, the file will be accessed by transferring the file through each of the named systems in turn (this is called *forwarding*). For example, the file name

```
seismo!zoo!/usr/spool/uucppublic/Xlib/Xlib.h
```

names a file Xlib.h located in the directory /usr/spool/uucppublic/Xlib on the remote system zoo. System zoo is not, however, directly reachable from the local system, so the file Xlib.h must first be transferred from system zoo to system seismo before it can then be transferred to your own system.

Each of the files named as *file1*, *file2*, ... on the uucp command can originate at a different system (local or remote), and the destination directory, *dir*, can be the same or different from any of the other files. With the uucp command, you can gather three files from three different remote systems and transfer the three files to a directory on a fourth system. None of the files have to originate from or be delivered to your own local system!

Note: The path name you give as *dir* (the receiving directory) has to end with a slash to indicate that it is a directory name. If you omit the slash, the uucp command might merge all the transmitted files into one file at the receiving system, store only one of the transmitted files, or behave in other strange and unpredictable ways.

For security reasons you normally cannot send a file directly to another user; instead, you must send it to a public directory specially reserved for intersystem communication. The correct naming convention for sending a file to a remote user is to send the file to

```
system!/usr/spool/uucppublic/receive/user/fromsys/
```

where *system* is the name of the remote system where the files are to be sent, *user* is the login name of the user to whom you are sending the files, and *fromsys* is your system's name.

Because usr/spool/uucppublic is the standard directory name for holding received directory files, the uucp command provides the abbreviation ~ for this portion of the file name. You can shorten the target directory name to system!~/receive/user/fromsys.

Rather than memorizing the proper format for the receiving directory name, you can use the uuto command, as in the following example:

```
$ uuto foo.h psycho!zoo!george
```

The uuto command lets you say who you want to send the file to, rather than the directory where the file is to be stored. uuto sends the file to the directory /usr/spool/uucppublic/receive/george/mysystem.

The easy way to receive files that are sent to you with uucp is to execute the uupick command. The uupick command works much like the mail command.

Sending Files Locally

The uuto command is useful for sending files to other users on your own system. Just as before, you usually cannot send a file directly to someone else's directories; you must transmit the file to the public directory, and the receiving user then must retrieve the file from there.

To send a file locally, execute the command

```
$ uuto -m foo.h george
```

Notice that you use no "bang" sequences (*system!system!...*) when you are sending to a local user. ("Bang" is the name for the exclamation point.) The -m option causes the system to notify George by mail that he has received files in the public directory.

George can receive his files by entering the simple command

```
$ uupick
```

Calculator

The dc and bc commands provide a powerful calculator you can use for many purposes.

> **Note:** See *The UNIX System User's Manual* by AT&T (Prentice-Hall, 1986; ISBN 0-13-938242-9) for more information on dc and bc.

The dc command uses Reverse Polish Notation—that is, it works like an old-fashioned calculator where first you enter the two operands, then press an operator key. The dc command is most useful for adding a column of figures, for example:

```
$ dc
c
2k
45.71
22.04+
7.16+
0.78+
p
75.69
^d
```

The c order tells dc to clear its registers. The 2k order tells dc to use two-place decimals. From there on, you enter a number and tell dc to add it in to the running result. The p order tells dc to print its register, but does not clear the register; you can use this fact to get subtotals. To exit dc, enter the EOF key sequence, usually ⌃d.

The bc command is no more powerful than dc, but easier to use for complex arithmetic. To use bc, you enter formulas. For programmers, the bc command is handy for its ability to convert between number bases. For example, to convert the hex number 3dc to decimal, use the following scenario:

```
$ bc
ibase=16
3DC
988
q
$
```

The ibase=16 line tells bc to use base-16 (hexadecimal) for its input. By default, both the input and output bases are 10.

File Finder

The ability to highlight the relationship of files by storing them in a common directory is unquestionably a wonderful feature of UNIX. Over time, an experienced user's home directory becomes a complicated structure of directories within directories containing hundreds or thousands of files.

What do you do when you forget where a file is located? You can always ask the UNIX file finder to locate it for you.

The `find` command searches a set of directories for files matching a set of criteria. The syntax of the command is fairly complicated, to allow a wide variety of search techniques.

2

> **Note:** For all the details, see *UNIX System V Bible: Commands and Utilities* by Prata and Martin (SAMS, 1987; ISBN 0-672-22562-X).

The simplest way to use `find` is to search a high-level directory for any occurrence of a file name. The following command searches all the directories under the home directory for the file name `chap01`:

```
$ find /u/jjv -name chap01 -print
```

You also can use wild cards in the name, but you want the `find` command to interpret the wild cards, not the shell, so you must quote a search parameter (quoting and wild cards are covered in Chapter 3).

If, rather than displaying the names of the files it finds, you would like a command to be executed for each file, you can use the `-exec` option. For example, the command

```
$ find memos notes -name 'chap*' -exec mv {} /u/jjv/doc \;
```

moves each located file into the directory `/u/jjv/doc`. Notice this example searches two directories, `memos` and `notes`. The special term `{}` is a placeholder that is replaced with the name of each file located. The ending, `\;` is a necessary delimiter to mark the end of the command to be executed.

Summary

In this chapter you looked briefly at the most commonly used parts of UNIX.

The section "The Shell" introduced the concept of a shell and explained that you can choose among at least two and possibly as many as three different shells as your UNIX command environment. The job of the shell is to read your commands, to interpret them into a series of basic system actions, and then to execute those actions. Your choice of shell determines the command language you must use, because the language supported by the sh, csh, and ksh shells differs from one another.

The section on "File Management" introduced you to the UNIX file system. Because the main purpose of a computer is to store and manipulate data, it is no exaggeration to say that its file system is the most important facet of the UNIX operating system. The UNIX file system is exemplified by its simplistic file structure, and by its organization of files into directories. Because UNIX is a multiuser system, interaction with files is always influenced by access permissions that govern your right to create, read, modify, and delete files.

The section on "Text Editors" provided an overview of commonly available UNIX text editors. You use a text editor to create and modify files for processing by UNIX commands. Because one of your earliest decisions as a UNIX user is to select a text editor and learn its operation, this section attempts to give you enough information to choose between the alternatives available to you.

The section on "Text Processing" intended to show you there are many commands to assist you in processing your files. Although some applications are sufficiently sophisticated that you must use a specialized program to do the file processing, many of the jobs you will want to do can be done with the existing UNIX commands. After reading this section, you should have some understanding of the kinds of file processing you can do with the existing UNIX commands.

The section on "Print Spooling" intended to give you an introduction to the subject of printing files. Because UNIX is a multiuser system, you usually will have to share the system's printer with other users. You will rarely be permitted to send information directly to a printer. Rather, you must use a system-wide printing service called lp that temporarily saves your printed information until a printer is available to print it. Your primary interface to the system printer service is the lp command.

The section on "Electronic Mail Service" provided an introduction to the complicated topic of exchanging information among UNIX users. The mail, mailx, and uucp commands provide ways to send files and messages to other users on your own system, as well as to users located on other systems that are connected by modem to your system. They also provide ways for you to retrieve and view messages and files that others have sent to you.

The sections on "Personal Calendar," "Calculator," and "File Finder" introduced you to some common productivity tools. Because UNIX is a personal computing system, allowing you to interact directly with the computer through a terminal, many people have found that the system can help manage their work in ways outside the traditional data processing framework. These personal productivity tools help you with commonplace jobs.

Now that you have some picture of the overall structure of UNIX and how to go about basic tasks, it's time to delve into the real subject of this book: the use of the UNIX shells. The shell is a language that uses the basic system commands as its verbs and operators. Trying to study the shell without first gaining some insight into UNIX commands would be like trying to learn a language without learning the verbs. Now that you've seen the verbs, you should look at the rest of the language.

2

Shell Basics

 n this chapter you will look at the basic concepts of the Bourne and Korn shells. These basic concepts enable you to understand command formats, to enter commands that say what you mean, and to interpret the results.

How a Command Is Interpreted

Every UNIX shell must perform three functions:

- *Read* the next line from the shell input file or command line

- *Analyze* the content of the line

- *Execute* the command(s) described by the input line

The *read* step is normally straightforward; its purpose is to acquire the raw text of the next command you want to be executed. The shell allows you to submit input from a file, from your terminal, or from any other source. How you specify the shell's input source and what it might be are determined by the shell itself.

3

The *analyze* step can be simple and straightforward. At a minimum, the shell must break the line into a series of words (called *parsing* the line). One of these words determines which command the shell will execute. Other words might be information you want passed to the command, such as file names and options. Depending on the sophistication of the shell, other words in the input line might control the manner in which the shell executes the command.

The *execute* step is where the action implied by the command you entered actually occurs. The shell must comply with strict UNIX requirements when invoking a command. Among other things, these indicate that the shell must provide a list of words to be passed to the command. The first word is the command name, and it tells UNIX which command to load. Any remaining words are passed to the command as data (these data words are called *arguments,* a term borrowed from mathematics). It is important to notice that bringing the command program into memory and starting it up are functions of the UNIX operating system, not the shell. The shell simply has to issue a *request* that supplies the required command name and argument words. The words supplied by the shell are normally those it extracted from your command line in the *analyze* step.

The simplest of all possible shells would pass every word you typed to UNIX. Although this process would get the job done, it would not provide you much flexibility. In fact, there are many useful services of the UNIX operating system you couldn't use if the shell did nothing more. All the UNIX shells provide a sophisticated command language that allow you do much more than execute commands.

To allow you to specify *how* to execute a command, the shell must recognize text in your commands that are actually instructions to the shell. Such instruction text have to be stripped from the command line before the command is executed. As a result, the list of words passed to the command is often not identical to the list of words you typed in your original command line.

As an example of how shell commands can differ from executed commands, consider the following Bourne shell command:

```
mail ted < message
```

This command contains four words: `mail`, `ted`, `<`, and `message`. All the UNIX shells allow you to separate words with one or more space characters. These spaces, also called *white spaces*, have a special meaning to the shell. They serve as word separators and are stripped from your input line before the command is invoked. After the *analyze* step, the shell has a list of four words comprising your original command, and the white space is gone.

The first two words constitute the command. The first word (`mail`) is the command name according to the UNIX convention. The second word (`ted`) is passed to the `mail` command as an argument. The shell has no idea what the `ted` argument means, but the `mail` command interprets its arguments as the log-in names of people to whom you want to mail a message.

The third word (<) is a shell *metacharacter* similar to the spaces. (A *metacharacter* is a character that has a special meaning assigned to it by the shell; other characters have no special meaning and stand for themselves.) This particular word tells the shell that the input to the `mail` command is to be taken from a file rather than from your terminal. The fourth word (`message`) tells the shell which file to use as the input for the `mail` command. The `message` word is not a metacharacter, but it still has special meaning to the shell because it follows the < symbol.

During the *analyze* step, the Bourne shell identifies the < character as a special symbol and arranges to have the `mail` command read the contents of the file called `messages`. After having made these arrangements, the shell discards both the < and `message` words and passes what's left to UNIX as the command to be executed (in this case, the two words `mail` and `ted`).

As you learn more about the UNIX shells, you will discover there are many special words and symbols you can type on the command line that actually control the behavior of the shell; these are stripped from the command line during the *analyze* step so the final list of words passed to the command contains only the command name and a list of arguments.

The shell supports many different kinds of special symbols on the command line. Some of these are:

- *Redirection* symbols that alter the default input source or output destination of a command.

- *Variable* symbols to which you can assign values—the shell substitutes the *value* of a variable symbol into the final command and deletes the original variable symbol name.

- *Command substitution,* where one or more arguments in the final command are actually the output of another command or group of commands.

- *Operators,* which allow you to combine several commands into a compound command that behaves differently than any of the individual commands taken alone.

Whenever you prepare a command for the shell, you will have to keep in mind the fact that the line you type often looks different when finally executed. In this chapter you will learn the rules and conventions for writing shell commands as well as writing the underlying basic UNIX commands.

The Standard UNIX Command Format

As mentioned in the previous section, the shell provides many features you can use to simplify command entry and to control the way in which a command is executed. After the shell has performed all substitutions, expansions, and redirections, a line of raw text remains that actually is executed. The shell does not understand the commands it ultimately executes, so you must. It is the syntax of the command line *as seen by the command itself* you examine in this section.

In the early days of UNIX, developers had no rigorous definition for the format of commands. In recent years, a preferred command line format has begun to emerge. This format, which I call the *standard* command format, is defined by the `getopt` command and C library function. Many of the older commands are still in use, however, so you find exceptions to these rules.

Words

The first step the shell performs in processing a command is to separate the command line into a series of words. It does this by scanning the line for *white space* characters. Blanks and tabs count as white space characters. Everything between white space characters is saved as a word of the command line. The white space characters themselves are discarded.

The first word of a command line (other than environment variable definitions and redirections; see the section "Simple Commands" later in this chapter) is always taken as the command *name*. The remaining words of the line are collectively called command *arguments*. A special type of argument, called an *option*, is recognized whenever the word begins with a hyphen (-).

The following sections describe the rules for writing command names, options, and arguments. In these sections, the word *argument* always refers to words not having a leading hyphen. In general, the term *argument* might refer to any word following the command name.

The Command Name

The command name is normally the first word of the command line. A command name is like a verb, because it tells the computer to do something. UNIX command names are often short, so you can type them quickly. Most names are mnemonics so you can easily remember them. Unfortunately, the meaning of many standard UNIX command names is not obvious due to their shortness.

Standard UNIX Command Format

verb -options arguments

The *verb* is the command name. It might be

- a simple word (set, ls, a.out)
- a path name (/bin/ls, ./who)
- a special symbol (:, #, .)

Command *options* are arguments that begin with a hyphen (-) and contain one or more *flags*, each consisting of a single letter. Each flag modifies the command's behavior in a specific way defined by the command. You decide which, if any, flags you want to specify on a command. An *option* might be:

- A single flag: ls -l -t
  Both options -l and -t are specified.
- Compound flags: ls -lt
  Both options -l and -t are specified.
- Flag with value: -Iinclude or -I include
  The name include is supplied to the command as the value of option -I. The value can be combined with the flag or stand as the next complete word.

Command *arguments* provide information to the command which it might require to do its job. Some commands require no arguments, others require a fixed number of arguments, and still others might take a variable number of arguments.

Example: diff -b *file1 file2*

File *file1* is compared to *file2* and a list of differences is printed. Due to option -b, variations in word spacing between the two files are ignored.

A command name is just a file name. The shell takes the first word of the command line and tries to find a file with that name. If the shell can find the file, and the file is marked executable, then the shell loads and runs the program in the file, passing the rest of the command line to the program.

Because the command name is just a file name to the shell, you can write a command name in any form that is valid for a file name. A full path name, such as /usr/games/dungeon, causes the shell to immediately run that specific file. A relative path name, such as ./dungeon or ../games/dungeon, also forces the shell to look in the named directory (. or ../games respectively) for the program file. A completely unanchored file name, such as games/dungeon or dungeon, forces the shell to search for the file in all the directories the shell knows about.

Command Options

Many UNIX commands support a number of command-line options that you can use to vary what the command does. By providing options, the command becomes more flexible, allowing you to tailor its actions to suit your needs.

Command-line options are never *required*; they are called options because you can choose to include them or omit them from the command.

In its most basic form, a command-line option is a separate word starting with a hyphen (-) and followed by a single character, usually a letter (*a* through *z* or *A* through *Z*). The option must be entered after the command name and must be separated from the command name by one or more white space characters. All command options should be entered before any of the command arguments.

For example, the command ls -l /bin lists the contents of the /bin directory in long form, one line per file. Without the -l option, the command lists only file names. The basic purpose of the ls command is to list the contents of directories. There are many different ways to format the listing, so the ls command provides options to enable you to select the listing format that most closely suits your needs.

When you want to enter several options on one command, you can either list them separately, as follows:

```
$ ls -l -a /bin
```

or combine the option letters into one word, like this:

```
$ ls -la /bin
```

The ability to combine option letters this way saves you time when typing the command. Unfortunately, some UNIX commands do not allow combined options, and the documentation is often vague on this point. You should generally assume that a command supports combined options unless its documentation specifically states otherwise.

Sometimes, a command option is provided as a way to give the command extra information. In such cases, the option requires you to specify a value after the option letter. A typical example is provided by the cut command:

```
$ cut -d: -f1,5 /etc/passwd
```

which prints the first and fifth fields of each line of the system password file.

The -d option specifies which character separates fields in each line of the file: The - introduces the option; the d marks this as the *delimiter* option; and the : is the value of the option—in this case, the character that separates fields in the input data. The option -f1,5 tells the cut command which fields of the input line are to be copied to output.

Notice the -d and -f options provide information to the command; namely, how fields are separated, and which fields to cut from the input line to yield the output lines.

Some commands permit you to enter an option and its option value as separate words. The standard command format requires new commands to support separated values; however, many older commands such as cut do not.

Command Arguments

Most commands use *arguments* to identify the files it's to work with, although some commands can use arguments for other purposes. The standard command format requires arguments to come after all options. Some commands, though, allow or even require options and arguments to be intermixed, so this is not a hard and fast rule. Arguments must be separated from each other and from the preceding command name and options by white space.

The Bourne and Korn shells allow a large number of arguments on a command, but there is a limit. If you try to put too many options and arguments on one command line, UNIX prints an error message and ignores the command.

Syntactically, arguments differ from options only by the leading hyphen. Because a leading hyphen signifies an option, you run into trouble if you try to use a file name beginning with a hyphen. The command ls -l always means you want a long listing of the current directory (option -l), never that you want the ls command to show the file named -l.

The Exit Value

Every UNIX command returns a numeric value to the shell. This value, called an *exit value*, indicates whether the command successfully performed the function you expected. If the exit value is zero, then no problems or errors occurred. If the exit value is any other number (from −128 to +127 inclusive), then the command partially or completely failed.

3

Sample Command

$ `make -n -f unix.mk less SHELL=/bin/sh`

make   is the name of the command.

-n   is the *no-execute* option; it restricts make to checking the
            syntax of its input.

-f   is the *file name* option; it tells make where to read its input
            from.

unix.mk   is the *value* of the -f option, in this case the name of the
            file that make should read. The make command does not
            mistake this option value as an argument because the
            command requires the -f option to be followed by a value.

less   is the first *argument*. It instructs make to build the program
            called *less* from its source code.

SHELL=/bin/sh
            is the second *argument*. Although not a file name, it is an
            argument form that the make command understands.

Often the exit value, if nonzero, indicates the nature of the problem.
For example, 1 might indicate an invalid option, and 2 might indicate a file
could not be opened. For many commands, though, no special significance
can be attached to a particular nonzero exit value. In all cases, the *meaning*
of an exit value is defined by the command that returned it, not by the shell.

Simple Commands

The most basic operation you can do with the shell is to execute a *simple
command*. The term *simple command* has a meaning special to the shell; it
refers to a single program call, possibly with options and arguments and
possibly with redirections, but not combined with any other command.
Simple commands are the basic building blocks of all shell statements.

The following are examples of simple commands:

```
$ pwd
$
$ cat myfile
$
$ echo "$0: error in `basename \`pwd\``" >&2
$
$ make -nd -f - 2>/dev/null </dev/null
```

As you can see, a simple command can actually be rather complex. In this chapter, you will look at the rules for forming simple commands.

Although you can enter commands literally as they are to be executed, the shell supports a much richer expression called *simple commands* that offers many useful features. The syntax of a simple command is as follows. You should notice that, in the following syntax description, all parts of a simple command can be omitted. This simply means that the shell will accept (and ignore) a completely blank line.

Simple Commands

`[ name=word ... ] [ word ¦ redirection ] ... [ ; ]`

Each `name=word` adds the variable `name` to the environment of the command. No white space can appear before or after the `=`. `name` must begin with an alphabetic letter or _ (underscore) and can be followed by any number of additional letters, digits, and underscore characters.

The first `word` in the command is the command name. A command name cannot be `if`, `then`, `else`, `elif`, `fi`, `for`, `while`, `until`, `do`, `done`, `case`, or `esac` unless quoted or escaped. A command does not have to contain a command name; if it does not, the Null command (see Chapter 10, "Built-In Commands") is executed by default.

A `word` is a list of one or more of the following:

A letter or digit:	`a-z, A-Z, 0-9,` or `_`
A special character:	`! @ # % - = + { } : , . /`
A *wild card*:	`* ? [expr]`
A variable:	`$name ${expr}`
A special variable:	`$? $@ $# $$ $* $-`
An escape sequence:	`\c`
A string in double quotations marks:	`"text"`
A string in single quotation marks:	`'text'`
Command substitution:	`` `command` ``

A command can contain any number of redirections (see the "Input/Output Redirection" section of this chapter). A redirection can occur as any word of the command, and is deleted before the command is executed.

The syntax of the simple command looks complicated, and it is. More than any other shell programming skill, the ability to fully use the simple command syntax distinguishes the shell expert from the beginner. In the remainder of this chapter, you will closely examine each of the syntax elements of a simple command, with the exception of variables, which are not fully discussed until Chapter 7, "Using Variables."

Regular and Special Characters

Words of a command can consist of the regular and special characters listed in the box "Simple Commands." An ASCII terminal, however, provides special characters not listed in the box. Special characters, specifically those not used as text characters (called *metacharacters*), are listed in the following box.

Shell Metacharacters

The following characters always have special meaning to the shell. They must be quoted or escaped when used as part of a command word:

$ ^ & * ( ) [ ] ; " ´ < > ? ` \

In addition, the following characters are metacharacters sometimes:

{ } when appearing by themselves
: inside a case statement
at the beginning of a word
~ at the beginning of a word (Korn shell only)
^ is not a metacharcater in the Korn Shell

These characters have a special meaning to the shell, and if written on the command line, cause the shell to take a special action. In other words, you cannot pass one of these characters through to the command you want to execute without taking special precautions. Because these characters have a symbolic meaning beyond their simple text meaning, they are called *metacharacters*. The use of some of these metacharacters is listed in the box. Others are discussed more fully in later sections of this chapter.

To use one of these characters as text (for example, as part of the file name lost+found, or in the message What is your name?) you must either *quote* or *escape* the character. Quoting and escaping are discussed in the section "Quoting" later in this chapter. If you have difficulty remembering which special characters are okay to use in text, quote or escape any character you are unsure of.

Comments

The shell allows you to add comments to your commands. Although comments are rarely used at the keyboard, they are helpful annotations in a shell program because they can be used to explain what portions of the shell program do. A shell program is a group of commands stored in a file. See Part III of this book for information about writing shell programs.

Whenever the shell sees a word beginning with #, it skips the rest of the word and the rest of the input line. The stripped words are discarded and never appear in the final command. If the first nonblank character of a line is #, then the entire line is considered a comment and is thrown away.

When added to the end of a command, a comment looks like this:

```
$ rm sample        # Remove the file "sample"
$ cp sample samp   # Now try to copy it
sample: not found
```

If you don't leave at least one blank or tab in front of the #, the shell sees the # as a regular character and not as the beginning of a comment:

```
$ rm sample#From current directory
sample#From: not found
current: not found
directory: not found
$
```

Wild Cards

If you have used MS-DOS, you're already familiar with *wild cards*, which provide a shorthand method for naming files. The UNIX shells also support wild cards. You will find using wild cards properly is essential to using UNIX effectively.

Most commands require their arguments to be the names of the files to be processed. Because most the typing you do involves entering file names, the Bourne and Korn shells provide some handy ways to abbreviate file names. The concept of abbreviated file names is similar to the joker in a deck of cards. You can write generic file names by using special *pattern* characters.

The shell replaces a word containing pattern characters with the names of all the files that match the pattern.

File Name Patterns

The Bourne and Korn shells replace a word of the command line containing any of the following *pattern-matching* characters with a sorted list of all the file names the word pattern matches:

*	Matches any string of zero or more characters
?	Matches any single character
[co]	Matches either the character c or o
[a-z]	Matches the character a, b, c, . . ., or z
[a-z0-9]	Matches any single lowercase letter or digit
[!co]	Matches any character except c or o
[!0-9]	Matches any single character except the digits

The following *tilde* sequences are recognized when they comprise a complete word, or occur at the beginning of a word followed immediately by /:

~	Replaced by the path name of your home directory
~name	Replaced by the path name of the home directory of user *name*
~+	Replaced by the path name of your current working directory
~-	Replaced by the path name of your previous working directory

---

The concept is best explained with an example. Consider the echo command, which types its command arguments. Look at the following dialog:

```
$ echo Hello there, Mr. Jones
Hello there, Mr. Jones
$
```

The command was entered with four arguments: Hello, there, Mr., and Jones. The command output that follows consists of those four words. The final line shows the shell *prompt* (see the section "Shell Prompts" at the end of this chapter).

Knowing that the echo command just types its arguments, you might find the following dialog a little confusing:

```
$ cd /usr/include
$ echo *.h
grp.h pwd.h stdarg.h stddef.h stdlib.h stdio.h time.h
$
```

Why didn't the echo command just type *.h?

The answer is that echo command never saw the argument *.h; what it saw was a list of five arguments: stdarg.h, stddef.h, and so on. (You might see a different list of file names if you try this example on your computer.) The shell *expanded* the argument *.h into a list of matching file names, in this case all file names in your current directory that begin with any sequence of characters and end with .h.

The Bourne and Korn shells permit the use of wild-card file names on *any* command. In fact, because wild card expansion is done by the shell and not by the command program, you can use wild card expansion anywhere in the command line, even where the command is not expecting file names.

Suppose you wanted to search a file for lines containing the character *. You could use the fgrep command to perform the search, as follows:

```
$ fgrep * sample.text
```

Unfortunately, the shell does not know that fgrep expects a search string in this position of the command, so the shell expands the * with all file names in the current directory. The fgrep command that is executed looks something like this:

```
$ fgrep foobar.text sample.text temp.text sample.text
```

As a result, the fgrep command searches the files sample,text, temp.text, and sample.text again for the string "foobar.text," which is certainly not what was intended.

The * Pattern

The character * is special to the Bourne and Korn shells. Beware of using the asterisk for any other purpose, because unless you take special precautions, the shell always tries to replace a word in the argument list containing * with a list of file names. To the shell, the * means "all file names that have anything in this position of the name."

Look at an example:

```
$ cd /usr/include
$ echo std*
```

```
stdarg.h stddef.h stdlib.h stdio.h
$
```

This time, only file names beginning with std were substituted for the argument std*. The asterisk doesn't take too many liberties though; file names must exactly match the pattern. From the previous example, you saw that one of the files in the /usr/include directory is stdlib.h. The following use of *, however, fails to find it:

```
$ cd /usr/include
$ echo *lib
*lib
$
```

Although the file name stdlib.h contains the characters "lib," the shell cannot match them with the pattern *lib because the pattern does not end with .h, but the file name does. Because the shell finds no file names ending in lib, it leaves the original argument unchanged, and that is what the echo command sees and types.

It is important to know that there is absolutely nothing wrong with the wild card format *lib. If you were to try the last echo command in another directory, you would get different results:

```
$ ls
glib            maclib
junk            payroll.lib
lib1            payroll.out
lib2            standard-lib
$ echo *lib
glib maclib payroll.lib standard-lib
$
```

This time all the files ending in lib were found and printed. The asterisk (*) wild card can match *any* character, including such commonly used punctuation as the hyphen (-) and the dot (.).

Notice that the shell matches the pattern character * with any number of characters, including zero, as long as the characters around * in the pattern also occur in the same positions in the file name. For example, the file names stdlib.h and stdio.h both match the pattern std* as well as the pattern std*.h. The pattern std* also would match the file name std because * can match zero characters.

If * occurs at the front of a pattern, then matching file names are selected based on the characters at the end of the pattern. The pattern *xyz selects files with names that end in xyz. The pattern *.o selects files with names that end in .o.

If * occurs at the end of a pattern, then the file names that begin with the same characters as the pattern are matched, and end characters are ignored. For example, the pattern my* matches all files having names that start with my. (Notice this handling differs from MS-DOS, where * can match either the file name or the extension, but not both. UNIX does not use file name extensions, so * can match . as well as other characters.)

If the * pattern character occurs as part of a path name—as in /usr /include/*.h—the shell searches the appropriate directories for matching file names, as in this example:

```
$ echo /usr/include/*.h
/usr/include/stdarg.h /usr/include/stddef.h ...
$
```

The line printed by echo is long indeed—too long to show on this page, because every matched file name generates a full path name as the replacement word. Notice the words substituted for a file name pattern always match the style of the pattern; if the pattern is a path name, the substituted file names are also path names.

The * pattern character can occur anywhere in a path name. Sometimes it is more useful to ask the shell to search for a middle or ending part of a path. The following example uses this technique to find all users' profiles:

```
$ echo /usr/*/.profile
/usr/barb/.profile /usr/fred/.profile /usr/jane/.profile
$
```

The use of embedded * works fine even when some of the directories searched do not contain the pattern. Thus, the shell ignores the directories /usr/lib and /usr/spool because they do not contain a file .profile.

The ? Pattern

The shell also provides a pattern character that matches only one character: the question mark (?). It matches any single character. Thus the pattern myfile.? matches any of the file names myfile.c, myfile.o, and myfile.y. The pattern myfile.? does not match myfile.sh because the pattern provides for only one arbitrary character after myfile., and myfile.sh has two. The pattern myfile.?h would match myfile.gh and myfile.1h as well as myfile.sh.

File-name matching has nothing to do with dot characters in the file name. Patterns work as well with file names containing no dot character. The pattern file? matches the file names file1 and fileb as well as file. because 1, b, and . are all acceptable matches for ?.

You also can string two or more ? pattern characters to mean any *two* or any *three* characters. For example, file?? matches fileAA, fileAB, fileCC, and file.x, where AA, AB, CC, and .x are all matches of ??.

Stringing several ? pattern characters together can give quite different results from the * pattern character. If your current directory contains the files

```
foo.1
foo.1a
foo.2
```

the pattern foo.?? matches only the file name foo.1a, whereas the pattern foo.* matches all three file names.

The [. . .] Pattern

When you get used to using file name shorthand on commands, having to enter long lists of file names becomes irritating. Thus, over the years, programmers have demanded more and more pattern-matching support from the shell. When you feel comfortable with using * and ?, you might want to try the [. . .] pattern.

The [. . .] pattern is written as a set of characters enclosed in brackets. The [. . .] pattern can match only *one* character in the file name, but the character matched can be any of those listed between the brackets.

For example, the argument myfile.[co] matches the two file names myfile.c and myfile.o. How convenient to be able to name two files precisely using only three extra characters. This kind of abbreviation is handy when removing files, as in the following example:

```
$ rm myfile.[co]
```

which removes both myfile.c and myfile.o.

This feature gets better. Suppose you want to print only the three files, foo1, foo2, and foo3, out of the list of files in your current directory. The command

```
$ lp foo[123]
```

does the trick. If you want to print all files starting with foo and ending in a lowercase alphabetic letter, you might think the following is the shortest command you can write:

```
$ lp foo[abcdefghijklmnopqrstuvwxyz]
```

Not so. You can use a character *range*, as in the following example:

```
$ lp foo[a-z]
```

which prints files in the series fooa, foob, fooc, ..., fooz.

When using a range, you type the beginning and ending characters of the range and separate them with a hyphen. To do this, you must know how the letters, numbers, and special characters are assigned to the ASCII character set. If you do not have such a table, you can always play it safe and list multiple ranges between the [ ] that you know works, as in the following example:

```
$ lp file[2-5c-m.,]
```

which matches `file2` through `file5`, `filec` through `filem`, as well as the two cases `file.` and `file,`, which are not part of a range.

Suppose you want to print all `file.x` except `file.c` and `file.o`. Is there a way to do that?

Sure. Use the *not* sign, as follows:

```
$ lp file.[!co]
```

to say *all files beginning with* `file.` *but not ending with* c *or* o. This technique also works with ranges; for example, `file[!2-5]` matches all file names starting with `file` and followed by any single character except *2, 3, 4,* or *5.*

Multiple Patterns

You can use more than one pattern character in a file name, and you can mix them any way you want. Consider the following examples:

Pattern	Matches These File Names	But Not These
abc*.*	abc1.h abc.ghk abc.ll.x	abc abcdef
junk	junk junk1 oldjunk.c	jink lotajun unk123
file*.?	file.c file241.o	file1.ly fileblock
file[123]*	file1 file20 file34.c	file file407

Another useful way to generate more complicated patterns is to use more than one pattern word in the command. You might overlook this simple strategy if you try too hard to do everything with one pattern. Consider the problem of listing all the program source files in a directory. Typically, these consist of files ending in `.c`, `.h`, `.l`, `.y`, and `.sh`, as well as a file called `makefile`. This combination cannot be represented with a single pattern, but the command

```
$ ls *.[chly] *.sh makefile
```

does the job nicely.

Tilde Expansion

The Korn shell adds a welcome extension to the wild card facilities of the Bourne shell. This extension is the use of the tilde (~) character to form some new abbreviations.

The tilde character, when used by itself at the beginning of a path, stands for the path name of your home directory. If, for example, your home directory is /usr/fred, you can form the path name of any of your subdirectories simply by using ~ to represent /usr/fred:

~/mail   is the same as   /usr/fred/mail

~/projects/lib   is the same as   /usr/fred/projects/lib

~   is the same as   /usr/fred

Using tilde expansion, you can jump to your bin directory from anywhere else easily:

`$ cd ~/bin`

Regardless of your current directory, you can list the contents of your bin directory easily with the command

`$ ls -x ~/bin`

There are other tilde expansions:

- the form *~name* expands to the home directory of user *name*. Example:
  `$ echo ~sam/projects`
  `/usr/sam/projects`
  `$`

- the form ~+ expands to your current directory. Example:
  `$ cd /usr/spool/uucppublic`
  `$ echo ~+/receive/fred`
  `/usr/spool/uucppublic/receive/fred`
  `$`

- the form ~- expands to your *previous* working directory. Example:
  `$ cd ~`
  `$ pwd`
  `/usr/fred`
  `$ cd /usr/spool/uucppublic`
  `$ pwd`
  `/usr/spool/uucppublic`
  `$ echo where is ~-`

```
where is /usr/fred
$
```

Notice that when you are using the Bourne shell, the tilde character is not recognized as a wild card.

Shell Variables

There are a number of pieces of information, called *variables*, which the shell provides to make your life easier. These tidbits include information such as the path name of your home directory, how often you want the shell to check for mail, and the list of directories you want the shell to search when looking for a command. They are called *variables* because they are similar to the *x* and *y* of algebra; the label of a variable has a fixed name, but it *stands for* information that can change from time to time. The information contained in a variable is called its *value*. Whenever the shell requires that a variable have a value, the shell arranges a default value until you supply your own value.

Table 3.1 identifies each of the shell variables and summarizes the usage or function of the variable. The Source column indicates *login* if the variable is set automatically for you when you login, *shell* if the shell initializes the variable itself, and *user* if the variable is unset (the corresponding function is inactive until you set its value).

Table 3.1. Shell variables.

Name	*Source*	*Usage*
CDPATH	none	Directory search path for `cd`
COLUMNS	shell	Width of edit window and `select` lists (Korn shell only)
EDITOR	none	Command editor (`emacs`, `gmacs`, or `vi`)
ENV	user	Setup script invoked for each command
ERRNO	shell	Last error code from a system call
FCEDIT	shell	Default `fc` editor
FPATH	none	Search path for function definitions
HISTFILE	none	File name to save command history
HISTSIZE	none	Minimum number of commands in history
HOME	login	Default argument for `cd`

continues

Table 3.1. continued

Name	Source	Usage
IFS	shell	List of word separator characters
LINENO	shell	Current line number in a shell script
LINES	shell	Number of terminal lines for `select`
LOGNAME	login	Your login name
MAIL	login	File to watch for new mail
MAILCHECK	shell	How often to check for mail (in seconds)
MAILPATH	none	List of files to watch for new mail
OLDPWD	shell	Previous working directory path name
OPTARG	shell	Current argument after `getopts`
OPTIND	shell	Number of arguments remaining after `getopts`
PATH	login	Search path for commands
PPID	shell	Process-ID of the parent process
PS1	shell	Primary shell prompt
PS2	shell	Secondary shell prompt
PS3	shell	Prompt string for `select`
PS4	shell	Debug prompt
PWD	shell	Current working directory path name
RANDOM	shell	A random integer from 0 to 32767
REPLY	shell	User input for last `select` statement
SECONDS	shell	Number of seconds since login
SHELL	login	Path name of shell to use for subshells
TMOUT	none	Delay before forcing log out (in seconds)
VISUAL	none	Command edit mode (`emacs`, `gmacs`, or `vi`)

Managing Shell Variables

With either the Bourne or Korn shell, you can display the defined shell variables and their current settings by entering the `set` command with no arguments. The following dialog shows the kind of output you receive:

```
$ set
CDPATH=:/u/jjv
HOME=/u/jjv
IFS=
```

```
LOGNAME=jjv
MAIL=/usr/mail/jjv
PATH=/bin:/usr/bin:/usr/local:.:/u/jjv/bin
PS1=$
PS2=>
SHELL=/bin/sh
```

A shell variable can be *local* in scope, in which case its value is known only to the current shell. It also can be *exported*, which means the shell automatically passes the variable and its value to other commands you invoke. The advantage in exporting a variable is it forces your environment to always appear the same with respect to that variable. If this is something you want, you should arrange for the variable to be exported (see the description of the export command in Chapter 10, "Built-In Commands").

To see only the list of exported variables, invoke the env command with no arguments:

```
$ env
CDPATH=:/u/jjv
HOME=/u/jjv
LOGNAME=jjv
MAIL=/usr/mail/jjv
PATH=/bin:/usr/bin:/usr/local:.:/u/jjv/bin
```

To display the value of one specific variable, use the echo command, as follows:

```
$ echo $PATH
/bin:/usr/bin:/usr/local:.:/u/jjv/bin
$
```

Notice the dollar sign ($) in front of the variable name PATH. The dollar sign tells the shell that the following word is a variable name and you want the shell to replace the name with the variable's value before executing the command. Without the dollar sign, the shell treats PATH as a regular word.

To assign a value to a shell variable, enter the variable's name and the new value, separated by =, on a line by itself:

```
$ PATH=:/bin:/usr/bin:/usr/local:/usr/fred/bin
$ echo $PATH
:/bin:/usr/bin:/usr/local:/usr/fred/bin
$
```

Do not put a $ in front of the variable name when setting the variable's value. Use it only when retrieving the value of the variable.

The rest of this section describes each of the variables that are special to the shell. (You can create other variables for your own use. See Chapter 7, "Using Variables," for additional information.)

CDPATH—The Directory Search Path

Format of CDPATH variable

CDPATH=[*path*][:[*path*]...]

The cd command uses the CDPATH variable. The value of CDPATH is the list of directories to be searched to locate the argument of the cd command. The *path* values must be directory names and must be separated by a colon (:). The cd command searches each directory *path* until a directory is found that contains the cd argument; the concatenation of *path* and the cd argument is the directory to which cd then changes.

The shell does not set the CDPATH variable automatically. You must assign a value to CDPATH if you want the cd command to use it. If the CDPATH variable is not set and you enter the command

$ **cd** *dirname*

the shell searches for *dirname* in the current directory. If, on the other hand, the CDPATH variable is set to

$ **CDPATH=:/u/mary:/tmp/mary**

the shell searches for the directories ./*dirname*, /u/mary/*dirname*, and /tmp/mary/*dirname* in turn. If it finds one of these, it changes to that directory. Notice an omitted *path*, such as follows = in the previous example, is treated as if . (the current directory) were specified.

COLUMNS—The Width of the Edit Window and the select Menus

ksh

Format of the COLUMNS Variable

COLUMNS=[*n*]

The COLUMNS variable specifies the width in columns of the display screen. The Korn shell initially assumes a default value of 80. The value of COLUMNS is used for command editing (see the section "Command Editing and Command History" in Chapter 5, "Special Features") and as the maximum width of select menus.

ksh | EDITOR—The Default Editor for the `fc` Command

Format of the EDITOR Variable

`EDITOR=.../[emacs¦gmacs¦vi]`

If the VISUAL variable is set, then the EDITOR variable is ignored. If neither the VISUAL nor the EDITOR variables are set, then by default the Korn shell does not provide command editing. You can still enable command editing with the set command.

If the EDITOR variable is set and ends with one of the words emacs, gmacs, or vi, then the Korn shell automatically enables the corresponding command edit mode. (See the set command in Chapter 4, "Compound Commands," and in the section "Command Editing and Command History" in Chapter 5, "Special Features.")

ksh | ENV—The Setup Script Invoked for Each Command

Format of the ENV Variable

`ENV=path`

If the ENV variable is set and non-null, the Korn shell attempts to execute the profile script file named *path* as the first step of command execution. The Korn shell provides no default for the ENV variable.

You might like to use the ENV profile to set aliases and options, define functions, and generally to establish a standard working environment in subshells that is consistent with your login shell environment. Typically, if you enter the shell from the vi, emacs, pg, mail or mailx, or cu commands, local settings from your login shell are not available. If you provide an ENV profile, you eliminate this inconvenience. For more information on aliases and subshells, see the section "Command Aliases" in Chapter 5, "Special Features," and the section "Statement Groups" in Chapter 4, "Compound Commands," respectively.

ksh FCEDIT—The Default Editor for the fc Command

Format of the FCEDIT Variable

`FCEDIT=path`

The Korn shell supports two kinds of command editing. The first, obtained when you execute the `set -o emacs` or `set -o vi` command, allows editing of command input as you type each command. The second type occurs only when you execute the `fc` command and is used only to edit a previously entered command.

The FCEDIT variable specifies which system editor you want to use to edit a previously entered command when you invoke `fc`. If the FCEDIT variable is not set, the Korn shell invokes the `ed` editor by default.

If you specify the `-e` option on the `fc` command, the FCEDIT value is ignored; for the command form `fc -e name`, the editor called *name* is used for that invocation of the `fc` command; for the command form `fc -e -`, no editor is invoked.

ksh FPATH—The Search Path for Function Definitions

Format of the FPATH Variable

`FPATH=[path][:[path]]...`

The Korn shell allows you to declare a name to be a function, even though the shell has not yet seen the function's definition. You do this with the command `typeset -fu name`, where *name* is the function name, `-f` declares the name to be a function, and `-u` declares it *undefined*.

Functions that have been declared undefined with `typeset` are resolved on the first attempt to execute the function. The Korn shell resolves a function by searching the list of directories given by the value of the FPATH variable for a file with the same name as the function name. If such a file can be found, the shell reads the file containing the function definition, stores the definition for later use, and executes the function call to start the search.

For the value of FPATH, specify a list of path names separated by colons (:). Each *path* must be the path name of a directory. If a path name is null, the shell searches the current directory.

HISTFILE—The Path Name of the Command History File

Format of the HISTFILE Variable

HISTFILE=*path*

If the HISTFILE variable is set when the Korn shell is invoked, then command history is initialized from the contents of the file. Before exiting, the Korn shell saves the current command history in the file named by *path*.

If the HISTFILE variable is not set, the Korn shell maintains all command history in memory, and when the shell exits, the command history is lost.

For *path*, specify the path name of the file where the Korn shell should save and retrieve command history.

HISTSIZE—The Minimum Number of Commands in History

Format of the HISTSIZE Variable

HISTSIZE=*n*

The HISTSIZE variable specifies the minimum number of lines of command history you want the Korn shell to maintain. The shell saves at least *n* lines of history, and might save more if there is additional space available to the shell.

For *n*, specify the number of lines of command history you want the Korn shell to maintain. If HISTSIZE is not set, the Korn shell saves at least 128 lines of history by default.

HOME—Your Home Directory

Format of the HOME Variable

HOME=[*path*]

The purpose of the HOME variable is to provide the cd command with a default argument when you provide none. The HOME variable is initialized to the sixth field of the /etc/passwd entry (the path name of your home directory) when you log in.

By definition the following two commands always have the same effect:

cd $HOME

cd

In general, you should not change the value of the HOME variable; a number of commands rely on its value, such as vi and mailx, and might not function properly after the change.

 The HOME variable and the ~ pattern character have similar meanings. However, the Korn shell replaces ~ with the path name of your home directory only when ~ appears as the first character of a word (~/bin for example), but both shells replace $HOME with the path name of your current directory wherever the variable appears in a word.

IFS—Internal Field Separators

Format of the IFS Variable

IFS='*char...*'

The IFS variable specifies the characters the shell is to treat as word separators in the second scan of the command line. The characters of IFS should be specified without separators of any kind, as in IFS=',:!'. If any of the characters to be specified in the value of IFS are metacharacters (see the section "Regular and Special Characters" in this chapter), the value should be enclosed in single quotations.

The IFS variable is initialized to the blank, tab, and newline characters at shell start-up time.

The shell performs two separate scans of the command line. In the first scan, words of the command are separated by white space (blanks and tabs). Wild card processing, command substitution, and variable replacement are then performed on each word. The words are then rescanned for the characters listed in the value of IFS, and split into new words although the IFS separators are discarded.

Because the shell initially divides the command line into words using white space as separators, the value of IFS usually has no effect on command input from the keyboard. However, a word on the command line that contains one of the IFS characters is further split for each IFS character found.

Using the default value of IFS, the command

```
$ rm foo.bar
```

is interpreted as two words: rm (the command name) and foo.bar (a file to be removed). If the value of IFS includes the period (.), the command is executed as follows:

```
$ IFS=.
$ rm foo.bar
foo not found
bar not found
$
```

You can use the IFS variable properly when writing shell programs, but you should leave its value unaltered when entering commands at the keyboard.

ksh | LINES—The Number of Terminal Lines for `select`

Format of the LINES Variable

LINES=[*n*]

The LINES variable specifies the number of lines on the display screen. The Korn shell initially assumes a default value of 24. The value of LINES is used only for command editing (see "Command Editing and Command History" in Chapter 5, "Special Features") and as the maximum length of `select` menus.

ksh LOGNAME—Your User Name

Format of the LOGNAME Shell Variable

LOGNAME=[*name*]

The login procedure establishes the value of LOGNAME as your login name. Some commands can use the value of LOGNAME to enter in system log files, to automatically send you mail and messages, and to otherwise answer the question *who are you?*

You can change the value of LOGNAME as shown in the following example:

```
$ echo $LOGNAME
mary
$ LOGNAME=tuttle
$ echo $LOGNAME
tuttle
$
```

However, commands that have to know who you are for purposes of system security are not fooled; such commands know you can change the value of LOGNAME easily so it uses other means to identify you.

The LOGNAME variable can be useful in shell scripts and in setting other variables such as PATH or MAIL. For example, you might easily set the MAIL shell variable to point to your system mail file with the following command:

```
$ MAIL=/usr/mail/$LOGNAME
```

MAIL—The File to Check for Mail

Format of the MAIL Shell Variable

MAIL=[*path*]

One of the services the shell provides is to periodically monitor the status of your system mail file, and to notify you when you have received mail. To do this, however, the shell must know the path name of the file where you normally receive mail. To allow you to receive notification when your mail file is not the standard path name, the shell uses the value of the MAIL variable as the path name of the file to watch.

For *path*, specify the path name of the file the shell is to watch for the receipt of mail.

The value of MAIL is set to /usr/mail/$LOGNAME automatically when you log in. Normally this is the path name of your system mail file.

If the last-modification time of the file changes between two successive checks, the shell issues the message You have mail after the completion of the next command you execute. The shell cannot write a message to your terminal when it is at a prompt so you do not receive notification until after the next command you enter.

MAILCHECK—The Frequency to Check for Mail

3

Format of the MAILCHECK Shell Variable

MAILCHECK=*n*

For *n*, specify the number of seconds you want to elapse before the shell checks your mail file again (see MAIL). By default the shell checks every 600 seconds (10 minutes). A value of 0 forces the shell to check for mail after every command.

Generally you want the shell to check for mail as frequently as possible, so you can see and respond to a message from someone else as soon as possible. However, if the shell must check for mail frequently, then you are forcing it to do extra work, which is usually wasted. The default value of 600 was chosen as a compromise. If the system seems to be responding slowly to your commands, one of the reasons might be that you have set a low value for MAILCHECK.

MAILPATH—A List of Files to Check for Mail

Format of the MAILPATH Shell Variable

MAILPATH=[*path*][:[*path*]]...

Older versions of the shell only supported the MAIL variable, which meant the shell could monitor only one file for the receipt of mail.

If you are sometimes logged in with different user names, and others know this, it could be difficult to predict to which user-ID others will send mail. You can use the MAILPATH variable to instruct the shell to watch several files rather than one.

The value of MAILPATH is specified in the same manner as for the CDPATH or PATH variables: enter a list of path names separated by colons. The path names you specify should name files, not directories, for several reasons. Mail is always posted to a file, so the ordinary use of the shell mail-checking facility is to watch for a change to a file. A directory does not necessarily show any change when data is appended to one of the files in the directory, so you might miss notification for path names that name a directory.

PATH—The Program Search Path

Format of the PATH Shell Variable

PATH=[*path*][:[*path*]]...

The PATH variable defines the set of directories the shell should search for a command name. To specify the value of PATH, write the list of directories as full path names and separate each path name from the next with a colon (:), as in the following example:

$ **PATH=/bin:/usr/bin:/usr/local:/u/mary/bin:.**

This example tells the shell to search five directories for commands: /bin, /usr/bin, /usr/local, /u/mary/bin, and the current directory (.).

If you write a colon separator without an intervening value, the omitted directory name is assumed to be . (the current directory); for example, PATH=:/bin:/usr/bin means the same thing as PATH=.:/bin:/usr/bin.

If the PATH environment has a null value or is unset, then by default the shell only searches your current directory for command names.

A default value for PATH is established when you log in.

PS1—The Primary Prompt

The PS1 variable specifies the shell's primary prompt string—See the "Shell Prompts" section later in this chapter. The shell writes the primary prompt string to your terminal before reading the first line of a new command. If *string* contains any characters special to the shell, *string* should be enclosed in either single or double quotations.

Format of the PS1 Variable

```
PS1=string
```

 Before issuing the prompt string, the Korn shell reevaluates any variable references and command substitutions contained in *string*. Using this feature, you can display the current directory as part of your prompt easily:

```
$ PS1='${PWD} $ '
/u/marty/src/payroll/weekly $
```

PS2—The Secondary Prompt

Format of the PS2 Variable

```
PS2=string
```

The PS2 variable contains the shell's secondary prompt string. The shell writes the secondary prompt string whenever keyboard input is treated as a continuation of an incomplete command. The shell initializes the value of PS2 to >.

PS3—The Prompt String for select

Format of the PS3 Variable

```
PS3=string
```

The value of PS3 specifies the prompt string written by the select command to solicit a menu selection. The default value of *string* is #?.

ksh | PS4—The Debug Prompt

> **Format of the PS4 Variable**
>
> PS4=*string*

The PS4 prompt is written before any shell output generated by the shell option -x. By default PS4 is not set. A typical value for PS4 is "$LINENO: " to display the current line number. By default PS4 is +.

SHELL—The Shell Path Name

> **Format of the SHELL Variable**
>
> SHELL=[*path*]

The system login routine sets the SHELL variable to the seventh field of the /etc/passwd entry, which is the path name of your login shell. If the seventh field is omitted, then SHELL is set to /bin/sh (the Bourne shell) by default.

If the file name of the shell is rsh (/bin/rsh is a link to /bin/sh) then a *restricted* shell environment is set that disallows the cd command and certain redirections. System administrators sometimes assign the restricted shell as a user's login shell to restrict that user's access to selected commands and files.

The shell only uses this variable to determine whether the environment should be normal or restricted. However, some other UNIX commands (such as make and vi) use the value of SHELL to determine which shell to call. Setting the value of SHELL has no effect on your current environment because the shell only checks it during start-up time and ignores it thereafter. You can change the value of SHELL to designate the shell you want to be invoked by commands that can, in turn, invoke the shell.

ksh | TMOUT—Delay before Forcing a Log Out

The TMOUT variable specifies a time limit in seconds for which the user session might be idle; after *n* seconds elapse with no terminal or command activity, the shell automatically exits. The timer begins to count when no command

programs are currently in execution; any command entry cancels the current
time-out interval.

Format of the TMOUT Variable

TMOUT=*n*

VISUAL—The Command Edit Mode

Format of the VISUAL Variable

VISUAL=.../[emacs¦gmacs¦vi]

If the VISUAL variable is set and ends with one of the words emacs, gmacs, or
vi, then the Korn shell automatically enables the corresponding command
editing mode. (See the set command in Chapter 4, "Compound Commands,"
and the section on "Command Editing and Command History" in Chapter 5,
"Special Features.")

Shell Prompts

When the shell is ready for you to enter a new command, it types a few
characters at the beginning of the line to let you know the shell is waiting for
you. These characters are called *prompts*. By default, the shell arranges for the
prompt to be the dollar sign ($). (If you are the superuser, the shell issues the
character as a prompt to remind you of the potential harm you can cause.)
You can change the shell's prompt to any sequence of characters you want.

If you issue the set command with no options, the shell shows you the
current settings of the various shell variables. Among these, you see the
variables PS1 and PS2:

```
$ set
CDPATH=.:...:/u/jjv
PATH=/bin:/usr/bin:/usr/local:/u/jjv/bin:.
PS1=$.
PS2=>
SHELL=/bin/ksh
TERM=ansi
$
```

Of course, you can see what the prompt is without using the set command, because the prompt is always shown at the beginning of the current line of your screen. Nevertheless, this exercise demonstrates that the shell gets its prompt character from the value of the PS1 variable.

You can change the value of the PS1 variable at any time by using the assignment command:

```
$ PS1=:
:echo hi
hi
:
```

If you want a blank space to follow the prompt, you must include the blank in the value of PS1:

```
:PS1="$ "
$ echo hi
hi
$
```

You might find it useful to have your prompt remind you of your current user-ID, especially if you can log in with any one of several user names. It is easy to arrange for your user-ID to be your prompt:

```
$ PS1="fred: "
fred: echo hi
hi
fred:
```

It is sometimes helpful to get the value of the prompt from the LOGNAME shell variable, as follows:

```
$ PS1="$LOGNAME: "
judy: echo hi
hi
judy:
```

Some other shells (such as the C shell, and the MS-DOS COMMAND.COM shell) allow the use of special replacement codes in the prompt string. These codes often are used to display the current directory as part of the prompt. The Bourne and Korn shells do not provide such a capability explicitly. In fact, if you have been an MS-DOS user, you must beware of trying to set the prompt as you are accustomed:

```
$ PS1=$p$g
echo hi
hi
```

What happened to your prompt? The shell took the $p and $g symbols as variables. Normally the p and g variables are undefined and therefore have no value. After substitution, the shell saw your assignment as PS1=, with nothing to the right of the = sign.

To get the current directory as a prompt, you must reset the prompt string every time you change to another directory. The cd command does not change the prompt for you; its job is to change the current directory only. To do more, you must embed the cd command inside another command (go, for example), and always change directories using the other command.

You can achieve the desired effect by entering the *function* definition in Listing 3.1 (see "Functions" in Chapter 4, "Compound Commands").

Listing 3.1. Shell function to show the current directory as the prompt.

```
go(){
cd $*
PS1="`pwd`> "
}
```

After entering the function definition shown in Listing 3.1, you have your prompt changed to the current directory every time you use go. Here is a sample terminal session:

```
$ go(){
> cd $*
> PS1="`pwd`> "
> }
$ go /usr/fred/lib
/usr/fred/lib> go
/usr/fred>
```

If you use the Korn shell, you can use a slightly more efficient version of go, as shown in Listing 3.2.

Listing 3.2. Korn shell function to show the current directory as the prompt.

```
$ go(){
> cd $*
> PS1="${PWD}> "
> }
$
```

You won't be learning how to write functions like this until later, so do not worry if you don't understand the code. Just type the function as shown (or add it to your .profile) and it will work fine.

Quoting

The wild-card file-naming capabilities of the shell are, without a doubt, a valuable time saver and a helpful feature. But every advantage has its price. The disadvantage of wild card support is that it is awkward to try to use the *, ?, and [ ] characters on a command line, except as wild cards.

Suppose you want to use a command that can calculate the value of simple arithmetic expressions. There is such a command, and its name is expr. To work a multiplication problem, you might want to enter the following command:

```
$ expr 27 * 4
```

If possible, the expr command displays the result of the multiplication. The previous example does not give the expected result though, because the shell recognizes the * as the wild card character and replaces it with the names of all the files in your current directory. The expr command sees something like this:

```
$ expr 27 bin calendar mbox sally.mail 4
```

To get around this problem, you have to have a way to tell the shell that the * character is to be passed to the expr command as is, without replacement. You must either *quote* or *backslash* the asterisk.

Quoting with \

The easiest way to avoid shell interpretation of the * on a command line is to precede it with a backslash (\).

The backslash is a shell metacharacter. (Recall that a metacharacter is any character that has special meaning to the shell, such as the *, ?, [, and] characters.) When the shell sees a backslash, it removes the backslash and ignores the character that follows it. If you rewrite your multiplication problem using the backslash, you now get the following result:

```
$ expr 27 \* 4
108
$
```

This time the command worked because the expr command saw three arguments: 27, *, and 4. When a blackslash hides a character from the shell, the character is said to have been *backslashed* or *escaped*. The backslash is the shell's standard escape character.

Because the backslash has special meaning to the shell, you must backslash it to pass a backslash to a command:

```
$ echo two \\backslashes
twoackslashes
$
```

You should have expected to get the output two \backslashes. The problem here is the echo command also processes backslashes. After the shell processes the line, it executes the command echo two \backslashes but then the echo command recognizes \b as a backspace sequence and deletes both the \b and the character preceding it.

This particular example shows the problems that can arise when both the shell and a command perform quoting substitutions on the input. It will be easier for you to cope with these situations by enclosing the arguments of echo in quotations, so the backslashes are processed only once.

Quoting with ´

The backslash character provides a useful way to quote a single character, but when both the shell and the command process the backslash, things can get confusing. You need a way to prevent any kind of shell manipulation of a command argument. The single quote (´) provides such a quoting mechanism.

Using Single Quotations

The following rule apply when you use single quotations:

- Use the single quotation (´) to protect text from any substitution. Backslashes, wild cards, variables, double quotations ("), and command substitution (`) are ignored in single quotations.

- Only another single quote can end a single-quoted string. Newline characters become part of the quoted string; a single-quoted string can span multiple lines.

- You cannot write a single quotation in single-quoted text: ´John´s violin´ and ´John\´s violin´ both produce unpaired single quotes and cause the shell to look for more input.

To mark a string of text together in a single word, and to prevent all shell substitutions on the text, enclose the text between single quotes. For example, you can write the previous echo command as follows:

```
$ echo 'Do you see a backslash \\ here?'
Do you see a backslash \ here?
$
```

The `echo` command still performs backslash substitution, but the command is easier to write because the effects of shell processing need not be taken into account in the single quotes.

You cannot include the single quote in an single-quoted string. You could try backslashing the embedded single quote—for example `'one \'` `quotation'`—but this does not work because the backslash is ignored inside the single quotes.

3

Quoting with "

Another way to hide characters special to the shell is to enclose them between double quotation marks ("). Text enclosed in double quotation marks is treated as one word, and wild card characters are treated as normal text. Other forms of substitution still occur for text enclosed in quotations.

Using Double Quotations

The following rules apply when you use double quotation marks:

- Use the double quotation (") to protect text from wild card expansion and from word splitting. To quote text, enclose the text between " marks:

  ```
  ls "*.c"
  echo "*** ERROR ***"
  ```

- The quotation marks are removed and only the quoted text is passed to the command.

- Variable replacement, backslashing, and command substitution are effective inside double quotations.

- You can write a " in double quotations by backslashing it:
  `"the \"big\" book"`

- Single quotations are treated as normal text inside double quotations: `"John's book"`

- Quoted text might span multiple input lines. The newline characters falling in the range of the quotation are included in the quoted text.

All the text enclosed in quotations is considered a single word by the shell, and is passed to the command as one argument. You must not include more text between quotations than is properly part of a single argument to the command. For example, the following is an attempt to avoid the `expr` problem:

```
$ expr "27 * 4"
expr: invalid expression
$
```

This "solution" does not work. Why not? Because `expr` is looking for three words: a number, an arithmetic operator, and another number. By enclosing the entire operand in quotations, the shell passes the character sequence "27 * 4" as one argument to the `expr` command.

The proper solution is this:

```
$ expr 27 "*" 4
108
$
```

By quoting only the asterisk, the `expr` command gets the right number of arguments and sees the * character rather than a list of file names.

It can be convenient to enclose more text in quotations than necessary. Consider this form of a previous example:

```
$ echo "Does the * print?"
Does the * print?
$
```

This time the shell does not notice either the * or ? pattern characters, so the message written by `echo` is the intended message.

Quotation marks are removed from the command line before the options and arguments are passed to the command. Of course, the text in the paired quotations stays together. (The shell scans the command line to determine the list of words to pass to the command. When the shell finds a quotation mark, it constructs the next word to be passed by reading to the ending quotation mark, then discarding both the beginning and ending quotation.)

You can include several lines of text in quotations simply by breaking each line as usual. All the text in the quotations, including the newline characters, becomes part of a single command argument. You can use this feature properly with a number of commands by writing a series of lines as a single argument:

```
$ fgrep -i "he
> him
> his" chapter.1
$
```

The resulting `fgrep` command searches the `chapter.1` file for all occurrences of the word he, `him`, or `his`.

What if you want to include a quotation mark inside the quoted text? If you take no precautions, the shell gets confused:

```
$ echo "Quotation " inside"
>
```

In this example, the shell has issued its secondary prompt (>), meaning that it is looking for more input. The shell considers the second quotation to end the argument, and the third quotation to start another quoted string. The shell now reads everything you type as part of a quoted string until you enter another quotation.

To include a quotation inside quoted text, you must escape the quotation, as follows:

```
$ echo "Quote \" inside"
Quote " inside
$
```

You could achieve the same result by using only the backslash:

```
$ echo Quote \" inside
Quote " inside
$
```

Notice that single quotes are ignored inside a double-quoted string; the shell does not nest quotations. Just as you can write double quotations inside a single quotation string, you can write single quotations in a double quotation string:

```
$ echo "CDPATH='$CDPATH'"
CDPATH='/u/jjv:/u/fred'
$
```

Mixing Quotations

It is always possible, if not necessarily convenient, to combine unquoted text and text quoted with " and ' to yield a desired argument value. Take the following command, for example:

```
$ make prog OPTIONS="-c -s -I'"$HOME/src"'"
```

This example passes two arguments to the `make` command. The first is *prog* and is a simple text string—actually a file name. The second is a compound string consisting of the following four text fragments:

Fragment as Entered	*Fragment as Seen by the Command*
OPTIONS=	OPTIONS=
"-c -s -I´"	-c -s -I´
$HOME/src	/u/jjv/src
"´"	´

The resulting set of arguments passed to make look like this:

$ **make** *prog* **OPTIONS=-c -s -I´/u/jjv/src´**

Remember that single quotes are ignored between double quotations, and the double quotations perform variable-symbol substitution. Therefore, the previous make command also could have been entered as follows:

$ **make** *prog* **OPTIONS="-c -s -I´$HOME/src´"**

This version of the command is worth close examination. You can see what appears to be a single-quoted string inside the OPTIONS argument. The shell, however, does not see it that way. Because the shell ignores single quotes inside double quotations, the shell sees the variable $HOME and makes the appropriate substitution.

To summarize, this section demonstrates two useful rules about quoting:

- Quotations do not nest.

- Any number of text fragments—some unquoted, some quoted with ", and some quoted with ´—can be combined to yield one argument for the command.

Command Substitution

Use command substitution to enter the output of a command as one or more arguments on the command line. A command substitution is enclosed between back quotations:

`` `shell-command` ``

The shell executes the *shell-command* between the back quotations (`) and captures the output of the command. The output text is separated into words using the IFS characters, and each word is checked for further substitutions. The resulting words replace the back-quoted expression in the command line.

Using Back Quotations

The following rules apply when you use back quotes for command substitution:

- The `shell-command` can be a simple or compound command (see Chapter 4, "Compound Commands") such as an `if` statement or a list of statements separated by semicolons (;).

- The shell executes the text between back quotations as a command.

- The standard output (see "Input/Output Redirection" in this chapter) of the back-quoted command replaces the back-quoted string.

The shell performs backslash substitution only on the text enclosed between back quotations. However, a second copy of the shell is invoked to execute the `shell-command`; the second copy performs all substitutions on the command because it does not see the back quotations. As a result, wild-card file names are expanded according to the environment in the back-quoted command, not according to the current environment. Look at the following command, for example:

```
$ ls `cd /usr/fred/src; echo *.c`
junk.c not found
temp.c not found
main.c
prog.c
$
```

This command lists all files ending in `.c` in your current directory that also occur in the /usr/fred/src directory. The error messages identify files in /usr/fred/src that do not occur in your current directory.

The output of a command substitution normally is broken into a list of words using the IFS characters. To prevent this tokenization, enclose the entire expression, including back quotations, inside double quotations, like this:

```
"`shell-command`"
```

The following is an example of command substitution:

```
$ cat group.1
mary
estelle
fred
bill
```

```
$ mail `cat group.1`
Hi, everyone!
Please plan to attend a meeting in the classroom at
2:30 this afternoon.
^d
$
```

This example demonstrates two commands. The first, cat, displays the contents of a file called group.1, which obviously contains a list of user names. The second, mail, sends a short message to the users named as the command's arguments. The example uses command substitution to list the names in the group.1 file in the mail command: The output of cat (a list of user names) replaces the expression `cat group.1`. The mail command, as executed, looks like this:

```
$ mail mary estelle fred bill
```

The Korn shell supports the following alternate syntax for command substitution:

```
$(shell-command)
```

This syntax has two advantages over the traditional back-quotation syntax. The first is that the $() notation is easier to read; the back quotation can be difficult to distinguish from the regular quotation, and $() can be printed by most printers, whereas " often can not. The second advantage is that the shell supports the nesting of command substitutions written with $(). Contrast the clarity of the following two commands:

```
$ echo `basename \`pwd\``
```

and

```
$ echo $(basename $(pwd))
```

Input/Output Redirection

Input/Output (I/O) redirection is perhaps the most useful feature of the shell. Redirection, of course, implies the action of directing something to a different location. Together, the terms describe the shell's ability to redefine the place where *standard input* is read from, or where *standard output* and *standard error* files are written.

Every time the shell invokes a program, it establishes default locations for the program's input and output. The shell does this by opening three files for the program. These three files are called standard input, standard output, and standard error. They are called *standard* simply because any command program can use these three files to read from or write to.

Input/Output redirection prepares *open file descriptors* for use by a program. (See the section "File Descriptors" in Chapter 1, "Introduction to UNIX," for an explanation of the concept of file descriptors.) Most commands that are supplied with UNIX use the standard Input/Output files for input, for output, or for both functions. In the following sections, you learn how to control where programs read and write information by using the standard Input/Output files.

Input Redirection

The standard input file is the default source of input to a command. Normally, the standard input file is assigned to your terminal keyboard.

You can change the assignment of the standard input file by including an input redirection operator on the command line. The valid input redirections are shown in Table 3.2. Each is discussed in detail in the following sections.

Table 3.2. Input redirection operators.

Syntax	Function
`< file`	Read input from `file`
`<&n`	Read input from file descriptor *n*
`<&-`	Close the standard input file
`<<tag`	Read up to the line starting with `tag`
`<<-tag`	Read up to the line starting with `tag`, discarding leading white space

Any of these operators can be prefixed by a file descriptor number from 0 to 9. If a file descriptor number is specified, that file descriptor is opened rather than standard input. Standard input is file descriptor 0, therefore `0<file` means the same thing as `<file`.

The < Operator

The < operator causes the shell to take the following word as the name of a file. The file is opened for reading and assigned to standard input. If the command normally reads standard input, it reads from the file you named following the < operator; if it does not, the redirection has no effect.

For *file*, specify a file name or a relative or absolute path name. The use of wild cards to generate the file name is not allowed, because wild card substitution implies the generation of a list of file names, yet only one file name is permitted following the redirection operator. The Korn Shell permits wild cards in the file name, but will expand only the first matching file name. Variable substitution, backslashing, and quoting are all permitted, however.

The placement of redirection operators on the command line is not particularly important; the shell simply strips redirections from the line before calling the command. The following sample commands all show valid placement of the input redirection to the cpio command:

```
$ cpio -itv < /dev/rmt0
$
$ cpio < /dev/rmt0 -itv
$
$ < /dev/rmt0 cpio -itv
```

In the previous examples, the redirection operator is written with a blank separating < and the file name; however, the blank is optional and the command can be written as

```
$ cpio -itv </dev/rmt0
```

If you have never used redirection before, you might try the exercise in Listing 3.3.

Listing 3.3. Preparing mail messages with an editor.

```
$ # Create the mail message:
$ ed msg.root
?
0a
Hi, root. This is a test of the mail command. Please send a
reply back to me.
.
w
61
q
$ # Now mail the message:
$ mail root <msg.root
$
```

By using input redirection, you can mail a message that you had prepared in advance using a text editor. Any text editor provides more flexibility for entering and editing text than the mail command, so you might prefer to create messages this way rather than by typing the message text directly into the mail command.

The <& Operator

The <&*n* operator changes the standard input of a command from your terminal to another file descriptor. (A file descriptor is a number assigned by UNIX to a file after it has been opened.) The number *n* specifies the file descriptor number as a single digit in the range 0 to 9.

Although syntactically valid, the <& operator is rarely used because there are usually no file descriptors open for input other than standard input itself. The shell automatically opens file descriptors 0, 1, and 2, which by convention are called standard input, standard output, and standard error, respectively. Other file descriptors must be opened either by a shell redirection or internally by a command program.

There are two situations where this operator can be useful.

The first situation arises when you are writing an application program in the C programming language. (If you do not write programs, skip this paragraph!) If you have already opened a file and want to pass it to a second program you are calling with the system function, you can do so as follows:

```
rc = system("prog2 <&3");
```

assuming that you already opened file descriptor 3 in your calling program and that you want prog2 to read 3 as its standard input.

In the second situation, assume that you wrote an application program (called formletter) and it takes a form letter and a name and address list and prints a customized form letter for each name and address. The program reads the form letter from file descriptor 0 (standard input), and the name and address list from file descriptor 4 (which has no generally accepted name).

To have the program read the name and address list from a file called names while you type the form letter, use this command:

```
$ formletter 4<names
```

This command tells the program to set standard input in the normal way (assigned to your keyboard), and to open file descriptor number 4 for input from the file called names. Please notice that no white space can appear between the 4 and the < redirection operator. If you put any blanks or tabs after the 4, the shell construes the 4 to be an argument of the formletter command and redirects standard input to the names file.

If you want the program to read the form letter from a previously stored file while you type the name and address list from your terminal, enter the following command:

```
$ formletter 4<&0 <form.1
```

The first redirection (4<&0) assigns file descriptor 4 to the place where file descriptor 0 (standard input) is already assigned—namely your terminal. The second redirection (<form.1) assigns standard input to the file form.1 that contains the form letter. Because the redirection of file descriptor 4 is performed before the redirection of file descriptor 0 (redirections are executed in left-to-right order), the redirection of file descriptor 4 is unaffected by the subsequent redirection of file descriptor 0.

The <&- Operator

Use the <&- operator to close an input file. The command gets an error condition if it attempts to read from the closed file descriptor.

The << Operator

The << operator must be followed by an arbitrary word, called a *tag*. << is like <, in that it causes the command to read its input from somewhere other than your terminal. However, the input for << does not come from an outside file; it consists of the following lines of shell input up to, but not including, the one containing *tag* as its first word. The shell reads the lines following in its input up to the tag line, and stores the lines it reads in a temporary file. The line containing *tag* as its first word is thrown away. The temporary file then becomes the standard input for the command.

The lines read ahead by the shell are called a *here document*, because the text of the input file occurs in-line in the shell input, rather than elsewhere in a file.

This operator is most useful in shell scripts, but it also can be used at the keyboard to prepare input for a command in advance of its execution.

Consider the following example:

```
$ mail <<END `who -q` &
Please get your timesheets to me by the end of the day.
END
$
```

You choose to execute the mail command as a background job (notice the ending &), probably because it takes a little time for the command to send a mail message to each user logged in. The command substitution `who -q` uses the who command to put a list of all the users currently logged in on the command line. The redirection operator <<END causes the shell to read the following lines up to, but not including, END, to store the lines (only one line, in this case) in a temporary file, and to set the standard input of the mail command to be that temporary file. You are free to go about other business while this command executes.

You can achieve the same effect by storing the mail message in a permanent file and redirecting standard input to that file:

```
$ cat >broadcast
Please get your timesheets to me by the end of the day.
^d
$ mail <broadcast `who -q` &
241
$
```

The version using a *here* document is not only shorter; in the second version, you have to come back later and delete the broadcast file, whereas the *here* document disappears automatically after the mail command completes execution.

The <<- Operator

The <<- operator is similar to << in that, for either operator, the shell reads ahead to *tag* (*tag* is an arbitrary word you choose), stores the lines in a temporary file, and assigns the temporary file as the standard input of the command on which <<- appears.

The - causes the shell to discard white space at the front of the lines it reads; the leading white space is not stored in the temporary file and is never seen by the command. This feature is most often used in shell scripts, where it is customary to indent commands for readability.

For example, consider this fragment of a shell script:

```
# Program to backup user directories
if [ $# -eq 0 ]
then
        cat <<-MSG >&2
        Usage: backup [ all ¦ uid ... ]
                all = back up all users
                uid = back up selected users
        MSG
        exit 1
fi
```

This fragment checks whether the right number of command arguments have been specified, and if not, it issues a message describing the script's proper usage. Although the details of the checking step involve shell facilities you have not learned yet, the cat command should be clear enough.

The <<-MSG expression tells the shell to read lines up to the one starting with MSG, and to present those lines as the standard input of the cat command. The lines down through MSG are not processed as shell commands—they are merely copied into a temporary file, to be read later by the cat command.

The >&2 expression is a simple redirection operator that causes the output of cat to be written to file descriptor 2, which is the standard error file. The output of cat is therefore treated as an error message by writing it to your terminal.

The next command executed by the shell is exit 1, because the lines intervening between the cat command and the exit command were stripped out as a *here* document file.

The advantage to using the <<- operator is that the shell strips off the excess blanks and tabs in the front of each line of the *here* document; the output that the cat command actually would write looks like this:

```
$ backup
Usage: backup [ all ¦ uid ... ]
all = back up all users
uid = back up selected users
$
```

Using the << operator instead, you would have to write the shell script fragment like this for the message to appear along the left edge of the screen:

```
# Program to backup user directories
if [ $# -eq 0 ]
then
        cat <<MSG >&2
Usage: backup [ all ¦ uid ... ]
all = back up all users
uid = back up selected users
MSG
        exit 1
fi
```

Notice that the lines of the *here* document must be left justified, which destroys the readability and clarity of the shell script.

Variable Replacement in *Here* Documents

The shell normally replaces occurrences of variables in a *here* document with their values. This is a handy way to generate customized text. For example, the command

```
$ cat <<END >&2
$LOGNAME: not authorized.

You are not allowed to access files in the `pwd` directory.
Contact your supervisor for assistance.
END
```

generates the following terminal output:

```
jones: not authorized.
```

```
You are not allowed to access files in the /usr/bin directory.
Contact your supervisor for assistance.
```

The $LOGNAME variable was replaced with the current user's login name: jones. The command substitution `pwd` inserted the current directory path name in the next to last output line.

If you want to suppress substitutions in the *here* document lines, you must quote all or part of the *tag* of the << or << - operator. Using the previous example, the command

```
$ cat <<'END' >&2
$LOGNAME: not authorized.

You are not allowed to access files in the `pwd` directory.
Contact your supervisor for assistance.
END
```

results in the following unaltered output:

```
$LOGNAME: not authorized.
```

```
You are not allowed to access files in the `pwd` directory.
Contact your supervisor for assistance.
```

All shell substitutions, except wild-card file-name generation, are performed on the lines of a *here* document unless the *tag* value is quoted, in which case no substitutions are performed.

Output Redirection

The standard output file is the default destination of output from a command. Normally, the standard output file is assigned to your terminal display. You can change the assignment of the standard output file by including an output redirection operator on the command line. The valid output redirections are shown in Table 3.3.

As with input redirections, any of these operators can be prefixed by a file descriptor number from 0 to 9. If a file descriptor number is specified, then that file descriptor is opened for output rather than standard output. Standard output is file descriptor 1, therefore 1>*file* means the same thing as >*file*.

Table 3.3. Output redirection operators.

Syntax	Function
`> file`	Write output into `file`
`>&n`	Write output to file descriptor *n*
`>&-`	Close the standard output file
`>> file`	Write output to the end of `file`

The > Operator

The `>file` operator causes the shell to take the following word as the name of a file. The file is opened for writing and assigned to standard output. If the command writes to standard output, it writes to the file you named following the > operator; if it does not, the redirection has no effect.

For `file`, specify a file name or a relative or absolute path name. The use of wild cards to generate the file name is not allowed, because wild-card substitution implies the generation of a list of file names, yet only one file name is permitted following the redirection operator. Variable substitution, backslashing, and quoting are all permitted, however.

The > operator is the most useful of all redirections; you use it frequently. The following are examples of using > to capture the output of a command in a file:

```
$ echo Please send me your timesheet. >msg
$
$ ls *.[ch] *.sh makefile >source.list
$
$ make -nd -f - </dev/null 2>/dev/null >defaults
```

The echo command is used in the first example to create a small file that could then be used as input to another command (such as mail). Using echo in this way is a common method of avoiding the use of a text editor for a small job.

The output of the ls command is captured in a file called source.list for later use, possibly with command substitution. For example, you could then use the tar command to back up only the source files in the current directory:

```
$ cpio: cpio -DC <source.list> /dev/rmt0
```

Finally, the make command provides an example of capturing useful information for later reference. When the -d option is specified, the make command writes a list of all its default rules and macros to standard output. The example uses output redirection to store this list in a file called defaults. The other options and redirections are needed to avoid having make do anything else.

The target of an output redirection does not have to be a disk file. The following command sends its output to a line printer:

```
$ fgrep -i nancy *.msg >/dev/lp
```

Alternatively, if you don't have a line printer reserved exclusively for your use, you use output redirection to save the command output for the lp command, like this:

```
$ fgrep -i nancy *.msg >cross-ref
$ lp cross-ref
lp-2051
$
```

Finally, the output redirection operator can be used to specify the destination of file descriptors other than standard output. Programs often write error messages to file descriptor 2 (commonly called *standard error*); you can capture such output in a file as follows:

```
$ cc newprog.c 2>newprog.errs
```

When the number of error messages exceeds one line, redirecting file descriptor 2 becomes a survival technique.

The >& Operator

The >&*n* operator allows you to redirect a command's output not to a named file, but rather to the same place as another open file descriptor. The >& operator must be followed immediately by a single digit that represents the file descriptor number. (For information about file descriptors, see the section "File Descriptors" in Chapter 1, "Introduction to UNIX.")

Redirection to a file descriptor is used to gather a program's output and error messages together in the same file. For example, the command

```
$ sh -x newscript >out 2>&1
```

often occurs when testing a shell script. The -x option causes the shell to print all commands it executes. The normal output of the executed script (newscript) is redirected to the file out. The shell's diagnostic output, normally written to standard error, is redirected to file descriptor 1. File descriptor 1 corresponds to standard output. As a result, diagnostic messages from the shell also are written into the file out.

Why redirect to a file descriptor number? Couldn't the command also have been written as

```
sh -x newscript >out 2>out
```

Yes, it could have, but the results would be undesirable. Even though both file descriptors are open on the same file, neither the shell nor the operating system realizes that this is the case; output to file descriptor 1 is managed independently of output to file descriptor 2. This means that two separate file pointers are maintained, and output to one file descriptor can overwrite output written to the other; lost and unreadable output are the likely results.

By using redirection to an already open file descriptor, you alert both the shell and the operating system that output is being written to the same file. They can and do take precautions that output occurs nondestructively. Lines written to file descriptor 1 and to file descriptor 2 are intermixed, but do not overlap; that is, only one file pointer is maintained for the two file descriptors.

In general, to capture several streams of output in the same file, you must open the first stream by using normal redirection (for example >*file*) and open the others by using file descriptor redirection (such as 2>&1).

The >&- Operator

Use the >&- operator to close an output file. The command cannot write to the closed file descriptor. To close a file descriptor other than standard input, specify the file descriptor as a digit from 0 to 9 immediately in front of the operator.

See the section "The <&- Operator" earlier in this chapter for a related discussion.

The >> Operator

The >>*file* operator works the same as the > operator, except that data is written to the end of *file*. Two or more programs can write to the end of a file using this operator without interference; the output of the programs is interleaved in the order written.

The >> operator is useful for accumulating the output of several consecutively executed commands in the same file. For example, the following commands print a listing of a file with each line numbered, add a cross-reference by line number to the listing, then submit the final result to the line printer:

```
$ pr -n text >pfile
$ fgrep -i king text >>pfile
$ lp pfile
$
```

You cannot use the >> operator to redirect to an open file descriptor; the expression >>&1 is invalid. You can achieve the desired result, however, by redirecting to a file descriptor that was opened for append:

```
$ cc myprog.c >>myprog.errs 2>&1
```

Because the cc command does not normally write to standard output, you could write the command as

```
$ cc myprog.c 2>>myprog.errs
```

with the same results.

Other Features

The redirection facilities of the shell are powerful, but do not provide every possible feature. This section covers some capabilities of the shell that are related to Input/Output redirection but achieved by other means. The Korn shell provides some features for Input/Output redirection that are not available with the Bourne shell, and these are described here as well.

Redirecting Input from Multiple Files

You occasionally might need to process several files with one command; input redirection does not provide this capability. However, the cat command together with a pipe can be used to the same effect. For additional information and examples, see the section "Pipes" in Chapter 4, "Compound Commands."

Avoiding Unintentional Overwrite with >

You might not always be aware of all the files in your current directory. If you name a file as the target of an output redirection and the file already exists, the new output overwrites the existing file. The Bourne shell does not provide a convenient way to prevent such an accident.

There are a couple of things you can do to avert a disaster:

- You can use the chmod command to withdraw write permission for *yourself* on important files you don't want to lose. To do this, enter the following command:

```
$ chmod -w file1 file2 ...
```

or use wild cards to protect a whole group of files:

```
$ chmod -w *.c
```

The disadvantage of this approach is that if you ever legitimately need to modify one of these files, you first must restore write permission, change the file, and, to be safe, remove write permission once again.

(You might be interested in the facilities of SCCS if you frequently need to protect a group of files. For additional information, see the admin, get, and delta commands in your UNIX system documentation.)

- You can set up a directory of your own to contain strictly temporary files, or use one of the system's tmp directories (either /tmp or /usr /tmp are usually available). Always send redirected output to one of these temporary directories, and move anything important to another directory for safekeeping.

To use this approach with relative ease, set a short variable symbol to hold the path name of your chosen temporary directory, like this:

```
$ tmp=$HOME/tmp
```

Then, whenever you want to redirect the output of a command, put it in your temporary directory:

```
$ fgrep -i nancy *.mail >$tmp/nancy
$ pg $tmp/nancy
```

 The Korn shell provides the noclobber option to prevent overwriting of files on an output redirection. To prevent opening an existing file for output, use the set command to set the noclobber option:

```
$ set -o noclobber
```

Attempting to write to an existing file with an output redirection results in an error message:

```
$ echo Categories: >list1
list1: file exists
$
```

To write to a file name even if it exists, use the >¦ operator:

```
$ echo Categories: >¦ list1
```

Writing the Output of Several Commands to a Single File

The shell provides a way to open a file for input to or output from a series of commands. Once opened for input or output, the file remains open for the entire command list. Use a *subshell* to achieve this effect (see "Statement Groups" in Chapter 4, "Compound Commands," for more information and examples).

Summary

This chapter has presented a large number of concepts, all of which are concerned with writing the so-called "simple" command. Actually, a simple command is called that because it is the basic unit of the shell language: it contains one action verb (usually the first word of the command line), a number of options and arguments, and possibly some modifiers. But the shell offers a rich variety of ways to write the command, options, arguments, and modifiers of the command line.

The various forms of expressions, wild cards, variables, and redirections are all intended to simplify your job of getting the computer to do what you want—the only problem is that they also make the shell language difficult to learn.

The opening section, "Standard UNIX Command Format," reviews the syntax of UNIX commands. The syntax of UNIX commands is much simpler than the syntax of shell commands, and more important for you to understand. The UNIX command syntax is the syntax actually understood by command programs themselves. Any shell command you enter using variables, wild cards, or other forms of shell expression must be reduced to the UNIX command format before invoking the command. Unlike some other operating systems (MS-DOS for example), UNIX commands understand nothing of wild cards, or any of the other expression forms; UNIX commands understand only options and arguments.

The UNIX command is a series of *words*. A word is any series of nonblank characters delimited by white space. To execute a command, the shell must break the command line into its component words. Any shell must do this. To invoke the command, the shell passes the list of words obtained after discarding any white space to the UNIX kernel, which takes over the job of loading and executing the command. The UNIX kernel always interprets the first word in the list as the name of the command and retrieves the program file with that name. The remainder of the words in the list is simply passed to the command program, which can interpret them in any way it wants.

The point of the standard UNIX command format is to try to impose some order and consistency to the way options and arguments are interpreted by the hundreds of UNIX commands. Fortunately for us, the standard command format is now followed by nearly all commands, but this was not always so. It actually has taken more than a decade for uniformity in command syntax to emerge as the UNIX operating system evolved.

The short section entitled "Simple Commands" presents the raw syntax of the simple command. The whole remainder of the chapter is needed to fully explain the implications of the syntax description presented in that section.

The next section, "Regular and Special Characters," introduces a theme that will hound you for the rest of your UNIX career, namely the *metacharacter*. These are characters that the shell uses to mark special syntax in the command line. For example, the dollar sign ($) introduces a variable reference; a double quote (") introduces a series of characters that must be interpreted as a single word even if the series contains embedded white space. These special characters pose a problem for you because there are often situations where these characters must be passed through to the UNIX command—for example, to form an unusual but legal file name. The problem then becomes to find a way to hide the character from the shell so that it will be passed to the command unmodified. Ways to solve this problem are described later in the chapter, in the section on "Quoting."

The "Comments" section introduces the brief subject of shell comment statements. These statements, always beginning with a # symbol (pronounced "hash," "sharp," or "pound" by various folks), provide a way to enter arbitrary text, usually into a shell script, to explain something to other people who may see the comment. The comment is used infrequently at the keyboard but is often sprinkled profusely throughout shell scripts.

The "Wild Cards" section explains how to use the shell's shorthand notation for writing file names in a command line. By the judicious use of wild cards, you can write one short "generic" file name which the shell will replace with dozens of file names. This is useful when you want to perform the same action on many different files—for example, to remove them or to print them out. If there is some pattern to the way the files are named, you can use wild cards to describe that pattern to the shell; then you don't have to type out each file name by hand. Experienced UNIX users like to use wild cards because wild cards greatly reduce the amount of typing you have to do.

The "Shell Variables" section introduces the concept of variables and presents a complete reference of all the variable symbols that are used or recognized by the shell. (In Part II, Chapter 7, "Using Variables," presents a much more detailed explanation of the concepts of variables.) The shell variables described in this section are used primarily to pass information to the shell. When you assign a value to the PATH variable, for example, the shell uses the value whenever it looks for a command. The relationship between a variable's name and its value is similar to the relationship between your name and yourself: it is a label used to identify a real object, except that for shell variables, the real objects are sequences of characters such as file or path names. For some shell variables, the total extent of your involvement with them is to set the value of a variable and let the shell use the value whenever it is needed. You can use other variables, such as the $HOME variable, in a command line as an abbreviation for a long path name.

The section on "Shell Prompts" explains all about the taciturn little dollar sign ($) that the shell prints in front of each of your commands. You can change the shell prompt to be something other than $ if you want, and sometimes it is helpful to do so. Many UNIX systems offer the ability to operate two or more login sessions from one terminal. If you're lucky enough to have such a system, you can use the prompt to remind you which login session you're currently working with.

The next section, "Command Substitution," addresses the remarkable capability of the shell to capture the output of a command and use that output as arguments in the command line of another command or as the value to be assigned to a variable. With command substitution, you can in effect use commands to write commands. For example, the wonderfully terse statement vi `grep -l george *.mail` at one stroke invokes the vi editor for all files whose name ends in .mail and that contain the word george anywhere in the file. The shell simply replaces the backward single quotes (`) and everything between them with the output of the command they enclose. Command substitution is similar to quoting but has a different purpose.

The final section of this chapter, "I/O Redirection," addresses the subject for which UNIX is best known: the ability to easily channel the input and output of a command to or from any file or device you want. Many UNIX commands provide no options to tell the command where to read its input from or where to write its output. By default, such commands read and write from your terminal. With the use of I/O redirection, you can cause such commands to read their input from an arbitrary file or to write their output to a file. For example, if you're a programmer, you occasionally may find it useful to redirect the compiler's error messages into a file so that you can examine them at your leisure. With redirection you can capture a listing of the files in your directory generated by ls, edit the list with vi, and then submit the list to the xargs command to remove, copy, or back up just the files you've selected. You can do many things with I/O redirection that are just not possible with any system but UNIX.

The remaining chapters in this book discuss the ways to combine simple commands into more complicated structures. Consequently, this chapter is perhaps the most important in the whole book. You should spend spend some time at the terminal trying out the many things this chapter has shown you how to do.

3

Compound Commands

The previous chapter examined the format of UNIX commands and reviewed the additional features of the shell for expressing a simple command: Input/ Output redirection, wild cards, variables, command substitution, backslashing, and quoting. This does not exhaust the capabilities of the shell. In addition, the shell supports the following statement types:

- Multiple commands per line, called *command lists*

- Background execution, where one or more commands execute invisibly while you continue to do other work at your terminal

- *Pipelines*, which allow the direct passing of data between two simultaneously active processes

- Conditional execution of a command list based on the success or failure of a command

- *Grouping*, which allows you to treat several commands as a unit

Although the previous chapter concentrated on *commands*, this chapter focuses on shell *statements*. Everything you type in response to the $ prompt is considered a shell statement. A statement can consist of one or several commands, or it can be a special construction that invokes a function or service built into the shell.

This chapter discusses the various methods for combining simple commands into larger units with new control and input/output capabilities.

Command Lists: ;

List

```
conditional-statement
or conditional-statement ; list
or conditional-statement & list
```

This chapter describes the syntax of shell statements. The previous box shows an example of syntax. Each box introduces a category of shell statement structures. Think of these categories as the parts of speech in the English language. The previous box describes the statement list, or *list*. Just as a *paragraph* in the English language is a list of basic elements called *sentences*, so too is the shell language *list* composed of basic elements, called *conditional statements*.

The name of a shell syntax structure is shown in the upper-left corner of a syntax box. The section containing the box defines this structure. The remainder of the box describes how the structure is built from simpler units.

When simpler syntax elements have to be be chained together to construct the larger unit, the elements are listed one after another on the same line. This process mirrors the English language, where one type of *sentence* can be formed by the list: *subject, verb, direct object.*

When a shell statement can be written in any one of several alternate forms, the alternatives are listed vertically and introduced with the word or. In the English language, for example, you know a *subject* can be any one of the following:

> *subject:*
> > *article noun*
> > or *noun-phrase*
> > or *gerund*

Of course, because each of the syntax items—*article, noun, noun phrase,* and *gerund*—are parts of speech, you should expect to find a similar syntax declaration for each in the text.

The previous syntax box shows that a *list* can take one of three forms. It can be a single *conditional statement*, or it can be a list of *conditional-statement elements* separated by a colon (:) or ampersand (&).

The text following a syntax box always explains the meaning of the syntax, but, because the syntax definition is intended for those experienced in using the shell, the explanation simply might mention some elements of the syntax that are discussed in depth elsewhere in the book.

The *command list* is, as its name implies, a list of statements to be executed one after another. Wherever the shell permits a single statement, it permits a list of statements.

In a command list, statements are separated by a semicolon (;) or by any number of newlines. The ampersand (&) also can separate consecutive statements (see the next section, "Background Jobs," for details).

The following is a command list:

```
cd worklib
grep nancy *.mail >xref
pg xref
```

This is also a list of these statements:

```
cd worklib; grep nancy *.mail >xref; pg xref
```

You can enter as many statements separated by semicolons as you want on a single line. Execution of the first statement does not begin until you finish the line by typing return; then each statement is executed after the previous statement finishes. Therefore, the statements of a list are executed consecutively.

Background Jobs: &

The shell normally waits for a command to complete execution before going to the next command. When you append the & operator to the end of a command, the shell goes to the next command immediately without waiting for the previous command to finish. When the shell does not wait for a command to complete, the command is said to execute in the *background*.

The terms *foreground* and *background* seem to imply different regions or areas of the computer where programs might run; in UNIX, however, these terms merely indicate whether or not a program is in communication with your terminal. A foreground program is one you are actively working with, such as a visual text editor; the key characteristic of a foreground program is that the shell waits for it to complete execution before issuing another prompt. A background program normally does not communicate with your terminal, and the shell does not wait for it to complete; you can enter other commands while the background program continues to run unobtrusively and unseen.

When the shell executes a command ending with &, it types the process-ID of the new process created to run the command. The shell then issues a prompt to your terminal immediately, without waiting for the process to finish. (The concept of a *process* is explained in Chapter 1, "Introduction to UNIX.")

When the shell initiates a background process, it normally redirects the standard input of the process to /dev/null. The /dev/null file is a special file that always looks empty. Reading this file returns end-of-file immediately; writing to it effectively discards the output. By setting standard input to the /dev/null file, the shell prevents the background process from trying to read from your terminal while you are using it for other things. If you want to provide a background process with an input file, you must redirect the command's standard input to that file (see "Input/Output Redirection" in Chapter 3, "Shell Basics").

This example invokes a command for background execution:

```
$ sort timesheets >tm.0626 &
8506
$ ps
    PID TTY        TIME COMMAND
     53 tty1      0:02 sh
   8506 tty1      0:00 sort
   8508 tty1      0:01 ps
$
```

If the timesheets file is large, it might take a long time to sort it. By running the command in the background, you do not have to wait for the sort to finish before doing other work. As the dialog shows, the shell starts the job, reports its process-ID, then issues a prompt immediately. You can do other work while the file is being sorted. The ps command shows the sort command is still running.

Using the ps Command

If you forget the process-ID of a background job but want to terminate it, or if you want to check whether a particular background job is still running, you can use the ps command to display a list of your currently active processes:

```
$ ps
   PID TTY        TIME COMMAND
    53 tty1      0:02 sh
    88 tty1      0:24 sort
   102 tty1      0:00 sh
   125 tty1      0:06 payw
   379 tty1      0:00 ps
$
```

The output of ps probably will show more processes than you expect, as in the previous example. You can clearly identify process 88 as the sort commands you previously entered. Process 379 is the ps command itself, which is of course active while it is producing this output. Process 102, however, might be somewhat mysterious; why is there another copy of the shell running?

The shell often has to invoke a subordinate copy of itself to manage the execution of a job. The second sh is actually a *subshell* of your login shell. See the section called "Statement Groups" later in this chapter for more information about subshells.

Using the kill Command

The shell reports the process-ID of the background job so you can terminate the job later if you want to. To cancel a background job already in progress, issue the kill command and specify the process-ID of the job to be terminated:

```
$ kill 8506
Terminated
$
```

To terminate all your background jobs at once, specify a process-ID of zero:

```
$ kill 0
sort: 88 Terminated
payw: 125 Terminated
Terminated
$
```

When you terminate more than one job, the shell reports the command name and process-ID (sort and 88, for example) of each job terminated. In this case three processes are terminated: the sort command, the payw command, and the subshell controlling payw. Thus the kill command is followed by three Terminated messages, not two.

When you terminate a job, you might receive only partial output or no output at all from the terminated job and you might damage files used by this job; for these reasons, you should use the kill command cautiously.

Using the nohup Command

When you log off, any background processes you are running at the time are automatically killed. Sometimes you might want to log off and let your background jobs continue to run until they are finished, perhaps long after you have gone home.

The nohup command disables the normal mechanism by which active processes are killed when you log off. If you use the nohup command to start a background job, that background job is immune to automatic logoff termination.

The format of the nohup command is:

```
nohup command &
```

You must enter the command that you want to protect as the argument of the nohup command. You can use redirections in the usual way:

```
$ nohup sort timesheets >tm.0619 &
```

This command runs sort as a background job, protects it from logoff termination, and sends the output of sort to the file tm.0619. After invoking the sort command this way, you can safely log off and the sort command continues to run.

If you do not redirect standard output, the nohup command automatically sends both output and error messages from command to the file nohup.out in your current directory.

Using the nice Command

When the system has to execute many processes simultaneously, the time available to spend working on each one diminishes accordingly. The decrease in the time the system spends per minute working on your own processes is regarded as reduced performance.

Reduced system performance is noticeable when it affects an interactive shell, because the shorter commands that users frequently execute take progressively longer to run, and your overall effectiveness decreases. Even if you like working with computers, taking longer than necessary to do a piece of work can be quite frustrating.

One way to minimize the impact of a heavy system load on the performance of interactive shells is to *prioritize* the system's work. Users like the system to give higher priority to shells that actually interact with users; background jobs—whose entire existence is somewhat ghost-like— can wait longer for their turn at the computer and thus avoid making users wait longer than necessary.

UNIX attempts to automatically bias its allocation of computer time toward preference of interactive processes. (An *interactive* process is one for which a user directly enters input or views output—that is, a foreground process.) However, distinguishing between interactive and non-interactive processes is tricky at best. You can help the system by actually telling it which processes should be executed at a lower priority.

Only you can decide when a process (typically a background job) can be executed at reduced priority without affecting your satisfaction with the system's performance. Whenever you are in no hurry for a background job to complete, you should use the nice command to invoke the background command at a reduced priority.

The format of the nice command is

```
nice [ -incr ] command &
```

Just as with the nohup command, the nice command internally invokes command. Before doing so, nice reduces the priority of the process by incr. For incr you can specify a value from 1 to 19; the larger the number, the less priority command has. If you omit the incr option, nice assumes a default value of 10.

When you invoke a command using nice, you do both yourself and everyone else a favor by reducing the degree to which your background jobs compete for system resources. Using the sort job as an example, the command

```
$ nice -15 sort timesheets >tm.0619 &
```

places less burden on the system than would the sort command executed by itself.

The bgnice option of the ksh command provides an automatic nice for each background command you execute. For more information, see Chapter 10, "Built-In Commands."

Conditional Statements: && and ¦¦

A shell conditional statement consists of two or more pipelines separated by the && (*and*) or ¦¦ (*or*) operators. A pipeline, by itself, is considered a degenerate case of a conditional statement. A pipeline can be a simple command. (The next section, "Pipelines," discusses pipelines in detail.

For now, it is only important to understand that a conditional statement is two or more simpler shell constructs joined by && or ¦¦.)

Conditional-statement

```
pipeline
or conditional-statement && pipeline
or conditional-statement ¦¦ pipeline
```

The ability to list more than one command on a line is a great convenience, but it also has its drawbacks. Consider the following command list, for example:

```
$ cd src/payw; rm main.c
```

There is no assurance the cd command executes successfully; your current directory might not be what you think it is, or you might mistype the directory name. If the cd command fails, the current directory remains unchanged, but the rm command is executed anyway. Failure of the cd command could result in removal of the wrong main.c file, which—depending on its importance and how well you keep backups—could be a disaster.

The shell provides a way to avoid the undesirable side effects of a command's failure by allowing you to condition the execution of a command on the success or failure of a previous command. You do this using the && and ¦¦ operators.

Using the && Operator

The && (called *and*) operator causes the shell to execute the command following the operator only if the command preceding it succeeded. You could rewrite the previous command list as follows:

```
$ cd src/payw && rm main.c
```

When rewritten this way, the rm command is executed only if the exit value of the cd command is zero (exit values are discussed in the section called "Standard UNIX Command Format" in Chapter 3).

The shell always interprets a nonzero exit value as an indication of the command's failure. By no coincidence, all UNIX commands and most user-written commands follow the shell's convention and return a zero exit value to indicate success, and a nonzero exit value to indicate failure.

The priority of the && operator is greater than that of the ; and & operators. Given a shell statement of the form

```
$ nroff notes.txt >notes.1st && lp notes.1st; rm notes.*
```

the shell always executes the nroff command; the lp command is executed *only* if the nroff command is successful; and the rm command *always* is executed. In other words, the shell treats the nroff and lp commands as one unit, and the rm command as another unit. In this particular case, it would have been better if the shell grouped the lp and rm commands together. There is a way to force the shell to use such a grouping—see the section "Statement Groups" later in this chapter.

Using the ¦¦ Operator

The ¦¦ operator (called *or*) is the opposite of the && operator; the shell statement following ¦¦ is executed only if the statement preceding it failed. The ¦¦ operator provides a way to specify an alternative action to be taken when a command fails.

The ¦¦ operator can be helpful at the keyboard when you prepare a background job. With the command

```
$ cc payw.c -o payw ¦¦ lint payw.c &
```

you can arrange to have the shell run lint if compilation of the source file payw.c fails. This way you obtain at least some useful output from the background job.

The ¦¦ operator is especially handy when you write shell scripts. The statement

```
$ test -d /tmp/pay ¦¦ mkdir /tmp/pay
```

creates the directory /tmp/pay only if that directory does not already exist.

When you cannot tolerate the failure of a command, a statement of the form

```
$ mkdir /tmp/pay ¦¦ exit
```

provides a convenient way to terminate a shell script if a command fails.

Combining the && and ¦¦ Operators

The && and ¦¦ operators have equal priority; a series of them are interpreted in left-to-right order.

For example, the command

```
$ cd src/payw && rm main.c ¦¦ pwd
```

is treated by the shell as if the left side of the ¦¦ operator were the cd and rm command group. The pwd command is executed if either the cd or the rm command fails.

For comparison, consider this statement:

```
$ test -d /tmp/pay ¦¦ mkdir /tmp/pay && payw -h >/tmp/pay/checks
```

The && and ¦¦ operators occur here in the opposite order as the previous example. Because the operators have the same priority, the shell proceeds as follows:

1. Execute the test command, which sets an exit value of 0 if /tmp/pay exists and is a directory.

2. If the test command fails (the exit value is nonzero), execute the mkdir command to create the /tmp/pay directory; the exit value is 0 if the mkdir command is successful.

3. If the last exit value is 0, execute the payw command.

If the test command succeeds, the mkdir command is skipped and the payw command is executed immediately. If the test command fails, the mkdir command is executed next, and the payw command is executed only if the mkdir command is successful.

Once again, the shell treated the first pair of commands as a unit. Because the first pair is joined with ¦¦, the pair are considered successful if either command is successful, and that in turn is sufficient to satisfy the && condition.

Pipelines: ¦

Pipeline

```
statement-group
or pipeline ¦ statement-group
```

This shell syntax box describes a *pipeline* as two or more *statement groups* separated by the ¦ operator (the symbol is pronounced "pipe"). The statement-group construct is fully explained in the next section. A simple command is one example of a statement group. A statement group, by itself, can be considered a degenerate case of a pipeline.

You establish a *pipeline* between two commands whenever you invoke the commands in the following way:

```
command1 ¦ command2
```

The shell starts both *command1* and *command2* for simultaneous execution. The standard output of *command1* is sent to one side of a pipe, and the other side is set up as the input to *command2*. In other words, everything written to standard output by *command1* appears on the standard input of *command2*.

The pipe mechanism is a basic UNIX facility. A pipe is like a file because commands can read information from it or write information to it. However, unlike most files, a pipe is not a permanent storage area for information. Information written to a pipe is held in system memory until another program attempts to read from the pipe; then the information held in memory is passed to the reading program. Normally a pipe is open by two different programs at the same time; one program opens the pipe for output, the other opens the pipe for input. The pipe therefore acts like a *conduit* for passing information directly between two programs.

The advantage of using pipes is that the data transferred through the pipe is never stored anywhere outside the computer's memory; it requires no disk space and almost no time to pass large amounts of data from *command1* to *command2*.

To simulate the effect of a pipe, you can use a temporary file and rewrite the pipeline as follows:

```
$ command1 >temp.file
$ command2 <temp.file
```

This rewriting has two disadvantages: first, the data must be written to disk and then read back in; second, the size of temp.file is constrained by the amount of disk space available. Any amount of data can flow through the pipe, and much faster than through a disk file.

A pipeline can consist of more than one pipe. If the commands used in the middle of the pipeline both read from standard input and write to standard output, a *multistage* pipeline such as

```
$ tbl chap1.txt ¦ nroff -mm ¦ col ¦ lp
```

is valid and quite useful. The tbl command reads text and formatting commands from the file chap1.txt; the output of tbl becomes the input of the nroff command; the output of nroff becomes the input of the col command,

and the output of col becomes the input of the lp command. Without using temporary files, the command formats an entire document and directs it to the printer in one continuous flow of processing.

Because pipes work only with commands that read from standard input or write to standard output, commands that work that way have extra value. A program that does both is called a *filter* because it can be used to easily transform data from one form to another. In the multistage pipeline shown previously, the nroff and col commands are examples of filters; they transform input data into another form appearing on standard output. Using filters, you can set up a multistage pipeline that performs quite complicated processing.

All four programs (tbl, nroff, col, and lp) are active and running at the same time. Conceivably, the first line of output from the tbl command could be processed by nroff and col, passed to lp, and be printed, all before tbl generates its next output line.

Simplifying a Pipeline

When the system is operating near capacity, it might not be able to set up a long pipeline. This is because the system's limit on the maximum number of processes that can be active at one time could be exceeded, or the pipeline might call for more files to be open at once than the system can support. These errors can occur only if the system is already running many processes or has many files open; no single pipeline you will build is likely to exceed the system's limits.

You can always simplify a pipeline so fewer simultaneously active processes or open files are required. The procedure is as follows:

1. Choose one pipe symbol (¦) from several in the pipeline where the pipeline could be split into two simpler statements. Delete the pipe symbol and break the line at that point into two lines. Example:

   ```
   tbl chap1.txt ¦ nroff -mm ¦ col ¦ lp
   ```

   becomes

   ```
   tbl chap1.txt ¦ nroff -mm
   col ¦ lp
   ```

2. Redirect the standard output of the first line to a temporary file:

   ```
   tbl chap1.txt ¦ nroff -mm >chap1.lst
   col ¦ lp
   ```

3. Redirect the standard input of the second line from the temporary file:

```
tbl chap1.txt ¦ nroff -mm >chap1.lst
col < chap1.lst ¦ lp
```

This procedure results in the pipeline being broken into two shorter pipelines (one or both of which can be a single command) and a temporary file being inserted to hold the intermediate data that previously flowed through a pipe.

Using Redirections with Pipes

A pipe is an implicit form of redirection. Consider the following pipeline, for example:

```
$ find /u -depth -print ¦ cpio -oc >/dev/rmt0
```

To set up the pipeline, the shell redirects the standard output of the find command to one side of the pipe, and redirects the standard input of the cpio command to the other side of the pipe. The cpio command is useful when backing up files because it copies large quantities of data from one place to another.

Because the syntax of pipes differs from that of redirections, you can specify redirections that conflict with the pipeline. For example, the command

```
$ find /u -depth -print >list ¦ cpio -oc >/dev/rmt0   #wrong
```

would not have the expected effect: the output of find would be written to the file list, and nothing would be written to the pipe. The first read by cpio would receive the end-of-file, and the backup tape /dev/rmt0 would be empty.

This confusion occurs because the shell first performs the redirections necessary to establish the pipeline, then performs any additional redirections you specified. (The subsequent user redirections override the pipeline redirections.) Neither the Bourne nor the Korn shell detects such conflicts; it is your responsibility to avoid them.

Operator Priorities

The priority of the pipe operator is greater than that of the && and ¦¦ operators, which are in turn greater than that of the ; and & operators. See the following statement, for example:

```
$ tbl mybook.txt ¦ nroff ¦ col >mybook.lst &
```

Here the ¦ operator has higher priority (binds more tightly together) than the & operator, so the `tbl`, `nroff`, and `col` commands all bind together into a unit to which the & operator is applied. The entire three-stage pipeline runs in the background. Similarly, the shell input

```
$ echo My Listing; pr mybook.1st ¦ lp
```

is actually two statements: the `echo` command is executed first, then the pipeline. The shell does not consider the `echo` command to be part of the pipeline, so the output of `echo` goes to your terminal and only the output of the `pr` command is piped to `lp`.

The && and ¦¦ operators also treat a pipeline as a unit. For example, a command of the general form

```
$ a ¦¦ b ¦ c && d
```

is interpreted by the shell as follows:

1. Execute command a.

2. If a fails, execute the pipeline b ¦ c.

3. If the previous command executed (a or c) is successful, execute d.

You can change the default interpretation by using the grouping operators. For more information see the section called "Statement Grouping" later in this chapter.

Processing Several Files with One Command

When describing Input/Output redirection in Chapter 3, "Shell Basics," the chapter noted the shell does not explicitly allow you to specify more than one file as the source of an input redirection.

However, you can use the `cat` command and a pipe to combine several files into one and then process the combined file with another command. It works like this:

```
$ cat file1 file2 ... ¦ command
```

The `cat` command lists the files named as its arguments to standard output; the standard output of `cat` therefore appears as one long file with the contents of *file1*, *file2*, and so on, strung end-to-end. Due to the pipe, the standard input of *command* appears to be only this concatenation of files.

Statement Groups: {} and ( )

Group

simple-command
or { *list* ; }
or (*list*)

The syntax of a statement group, as shown in the previous box, allows you to enclose any statement *list* (lists are explained at the beginning of this chapter) in parentheses (( )) or braces ({}). The group of enclosed statements is treated syntactically by the shell as a single statement for the purpose of setting pipelines and redirections, or for establishing the order of evaluating conditional statements. Syntactically, a simple command is a degenerate case of a statement group.

In the previous sections, you have been examining the way the shell groups statements combined with the ; , &, ¦, &&, and ¦¦ operators. The default grouping is not necessarily the one you would always want. The grouping operators provide a way to override the shell's default grouping.

Grouping operators provide one more capability; the ability to apply a redirection to an entire group of statements rather than just one statement.

Grouping with { }

The { (left brace) and } (right brace) are operators only when they are not combined with any other characters, and only at the beginning of a command. When embedded in a word, or when appearing as a command argument, the braces are treated as ordinary characters.

All the commands and statements appearing between braces are treated as a unit when evaluating operator priorities, and with respect to redirections.

Using Nested Redirections

You can use redirections on individual commands inside the braces and on the entire brace group as well. When conflicts occur, a redirection on an inner command takes precedence over a redirection applied to the group. The following command shows how overriding redirections can be used effectively:

```
${
$   echo "NAME      UID GID IDENT"
$   sort -t: +0 -1 /etc/passwd > /tmp/users
$   who ¦ cut -d' ' -f1 ¦ sort -u ¦
$     join -t: -j1 1 -j2 1 - /tmp/users ¦
$     awk -F: '{printf "%-8s %3d %3d %s\n", $1, $3, $4, $5}'
$   rm /tmp/users
$} >who.o
```

The purpose of this command is to display a sorted, annotated list of the users who are currently using the system. The overall output of the command is written into the file who.o, which could later be printed, viewed, edited, or used as input to some other command. The output of the command looks like this:

```
NAME      UID GID IDENT
fred      105   7 Ferdinand Foobar
marianne 100   7 Marianne LePesque
src       106   2 Source Administration
```

The echo command writes a heading line to label each column of the report. Because the output of the echo command is not redirected, the output redirection for the command group applies, and the message is written into who.o.

The sort command produces a sorted version of the /etc/passwd file. Standard output is redirected to the /tmp/users file so the sorted file can be captured for later use by the join command. Although standard output has already been redirected to the who.o file for the group of commands, it is redirected separately for the sort command.

The pipeline that follows gets a list of the currently active users from the who command, discards all but the first field of each line using cut, sorts the user list, and then uses the join command to select lines with the same user name from the /tmp/users file. The awk command is used to convert lines in the /etc/passwd file format to a format that is easier to read.

The output of the final stage of the pipeline (the awk command) is not redirected, it is written to the who.o file. As the last step in the command group, the temporary file /tmp/users is deleted with the rm command.

Although this example demonstrates only the redirection and re-redirection of standard output, the same principle applies to the standard input and standard error files.

Command groups can be nested within command groups; inner command groups can be redirected, and commands in inner groups can be redirected again. The shell does not lose track of the current redirections at each group and command level, no matter how complicated the statement.

Overriding Operator Priorities

Braces can change the shell's interpretation of a series of commands. In the section called "Using the && Operator" earlier in this chapter, you looked at the shell's interpretation of the command

```
nroff notes.txt >notes.lst && lp notes.lst; rm notes.*
```

By default, the rm command is executed whether or not the nroff command succeeds. However, by using braces, you can force the shell to treat the lp and rm commands as a unit, both of which are dependent on the success of the nroff command, as follows:

```
nroff notes.txt >notes.lst && { lp notes.lst; rm notes.*; }
```

Now, if the nroff command fails, nothing else happens; but if it is successful, the lp command prints the nroff output, and the rm command removes your temporary working files.

You do not have to write the entire command on one line; the newline character also can be used to separate commands, like this:

```
$ nroff notes.txt > notes.lst &&
> {
> lp notes.lst
> rm notes.*
> }
lp-251
$
```

Notice how the shell uses the secondary prompt character (>) to remind you that you have not finished the command yet. For more information about prompts, see the PS1 and PS2 shell variable descriptions in Chapter 3, "Shell Basics."

Braces also affect the interpretation of commands combined with &&, ¦¦, and ¦ operators. In the previous sections "Pipelines" and "Operator Priorities," you looked at the following command form

```
a ¦¦ b ¦ c && d
```

and noted the shell would, by default, group the commands as if

```
a ¦¦ { b ¦ c; } && d
```

were written. Using braces, you can change the shell's interpretation of the command to

```
{ a ¦¦ b; } ¦ { c && d; }
```

which might be more useful; as regrouped, the shell executes a pipeline between two conditional commands. Consider the following application for example:

```
{ pr monthly.pay || pr weekly.pay } | { lp && rm *.pay ; }
```

If the monthly payroll file exists, it is printed; otherwise the weekly payroll file is printed. In either case, the file is removed after printing.

For another example, look at this command:

```
a && { b || c; }
```

Its operation is quite different, in some circumstances, from the unadorned command:

```
a && b || c
```

In the first case, if the a command fails, then both the b and c commands are skipped. In the second case, if the a command fails, the c command is executed. Consider the following experiment:

```
$ false && echo b || echo c
c
$ false && { echo b || echo c; }
$
```

The false command always returns a nonzero exit value, but performs no other action. The first command displays c because, by default, the shell interprets the statement as

```
$ { false && echo b; } || echo c
```

Grouping with ( )

The parentheses ( ) group commands much like braces; however, they differ in the following respects:

- Parentheses do not have to be separated from other characters by white space, as do braces. Parentheses are full metacharacters, and are recognized as grouping operators by the shell wherever they occur in the command line, unless quoted or backslashed.

- A command group enclosed in parentheses is executed by a *subshell*; in other words, by a copy of the shell as a new process. Commands that change the process environment have no effect outside the parentheses.

Because parentheses initiate a subshell, commands that would be awkward to use inside {} groups are convenient inside () groups. Consider the following command:

```
$ (cd /usr/src/pay; pr main.c; cc main.c -o main 2>&1) | lp
```

Because the effect of the cd command ends with the closing parenthesis, you do not have to cd back to your original directory after this command.

Redirections applied to a subshell apply to all commands in the subshell, just as with {}. In the previous example, the output of pr is written to the pipe and both the standard output and standard error of the cc command also are written to the pipe. The lp command therefore prints a listing of the main.c file, followed by any error messages written by cc.

Functions

This section discusses concepts related to shell programming. Although functions enable you to create handy abbreviations for commands, full use of these functions requires some knowledge of shell programming.

> **Function**
>
> *name* () { *list* ; }

A shell *function* is a named collection of commands that can be executed simply by entering the function name. A function definition consists of three parts: a *name*, a pair of parentheses, and a command list enclosed in a pair of braces.

The function's name must conform to the shell rules for variable names: it must begin with an alphabetic letter or the underscore (_), and can be followed by any number of letters, digits, or the underscore character.

The () characters following the function name alert the shell that this is a function definition. White space can appear between the parentheses, but is not required.

The following command list constitutes the body of the function definition; it must comply with the rules for forming a statement group with braces. Some versions of the shell permit the braces to be omitted when the function body consists of only one shell statement; however, this usage is non-standard and does not follow modern usage. Even when the function body contains only one statement, you should enclose it in braces.

Functions are often a handy way of abbreviating commands for use at the keyboard. For example, the following defines a new command named man that displays on-line help information using a full-screen pager:

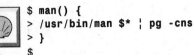

```
$ man() {
> /usr/bin/man $* ¦ pg -cns
> }
$
```

After entering the man function definition, the command

```
$ man grep
```

displays help information for the grep command using pg; you can page backward and forward through the display at your leisure, and the information does not scroll off the top of your screen as it used to.

If the function name duplicates the name of another function, a built-in shell command, or a regular command, then that function or command can no longer be invoked by its name. A function or built-in shell command becomes inaccessible because there is no other name by which it can be accessed. A regular command can still be accessed by using its full path name, as the function definition of man demonstrated.

Notice that shell functions can do things that are difficult or impossible to do with *aliases*. The Korn shell alias command allows you to abbreviate a command and its options to a single short word, but the function (supported by both the Bourne and Korn shells) allows you to execute multiple commands with one command entry, and to use the command arguments wherever appropriate.

Defining Functions

A function must first be defined before it can be used. To define a function, you must arrange for the shell to execute the function definition. When executed, the shell stores the pre-processed function definition in memory; in effect the function definition becomes a user-written built-in command.

The following shell input defines a function:

```
$ lx() {
> /bin/ls -FC $*
> }
$
```

The following shell input does *not* define a function:

```
$ true ¦¦ lx() {
> /bin/ls -FC $*
> }
$ lx $HOME/bin
lx not found
$
```

Because the `true` command always returns an exit value of 0, the function definition of `lx` never is executed; a subsequent attempt to invoke the function fails with the message `lx not found`.

In a shell script, it is usually best to locate all function definitions at the beginning of the script file. If you place function definitions at the end of the script file, the functions are not defined until after all other commands in the file have been executed—probably not what you intended.

Calling Functions

To invoke a function, simply enter its name:

```
$ lx
adm/              lib/              terminfo/
bin/              mail/             tmp/
etc/              mbox
$
```

A function also can be invoked with arguments. In the function definition, the arguments are accessible in the special variables $1, $2, $3, and so on. For more information about using arguments, see Chapter 7, "Using Variables."

For good or ill, the arguments of a function call replace the current shell arguments. If you later have to refer to the current shell arguments, you must save them before calling a function; they can later be restored with the `set` built-in command:

```
args="$*"
fun
set $args
```

Function Execution

When you call a function, the shell simply executes a list of statements stored out-of-line from the current shell input. No subshell is invoked and no new process is created. As a result, any changes to the shell environment remain in effect after the function exits. Specifically, the following actions have lasting effect:

- Any change of the current directory.

- Any change of the file-creation mask with `umask`.

- Any change of process limits with `ulimit`.

- Any creation, setting, unsetting, or exporting of shell variables.

- Any alteration of the shell arguments by set or shift.

  In addition, a function call always has the following effects:

- The last exit value ($?) is changed by return or by reaching the end of the function.

- The argument list ($* and $@) is the list of arguments from the function call.

- The number of arguments ($#) is the number of arguments that appeared on the function call.

A redirection applied to a function call is in effect for the entire function body; this is equivalent to applying a redirection to a statement group (see "Statement Groups" earlier in this chapter).

Some Useful Functions

Functions can be a great time saver at the keyboard. You can add any number of functions to your .profile, as in the following examples. You can use these specific functions, or they might suggest to you some shell functions that would save you time.

Directory Push and Pop: pushd and popd

The two functions pushd and popd (Listing 4.1) go together. The pushd function acts like cd, but saves the path name of your current directory on a stack. The popd function returns you to the directory on the top of stack (the most recent directory saved by pushd). You can use them to move from directory to directory without getting lost, and popd enables you to return to a directory you have previously visited without having to type the directory's path name or even remember where you were.

Listing 4.1. The pushd and popd functions.

```
# pushd - save current directory then cd
pushd() {
    DIRS="`pwd` ${DIRS}"
    cd $1
}
# popd - return to previous directory
popd() {
    set -- ${DIRS:-.}
```

```
    cd $1
    shift 1
    DIRS="$*"
}
```

The following function, up, also is helpful for directory management. Use up to change to the immediate parent of your current directory. Though simple, this function saves keystrokes, which is after all the purpose of shell functions.

```
up() {
    cd ..
    pwd
}
```

The to Function

Many find the cd command to be somewhat inadequate by itself. Frequently, changing to a new directory immediately raises the question of what files are contained in the directory, so you often might find yourself issuing the ls command after a cd. The following function combines cd with ls and also provides a facility for managing your shell environment.

When you use a directory for a specific purpose—such as to develop a program for an application or to hold mail messages you have received—you immediately want to do certain things when switching to that directory. The to function enables you to set up an environment file in such directories. The file, which must be named .i, should contain the shell commands you want executed whenever you switch into that directory. The to function automatically executes the commands in the file whenever you use to to switch to that directory.

As shown in Listing 4.2, the to command executes the ls command unless a .i file is present.

Listing 4.2. The to command.

```
to() {
    cd $1
    if [ -s .i ]
    then . .i
    else /bin/ls -bCF
    fi
}
```

Miscellaneous Functions

Listing 4.3 is a collection of shell functions that are straightforward and helpful.

The `cls` function clears the display screen. The `pg` function redefines the `pg` command to act as a full-screen pager. The `lx` function provides a multiple-column directory listing, and the `ll` function provides a long listing.

Listing 4.3. Miscellaneous functions.

```
# some handy shell functions
cls() { echo `\033[H\033[J\c´ >/dev/tty ; }
pg() { /usr/bin/pg -cns -p´Page %d:´ $* ; }
lx() { /bin/ls -bCF $* ; }
ll() { /bin/ls -lb $* ; }
```

4

Summary

This chapter provides a technical description of the shell syntax. The Bourne and Korn shells are complex languages with many nuances and peculiarities. You should not expect to completely understand what you read in this section if you are new to UNIX. Unfortunately, each part of UNIX is intertwined. No one can fully understand how to use the shell without also understanding the underlying paradigms of the UNIX kernel, including such baggage as process scheduling, permissions, and the like. Also, the design of the shell influenced many UNIX commands that were developed after the shell, so there is an intimate relationship between the way commands and shells work.

The simple command is the shell syntax's most elementary structure. The previous chapter covered the syntax of the simple command. This chapter discussed the facilities of the shell that combine several individual commands into a single larger, compound command. The structures discussed were lists, conditional statements, pipelines, statement groups, and functions.

The *list* is a rather simple concept enabling you to enter several commands at a time. Some other operating systems restrict you to entering one command at a time (MS-DOS is an example of such an operating system). UNIX, on the other hand, lets you enter several commands before hitting Return. Although this might not seem like a great advantage, it actually makes the shell much easier to use.

The *conditional* statement provides a way to execute (or not to execute) one statement, depending on the success or failure of a previous command. Although conditional statements are not often used with the keyboard, most experienced users would admit they should use the conditional statement more often for their own protection. Conditional statements are also an essential part of writing shell scripts.

The *pipeline* statement provides a fundamental UNIX capability—that of passing the output of one command directly to the input of another command without storing the data in an intermediate file. Although you might find pipelines to be unessential and maybe even peculiar at first, as your experience with UNIX increases, you will find yourself using pipelines more and more frequently.

The *statement-group* constructions are not used as often as the other structures, but they provide an important capability: enabling you to temporarily change your execution environment for the execution of a few commands, after which the previous environment is restored automatically. Many UNIX commands, such as cd or ulimit, change the execution environment. With the use of statement groups, you can change the environment temporarily and, therefore, avoid restoring an environment by hand.

This chapter completes your study of the shell syntax used at the keyboard. The next chapter ends Part I by presenting shell facilities you can use at your keyboard without introducing any new syntax. After that, you will be ready to plunge into Part II, "Shell Programming," where a new set of shell commands and syntax structures awaits you.

## Chapter 5

Special Features

Although the previous chapters have covered all the basic features of the shell, a number of shell features are not directly involved with the execution of commands. This chapter ties up those loose ends by examining the following:

- Invocation of the shell

- The shell options

- Command aliases (Korn shell only)

- Command history and command editing (Korn shell only)

After completing this chapter, you will have learned enough about the shell to use it effectively at your terminal. Remember, though, the shell is only a vehicle for entering and executing commands. To use UNIX like a pro, you must become familiar with the UNIX commands as well. The easiest way to do that is to sit down at your terminal with a good book about UNIX commands, such as *Using UNIX* (Que, 1990; ISBN 0-88022-519-X), and experiment. There is no substitute for hands-on experience and, with a little patience and a few good books, you can be your own guide to the UNIX environment.

From time to time, this book mentions UNIX facilities too advanced for the scope of this book to discuss in great depth. A companion volume, such as *UNIX Programmer's Reference* (Que, 1991; ISBN 0-88022-536-X), covers many topics that are discussed briefly in this book.

Shell Invocation

When you log in, the system automatically invokes the shell for you. You also might want to invoke the shell from time to time to:

- Execute a prepackaged stream of commands stored in a file

- Preserve your current process environment (working directory, file-creation mask, arguments, variables, and so on) while temporarily changing the environment to execute a command or series of commands

- Temporarily or permanently use a different shell

Despite its special importance, the shell is just a command like any of the hundreds of other UNIX commands. To execute it, you only have to type its name, followed by any options you want to use, followed by any arguments.

The name of the Bourne shell is sh; for the Korn shell, it is ksh. To execute a new, interactive copy of the shell, you only have to enter the name of the shell as a command:

```
$ sh
$
```

Now, although your prompt might look the same, you are executing a new copy of the shell. To prove this, execute the ps command to display the current list of processes:

```
$ ps
    PID TTY      TIME COMMAND
     53 cons1    0:02 sh
     66 cons1    0:00 sh
     67 cons1    0:00 ps
$
```

The output of ps shows that two separate processes, 53 and 66, are both executing the sh command. Your terminal communicates with the new shell until it terminates, at which time you once again will be in your original shell.

When running a second copy of the shell, you might want to change the prompt. This is easily done by assigning a new prompt string to the shell variable PS1 (see "Shell Variables" in Chapter 3, "Shell Basics," for more about the PS1 variable):

```
$ PS1="level 2: "
level 2:
```

To exit the second copy of the shell, use the `exit` command. (You also can press the EOF key—usually ^d—to send the shell an end-of-file on its input; the shell always exits when it reaches the end of its input file.)

```
level 2: exit
$
```

The prompt automatically returns to the original value of PS1 when you return to your top-level shell.

Shell Options

The shell supports a number of options that you can specify on the sh or ksh command. This section describes the supported options. To help you remember the various options, a mnemonic phrase in italics is provided for each key letter.

You can reverse the effect of an option by specifying +x rather than -x (where x is any option key letter) on the set command. For example, sh -e sets the error exit option, and set +e would unset the option. You cannot use the set command to set or unset the -c, -i, -p, -r, or -s options.

The -a Option *(All Export)*

When the -a option is set, any change to a variable causes the shell to automatically export it. The effect is that all variables defined or changed from the time the option is set are exported. Use +a to disable automatic exporting.

The -c Option *(Command)*

This option can be specified only on the command line; it cannot be set with the set command. The next argument is taken as a command and executed, after which the shell exits. This option is usually used in the form sh -c `"command"`.

The -e Option *(Exit on Error)*

This option causes the shell to exit immediately when a command returns a nonzero exit value. With this option you can execute a series of commands without having to test each command's exit value explicitly. Once the option is set, you can disable it by executing set +e. Note: Commands executed as the operand of if, while, or until do not affect the -e option.

The -f Option *(File Name Generation)*

When set, the -f option prevents the shell from expanding wild cards; the *, ?, and [ ] characters are treated as ordinary data characters. To resume normal wild-card expansion, issue the command set +f.

The -h Option *(Hash Functions)*

Use the -h option to cause the shell to define a function when the definition is read. Ordinarily, the shell considers a function to have been defined only when its definition has been executed. (See "Functions" in Chapter 4.) To revert to the standard action, issue set +h.

In the Korn shell only, the -h option causes each command encountered to be treated as a *tracked alias;* that is, as an alias for the full path name of the command. This is equivalent to the hashing facility of the Bourne shell. When the option is not set, or when set +h is issued, each invocation of a command other than an explicitly tracked alias results in a full search of the directories named in PATH. Setting the -h option usually improves the performance of the Korn shell.

The -i Option *(Interactive Shell)*

The interactive option causes the shell to issue a prompt before each read of standard input and to ignore signals to protect the shell from termination. The interactive option is assumed by default when the shell is invoked without the -c or -s options, and standard input is a terminal. The -i option cannot be set or reset with the set command.

The -k Option *(Keywords)*

Use the -k option to add keyword arguments occurring anywhere on the command line to the environment of the called command. When the -k option is not set, only keyword specifiers appearing before the command name are added to the environment of the command. Use set +k to cancel the effect of option -k and revert to standard shell handling of command arguments.

The -k option was intended to simplify the coding of shell scripts to support keyword operands on the command line. For example, if the -k option is set and the user issues the command copy /dev/rmt0 BLKSIZE=512, the variable BLKSIZE is set and has the value 512 when the shell script copy begins execution. However, because most users do not set the -k option, this facility usually is not available to shell script programmers.

The -m Option *(Monitor)*

The -m option causes a background command (a command ending with &) to be run in a separate process group. Such a command is immune to the kill 0 command, to the effects of the INTR key, and to logoff termination, and you get a message when the job finishes.

The -n Option *(No Execute)*

When set, the -n option prevents the shell from executing commands, although the commands can still be traced by the -v and -x options. The -n option is intended to facilitate testing of the logic of a shell script. Shell commands and built-in commands are executed even when the -n option is in effect. Issue set +n to cancel the no-execute option.

The -o Option *(option)*

The -o option allows the setting or unsetting of options by name. The allowed values of *option* are shown in Table 5.1.

Table 5.1. Options specifiable with -o.

Option Name	Effect
allexport	Same as -a
bgnice	Run background jobs at reduced priority. The bgnice option causes the Korn shell to execute background commands at a reduced priority as if the nice command had been used to invoke the command. You do not have to use the nice command when this option is set.
errexit	Same as -e
ignoreeof	Ignore the EOF key. The ignoreeof option prevents an accidental entry of the EOF key (usually ^d) from terminating the shell. When this option is set, you must use the exit command to terminate the shell.
keyword	Same as -k
markdirs	Append / to generated directory names
monitor	Same as -m

continues

5

Table 5.1. continued

Option Name	Effect
noclobber	Prevent overwriting an existing file. The `noclobber` option prevents overwriting an existing file with the > output redirection operator. To write to an existing file, you must use the >¦ operator.
noexec	Same as `-n`
noglob	Same as `-f`
nolog	Do not save function definitions in the command history file
nounset	Same as `-u`
privileged	Same as `-p`
trackall	Same as `-h`
verbose	Same as `-v`
vi	Use the Vi command-line editing mode
viraw	Process each character as it is typed
xtrace	Same as `-x`

The `-p` Option *(Privileged)*

When the shell is invoked explicitly with this option, and the real user-ID or group-ID of the process is not the same as the corresponding effective ID, then the `.profile` file is not executed, and the system file `/etc/suid_profile` is executed whenever the ENV profile would have been executed. To apply this option to a user's login shell, it must appear in the shell command field of the user's `/etc/passwd` entry.

The `-r` Option *(Restricted Shell)*

When appearing on the command line of the sh or ksh command, the `-r` option forces the shell to be a restricted shell. The following actions are disallowed by a restricted shell:

- The cd command cannot be used
- The shell variables SHELL, ENV, and PATH cannot be set or modified
- Command names cannot contain the / character

- Output cannot be redirected (>, <>, >¦, or >> are treated as illegal operators)

You also can initiate a restricted shell by executing the command rsh (or, for a restricted Korn shell, rksh). The system administrator can specify a restricted shell as a user's login shell to establish a specialized environment for that user.

The restricted environment does not apply to commands invoked by a restricted shell; therefore, users can execute any command to which they have access. Users can bypass the restricted environment if they are granted write access to their home directory or any directory in the path.

The -r option cannot be set or unset with the set command.

The -s Option *(Standard Input)*

The -s option forces the shell to read commands from the standard input file. Any arguments of the sh or ksh command are assigned to the variables $1 through $9. The -s option cannot be set or reset with the set command.

The -t Option *(Temporary)*

When specified on the sh or ksh command, the -t option causes the shell to exit after executing the first command found in shell input. The -t option is tacitly assumed when the -c option is specified.

The -u Option *(Unset Error)*

When the -u option is set, the shell considers a reference to an unset variable to be an error; the shell issues an error message and exits immediately if such a reference occurs. Use the command set +u to disable this option.

The -v Option *(Verbose)*

When set, the shell prints each input line before any parsing, variable substitution, or other processing is performed. Output generated by the -v option is written to the standard error file. Use the command set +v to disable the printing of shell input.

The -x Option *(Extra Output)*

When this option is set, the shell prints each command immediately before executing it. The printed command shows the result of file name generation, variable replacement, and command substitution. The image printed shows the command exactly as it actually is invoked. Output generated by the -x option is prefaced by the string "+ " (plus sign followed by a space) and is written to the standard error file. The -v and -x options print different information; therefore, either or both options can be specified. Use the command set +x to disable the extra output.

Lines generated by the -x option are written to standard error and are prefixed with the string value of PS4. By default the value of PS4 is "+ ".

Command Aliases

Command aliases, a feature of the Korn shell not available to Bourne shell users, enables you to define shortened forms or a nickname for commonly used commands.

The command alias facility of the Korn shell is based on a similar feature of the older C shell developed for the BSD version of UNIX and is intended to provide a measure of compatibility for those accustomed to the C shell. Users of both the Bourne and Korn shells should notice, however, that shell functions provide more flexibility and functionality than command aliases.

The alias facility is based around the alias command (defined in detail in Chapter 10, "Built-In Commands"), which associates a single word with a command name and as many options and leading arguments as you want. The facility also includes the unalias command, used to delete a previously defined alias.

An alias can be defined as simply as this:

```
$ alias pg='/usr/bin/pg -cns "-pPage %d"'
```

After executing this alias command, entering pg as a command name is equivalent to entering the entire text /usr/bin/pg -cns "-pPage %d", obviously saving a considerable number of keystrokes. Any arguments entered after pg are tacked onto the alias text to generate the command actually executed. For example, the simple command

```
$ pg myprog.c
```

after alias substitution is executed as if

```
$ /usr/bin/pg -cns "-pPage %d:" myprog.c
```

had been typed.

The arguments of the `alias` command are *name=value* pairs, where *name* is the new command name to be defined, and *value* is the text to be substituted for *name*. You can specify any number of command aliases on one `alias` command simply by listing them with blanks or tabs between each *name=value* pair.

The *value* string is commonly enclosed in double quotation marks, which are required whenever the substitution text contains white space or special characters.

Notice that the alias facility provides no way to substitute keyboard entries *into* the substituted text. The `pg` example shows the use of aliasing to provide an abbreviation for the front part of a command; additional text entered after the alias name is simply appended to the substitution text to form the final command. For example, most users would prefer to display command help information with the command

```
man command-name ¦ pg
```

but it is not possible to define an alias for the `man` command that sets up the pipe. A shell function can do the job handily, however:

```
man(){
    /usr/bin/man $* ¦ pg
}
```

Tracked Aliases

The `alias` command supports a `-t` option that designates the following command names as *tracked aliases*. A tracked alias is a simple command name; its value is the full path name of the command file, or the *value* in the *name=value* pair. Tracked aliases execute faster because the shell does not have to search for the command.

Unlike a conventional alias, a tracked alias does not require that you define its value; the Korn shell assumes that responsibility. Therefore, when you specify the `-t` option on the `alias` command you should only list command names without values, like this:

```
$ alias -t vi awk pg more make cc
```

When you enter the `alias` command with the `-t` option, you define specific command names to be tracked. Alternatively, you can ask the Korn shell to track all command names by setting the `-h` option (either with the

ksh

set -h command or by specifying the -h option on the ksh command); this is called the *trackall* mode. In trackall mode, the shell automatically adds every command name you enter into the alias table as a tracked alias.

A tracked alias can be in one of two states: defined or undefined. The first time the Korn shell attempts to invoke a command and its name is found to be an undefined tracked alias, the Korn shell searches the directories listed in PATH for the command file and stores the path name of the file as the value of the tracked alias; the alias is then considered defined. If you execute the command again, its name is recognized as an alias for the full path name of the command file, and the shell can skip the directory search. A command name set as a tracked alias can therefore be executed more quickly than other command names.

You cannot define the value of a command alias and set the command as a tracked alias both at once. To achieve best performance, you should supply the full path name of commands used in the value of the alias. For example, the definition

```
$ alias pg='/usr/bin/pg -cns -p"Page %d"'
```

executes more efficiently than the equally valid definition

```
$ alias pg='pg -cns -p"Page %d"'
```

This caveat applies only to aliases where the command to be executed is the same as the alias name. In other cases, tracking can still be used. For example, the following two alias definitions are compatible with one another:

```
$ alias -t pg
$ alias list='pg -cns'
```

You also could use trackall mode to let the Korn shell determine the full path name of the pg command file.

Exported Aliases

Normally a command alias is known only to the one copy of the shell that processed the alias command. This means an alias you can use at your keyboard is unknown inside any shell scripts you invoke.

At first glance, you might think shell scripts should avoid the use of aliases defined by the user; such definitions are outside the control of the shell script programmer and cannot even exist.

For aliases having arbitrary names, this is true. An alias for a standard command name might be something you would much want to affect shell scripts. Consider, for example, a script that displays a file with the pg command, such as Listing 5.1, which is used to display the current version of an SCCS (Source Code Control System) file (an SCCS is a collection of UNIX commands used to manage various versions of text files):

Listing 5.1. A command to display an SCCS file.

```
# ver - display an SCCS file version
if [ $# -ne 1 ]
then
    echo "Usage: ver filename"
    exit 1
fi
get -p -s s.$1 ¦ pg
```

After checking for the right number of arguments, the script pipes the output of the get command (which retrieves an SCCS file version) to the pg command (which displays a file on the terminal screen). The program is simple and, in particular, provides no way to specify options on the pg command.

Without options, the pg command simply scrolls the displayed file, letting lines rapidly roll off the top of the screen. With the proper options, though, pg can act as a display pager, letting you page back and forth through a file. The problem then is, how do you get the shell script to issue the pg command with the proper options?

The alias command can provide a solution. If you enter the following alias

```
$ alias pg='/usr/bin/pg -cns -p"Page %d"'
```

then any pg command you issue from your keyboard does pages rather than scrolling. The pg command in the ver shell script still scrolls. Can you get the alias for pg to apply inside the shell script as well as outside?

Yes. Simply include the -x option on the alias command, like this:

```
$ alias -x pg='/usr/bin/pg -cns -p"Page %d"'
```

The -x option tells the Korn shell to define an *exported alias*, which simply means the alias is passed to subshells through the command invocation mechanism. If a called shell script in turn invokes a shell script, that shell script also inherits the exported alias.

Exported aliases cannot be propagated to shell layers initiated by an explicit call to the shell. An explicit call occurs when you issue the ksh command, or when you escape to the shell within a command such as vi. You can, however, put alias definitions that should always be available into a file

ksh

and specify the full path name of the file as the value of the ENV shell variable. The Korn shell automatically executes the contents of the ENV file when it starts.

Preset Aliases

The Korn shell automatically defines a number of standard aliases at start-up. Some of these aliases define names that were built-in commands in the Bourne shell but have been replaced in the Korn shell by new, different commands with additional functionality. Others are provided for convenience.

Preset aliases are not special; you can change them with the `alias` command or delete any preset alias with the `unalias` command.

5

Preset Aliases

```
autoload='typeset -fu'
false='let 0'
functions='typeset -f'
hash='alias -t'
history='fc -l'
integer='typeset -i'
nohup='nohup '
r='fc -e -'
stop=kill -STOP
suspend=kill -STOP $$
true=:
type='whence -v'
```

Command Editing and Command History

ksh

For many programmers, the most important new feature of the Korn shell is its command history and command editing capability.

The command history feature provides a record of previous commands you have entered. You can call a command from the history and reexecute it without having to retype it. The shell does not save commands issued from shell scripts; only commands you enter from the keyboard are stored in the command history. Although the command history can be useful by itself, the primary use of this feature is to provide a basis for command editing.

Command editing enables you to retrieve a previously entered command from the history file, modify it, then reexecute the command. It also provides a means to modify a command while you are entering it, as if you were using a text editor.

About Command History

An interactive Korn shell saves all commands you enter in a disk file. The HISTFILE shell variable specifies the name of the file, and HISTSIZE specifies its minimum size in lines.

You should set the value of HISTFILE to the path name of a file where the Korn shell can save command history. Typically, you choose to place the file in your home directory. If HISTFILE is unset or is not a valid path name, then the shell assumes a default path name of $HOME/.sh_history.

For HISTSIZE, specify the minimum number of lines of command history you would like the shell to keep. The shell does not delete old lines until the total number of history lines saved exceeds the numeric value of HISTSIZE. If enough space is available, the shell might save more lines than you request.

If you have a shell profile in your home directory (its standard name is .profile), you can add your specifications for HISTFILE and HISTSIZE to your profile by inserting the following commands anywhere in it:

```
HISTFILE=$HOME/.hist
HISTSIZE=125
```

Although you can export these variables, it's usually not necessary because only the login shell uses their values; subshells and noninteractive shells do not save command history.

When the shell exits (when you log out, for example), it records any command history in memory into the history file before terminating. When you next log in, the shell automatically reloads the history file into memory. The history file, therefore, provides memory of your activities from one login session to the next. In practice, this turns out to be a nice feature because it helps you remember today what you were doing yesterday.

You can use the fc command to display all or portions of the command history. To list the history, specify the -1 option or use the built-in alias history, and indicate the range of lines to be displayed.

ksh

The following example shows the use of the `fc` command to redisplay previously entered commands. In this case, the chosen command restricts the display to the last ten lines to avoid a long—and otherwise meaningless—list of commands.

```
$ fc -l -10
make label
rm label;make label
label&
kill %1
pwd
cd bbs/cis
lx
pg capture.log
view capture.log
cd -1
fc -l -10
$
```

The output from the `fc` command lists history; beginning with the oldest selected line and ending with the most recently entered command (not coincidentally, the most recent command will always be an `fc` command).

5

---

fc Command Format

`fc [-nlr] [ first [ last ] ]`

Options	Meaning
`-n`	Suppress printing of line numbers
`-l`	List only; do not execute the lines (or use alias `history`)
`-r`	Reverse the order of the lines

The `first` and `last` options select a range of lines to be printed. If you omit `last`, it defaults to –1 (prints from `first` through the most recent command). For either `first` or `last` you can specify the following:

- A positive number representing the *n*th line of history. Each line is numbered as it is stored in the history file. When older lines are deleted, the remaining lines are *not* renumbered; they retain their originally assigned line numbers.

- A negative number representing the *n*th line of history counting backward from the current line. Thus, –1 designates the most recent command you entered, –2 designates the line before that, and so on.

- A character string. The most recently entered command starting with the given string is selected.

If you specify neither *first* nor *last*, then the last 16 lines of history are printed.

The following examples show some of the ways you can select a range of lines to be displayed:

- `fc -nl` displays the last 16 lines of history without line numbers.

- `fc -l 316` displays lines 316 through –1.

- `fc -l 316 424` displays lines 316 through 424 inclusive (109 lines).

- `fc -l -5` displays the fifth most recent line and all following lines; that is, the fifth one back counting the last line you entered as –1.

- `fc -lr vi cc` displays lines starting with the most recent `vi` command you entered through the most recent `cc` command you entered. Due to the `-r` option, the lines are listed in reverse order with the most recently entered commands at the top of the list.

Reexecuting Commands

When you enter the `fc` command without the `-l` option, the lines you selected with *first* and *last* are not displayed; rather, they are copied to a temporary file, an editor is invoked, and you are given an opportunity to modify the commands as you want. Then the modified commands are executed.

Format of `fc` Edit Command:

`fc [ -e editor ] [ first [ last ] ]`

If you specify the `-e` option, the editor you name as `editor` is invoked. If you do not provide an explicit editor name with the `-e` option, the shell takes the value of the `FCEDIT` shell variable as the name of the editor to be invoked. If `FCEDIT` is null or unset, the shell uses a built-in default of `/bin/ed`, the system's basic editor.

The following examples show the use of the `fc` edit command:

- `fc make` invokes the default editor to edit the single command line most recently found in the history file, starting with the command name `make`.

- `fc -e emacs make` invokes the Emacs editor, regardless of the `FCEDIT` value, to edit the single most recent line from the history file that begins with `make`.

| ksh |

- `fc -5 -1` invokes the default editor to edit and reexecute the previous five commands you have entered.

Alternatively, you can skip the editing step and reexecute a previously entered command immediately. Although you are not given the opportunity to edit the command, you can replace any substring of the command with a new string by using the *old=new* argument.

Format of fc Substitute Command

`fc -e - [ old=new ] [ command ]`

Notice that you *must* supply the arguments `-e -` (indicating you do not want to use an editor) to reexecute a command immediately. The Korn shell provides a preset alias to reduce the amount of typing required:

`alias r='fc -e -'`

Any change made to the command by the *old=new* parameter affects only the new command executed; the original line in the history file remains unchanged.

5

The following examples show the effect of entering the `fc` command for substitution:

- `r checks=vouchers` reexecutes the previous command you entered, changing the word `checks` in the command line to `vouchers`. If the previous command had been `cd /usr/applib/checks`, the new command executed would be `cd /usr/applib/vouchers`.

- `r checks=vouchers 5` reexecutes history line number 5 after changing the word `checks` to `vouchers` in the command. (Notice that this code specifies 5 as the value of the *command* argument of `fc`. This is because 5 designates the command in the history file that should be reexecuted.)

- `r checks=vouchers fgrep` reexecutes the most recent `fgrep` command you entered, changing the word `checks` in the command line to `vouchers`.

- `r` reexecutes the last command you entered without any changes.

Command Edit Mode

The older Bourne shell provides you a limited ability to correct keystroke errors while you are typing a command; you can backspace over the error and retype the rest of the line, or you can press the KILL key (usually ^ @) and type the whole line over.

The Korn shell provides a command entry mode that makes keying in commands as easy as using a text editor. This facility differs from the command editing capability provided by the `fc` command in the following ways:

- Editing with `fc` invokes a separate editor utility, whereas command edit mode is built into the Korn shell.

- You can use any editor with the `fc` command, but command edit mode provides only specific editing interfaces.

- With `fc`, you can edit a command only after a command has been entered and executed, whereas command edit mode lets you modify a command "on the fly."

- Command editing with `fc` is always possible, but command edit mode must be turned on before you can use it, and cannot be started in the middle of a command you have already started to type.

The Korn shell provides three command-editing interfaces: the Vi edit mode, with the look and feel of the Vi editor; the Emacs edit mode, a simulation of the Emacs editor; and Gmacs, a variation of Emacs mode.

How To Activate Command Edit Mode

You can activate command edit mode with any one of these three methods:

1. Invoke the shell with the appropriate option: `ksh -o` *mode* where *mode* is `vi`, `emacs`, or `gmacs`.

2. Turn on the desired mode with the `set` command: `set -o vi`, `set -o emacs` or `set -o gmacs`.

3. Set the `VISUAL` or `EDITOR` shell variable to designate the editor you want to use before invoking the shell, or any time thereafter; for example, `VISUAL=vi` or `VISUAL=emacs`. The shell checks the `VISUAL` variable before checking the `EDITOR` variable; either variable can specify the command edit mode.

The shell monitors any assignment to the `VISUAL` or `EDITOR` variables to check whether the assigned string value ends with a mode name; if it does, the command edit mode is automatically activated as if the command `set -o` *mode* had been executed. The shell also checks the initial value of these variables when it begins; if the variable is exported and has a non-null value and its value ends in the string `vi`, `emacs`, or `gmacs`, the shell comes up in command edit mode with that interface selected.

ksh

In addition to the vi option, you also can set the viraw option (viraw is ignored if vi is not also set). Without viraw, the shell does not receive input until you press Return or Esc; also, the ERASE and KILL keys retain their usual function. When viraw is set, the shell reads each character as you type it, and the ERASE and KILL keys enter data; their usual control function is disabled.

Although viraw mode provides an interface closer to the real Vi editor, it imposes an additional load on the system because the shell must be interrupted to process each character you type. If the system load is too great, you might notice a pause between pressing a key and its output to the screen, or experience delays when the system cannot accept another character from you. In such cases you should turn off viraw mode by entering the command set +o viraw. In general, you should avoid using the viraw mode.

The Vi Edit Mode

The Vi edit mode duplicates the editing interface of the Vi editor. The interface is in one of two states at all times: *input* or *command* mode.

When the shell issues a prompt, it places your terminal in *input* mode; every character you type is treated as data and is appended to the current input line. You can perform only limited editing operations in input mode. The Return key notifies the shell that you have finished typing the command, and the shell responds by executing the command.

When you press the Esc (escape) key, the edit interface leaves input mode and enters *command* mode. In command mode, the alphanumeric and control keys of your keyboard are treated as commands, not as data; pressing the a key, for example, causes the shell to perform the add-after function (see table 5.3.) and does *not* insert the letter *a* into the command line. Some commands return your terminal to input mode. You can therefore switch back and forth between input and command modes by using the Esc key and edit commands.

Edit Window

Normally the system allows you to type past the end of a line—the screen scrolls up one line and the cursor wraps to the beginning of the next line. In command edit mode, the line containing your cursor is treated as a *window*, and all cursor motions are constrained to that line.

The shell variable COLUMNS specifies the width of the edit window. If COLUMNS is not set, a value of 80 is assumed. When displaying a line longer than the number of characters the COLUMNS variable specifies for the edit window, the shell scrolls the text left and right so the displayed portion always includes the cursor position. In input mode, typing beyond the rightmost position causes the line to slide to the left. In command mode, moving the cursor beyond the left or right limits of the window causes the line to scroll to the right or left as appropriate.

Using cursor motion commands, you can move the edit window left or right to view any portion of a long command, or up and down to view any line in the command history file. The edit window therefore provides access to the entire history file. If you press Return while viewing or editing a line, that line is executed. This action enables you to execute previously entered commands without resorting to the use of `fc`.

Input Mode Commands

When in input mode, such as when entering a new command in response to a shell prompt, you can perform basic editing operations on the text as you type it. Table 5.2 lists the input mode edit commands. As the table indicates, an edit command is quite different from a shell command; edit commands are usually single keystrokes or control characters.

Table 5.2. Input mode edit commands.

Command	Action
Return	Execute the command displayed in the edit window
Esc	Leave input mode, enter command mode
ERASE	Backspace over the previous character
^w	Delete the previous word
^d	Terminate the shell (command has to appear as first character on the line)
^v	Ignore the control function of the next character typed
\	Enter the next ERASE or KILL key as text

The ^V key (hold down Ctrl while pressing the v key) tells the shell that the next keystroke is intended as text input even if it normally would be taken as a control operation. For example, you can enter a literal escape character by typing ^v and then pressing the Esc key.

The backslash (\) key normally results in entering a backslash into the current command at the cursor position. When the next keystroke is the backspace (ERASE) or KILL key, the corresponding ASCII code (usually ^h

ksh

and ^@ respectively) is entered as text rather than as the normal control operation—the backslash character discarded in such a case.

Only the keys listed in Table 5.2 are recognized as control operations when in input mode. Any other keystroke is taken as a text character and is inserted into the command line at the current cursor location.

Command-Mode Commands

In command mode, all keystrokes are interpreted as editor commands and either perform the corresponding action or cause a beep if no editor command is defined for that key. To get into command mode, press the Esc key.

Although edit commands are a single character, most commands can be preceded by an optional *count*, and some commands require a single-character *argument*. The general format of a command is [n]xc, where n is the count, x is the command, and c is the command argument. A count repeats the action of the command that number of times. For example, to skip the cursor ahead 3 words, enter the command 3w; to skip ahead 12 words, enter the command 12w.

You might find command mode disconcerting at first because commands are not displayed as you type them. Nothing is shown on the screen as you type the command 12w, but when you press the w the cursor suddenly jumps ahead 12 words.

In the command descriptions in Table 5.3, the notation [n] appears in front of the command code when a command allows an optional count. When a command requires an argument character, it is shown as c following the command code. Commands that do not accept a count or an argument are shown without the notation. Any count you might have entered in front of the command is discarded; any argument character you type after the command is taken as another command.

The term *word* refers to any alphanumeric string of characters delimited by the beginning or end of line, or by any punctuation character. Some commands treat a word as a series of characters between white space; these describe the command action relative to a *blank-delimited* word.

Some commands switch from command mode to input mode to let you enter new text into the current line. In such cases, the operation is not considered to end until you press Esc to leave input mode and return to command mode.

Table 5.3. Vi command mode editing commands.

Command	Action
a	Add text *after* the current character. The terminal is put into input mode to allow you to enter text.
A	Add text after the end of the line. This command moves the cursor to the position following the end of line and puts the terminal into input mode. Equivalent to $a.
[n]b	Move the cursor backward to the beginning of the previous (nth previous) word.
[n]B	Move the cursor backward to the beginning of the previous (nth previous) blank-delimited word.
c[n]motion [n]cmotion	Change text from the current cursor position through the character to which motion would move. For motion, specify a cursor movement command, optionally including count and argument. You can supply a count with either the c command or the motion command, but not both. For example, either 3cfh or c3fh would change characters from the current position through the third occurrence of an *h* to the right of the current position. The change operation logically deletes the selected characters, then enters input mode to let you enter the replacement text.
cc	Delete the entire line and enter input mode.
C	Change text from the current position through the end of the line. Equivalent to c$.
[n]dmotion d[n]motion	Delete characters from the current cursor position through the character to which *motion* would move. For motion, specify any cursor movement command, optionally including count and argument. You can specify a count on either the d or the motion command, but not both.
dd	Delete the entire line.
D	Delete text from the current position through the end of the line. Equivalent to d$.
[n]e	Move the cursor forward to the end of the current (nth following) word.
[n]E	Move the cursor forward to the end of the current (nth following) blank-delimited word.

continues

ksh

Table 5.3. continued

Command	Action
[*n*]f*c*	Move to next (*n*th) character *c*.
[*n*]F*c*	Move the cursor backward to the (*n*th) previous character *c*.
[*n*]G	Move the cursor to line *n* of the command history file. If *n* is omitted, move to the first (least recently entered) command.
[*n*]h	Move the cursor left one (*n*) character(s).
i	Insert text *before* the current character. The terminal is put into input mode to let you enter the new text.
I	Insert text at the beginning of the line. Equivalent to 0i.
[*n*]j	Move the cursor down one (*n*) line(s). The target line is retrieved from the command history file and displayed in the edit window. Each execution of the j command moves forward through command history to successively more recent commands.
^J	Same as Return. The current line is executed immediately.
[*n*]k	Move the cursor up one (*n*) line(s). The target line is retrieved from the command history file and displayed in the edit window. Each execution of the k command moves backward through command history to successively earlier commands.
[*n*]l	Move the cursor right one (*n*) character(s).
^L	The cursor skips to a new line and the current line is redrawn. This command is useful when the terminal display has become scrambled.
^M	Same as Return. The current line is executed immediately.
n	Repeat the last / or ? command.
N	Repeat the last / or ? command, but in the reverse direction.
[*n*]p	Insert the characters deleted by the last d or D command, or yanked by the last y or Y command, after the current cursor position. To copy characters from one place to another, yank them with y and insert them with p or P; to move characters by (*n*) characters, delete them with d before inserting them with p or P
[*n*]P	Same as the p command, but places the inserted characters before the cursor position rather than after.

Command	Action
[*n*]r*c*	Replace the current (next *n*) characters with *c*, then move the cursor to the next position. If a count is specified, that number of characters in the line, starting at the current cursor position, are replaced with *n* repetitions of *c*.
R	Replace characters. The terminal is put into input mode. As characters are typed, they overlay existing characters in the line.
S	Equivalent to cc.
[*n*]t*c*	Move the cursor to the character immediately preceding the next (*n*th) character *c* in the line. The t command is most often used to specify motion for the c and d commands, because in that context it means *up to but not including*.
[*n*]T*c*	Move backward to the character following the (*n*th) previous character *c*. The T command is most often used to specify motion for the c and d commands because in that context it means *back to but not including*.
u	Undo the effects of the previous text modification command, restoring the line to its prior image. Cursor movement commands cannot be undone. The u command can be undone, in effect toggling between two alternative line images.
U	Undo any and all text modifications to the current line. Successive U commands have no effect, but u can undo the effect of U.
[*n*]v	Invoke the command editor specified by the VISUAL or EDITOR variable to edit the current line. If the count field *n* is specified, then edit that line of the history file. Note that the v command in Vi command edit mode is equivalent to entering the command fc -e ${VISUAL-${EDITOR}} *n*.
[*n*]w	Right one (*n*) words.
[*n*]W	Move the cursor right one (*n*) blank-delimited word(s).
[*n*]x	Delete characters at and to the right of the current cursor position. Text to the right of the deleted characters is shifted left.
[*n*]X	Delete characters to the left of the current cursor position. Text to the right of the deleted characters is shifted left.

continues

ksh

Table 5.3. continued

Command	Action
[n]ymotion y[n]motion	Copy text into the delete buffer from the current cursor position through the character to which *motion* would move. The copied text is not deleted from the current line. For *motion* specify a cursor movement command, optionally including count and argument. You can supply a count with either the y command or the motion command, but not both. Example: yw yanks the current word; y$ yanks the rest of the line; y3l yanks the next three characters.
Y	Copy characters from the current cursor position through the end of the line into the delete buffer. (See also p and P.) Equivalent to y$.
[n]yy	Yank the current (last *n*) lines into the buffer. Use the p command to insert the yanked line(s) into a line.
0	Move the cursor to the first position of the current line.
[n]¦	Move to column *n* of the line.
[n]+	Same as the [n]j command.
[n]-	Same as the [n]k command.
/string	Search backward through the history file for a line containing *string* in any position. The first such line found halts the search, the line is displayed in the edit window, and the cursor is placed at the beginning of the line. The notation ^string requires the string to be found at the beginning of the line. Note: You cannot use a regular expression in *string*.
?string	Same as / but searches in the forward direction (toward the most recently entered command).
[n];	Repeat the previous f, F, t, or T command (*n* times).
[n],	Repeat the previous f, F, t, or T command (*n* times) but in the reverse direction.
[n]~	Convert characters from upper- to lower- or lower- to uppercase.
^	Move the cursor to the first nonblank character of the line.
$	Move the cursor to the end of the line.
.	Repeat the previous text modification (not cursor movement) command.

Command	*Action*
#	Insert a # in front of the current line and save the modified line in the command history file. This operation converts a command into a comment that has no effect if executed, but can later be retrieved from the command history file for further editing and execution.
[n]_	Insert the last word of the previous line at the cursor position. If *n* is specified, then word *n* of the previous line is inserted. Thus, 2_ would insert the second word of the previous line. (A *word* in this context is alphanumeric text bounded by punctuation characters.)
*	Replace the current word with the list of files obtained by doing a wild-card search for *word**. For example, the input echo /stand/unix[Esc]* is changed to read echo /stand/unix /stand/unix.old. The cursor is positioned after the last file name and the terminal is in input mode.
\	Replace the current word with the first file name found that starts with the same characters. Thus, vi pr[Esc]\ might be completed as vi prog.c. If no matching file can be found, the terminal beeps; otherwise the cursor is placed after the file name in input mode.
=	Search for all file names beginning with the same characters as the current word. The list of matching file names is printed, and then the input line is redrawn. The terminal remains in control mode. For example:

```
$ vi prog[Esc]=
1) prog1.c
2) progmain.c
$ vi prog
```

| @*letter* | If an alias named _*letter* exists, its value is executed as a sequence of control commands. |

The Emacs and Gmacs Edit Modes

The Emacs edit mode simulates the editing interface of the Emacs editor. The Emacs editor itself is not included as a standard component of UNIX System V. The Korn shell, however, supports a look-alike command edit mode because Emacs is a familiar add-on package to many users.

ksh

The Gmacs edit mode is nearly identical to Emacs mode, differing only in the action of the ^t command; for that reason, both interfaces are described together.

Unlike the Vi edit mode, the Emacs (and Gmacs) edit interface is not *modal*. All edit commands are formed as a two- or three-stroke sequence starting with the Esc key or the Ctrl key. When you press an alphanumeric character, it always results in adding text to the current command line.

The Emacs interface provides the commands listed in Table 5.4. The notation [Esc *n*] describes an optional count prefix which, if present, executes the command *n* times. The code ^f means hold down the Ctrl key and press f; Esc x means to press the Esc key, then press x.

In general, a Ctrl-letter key operates on a single character and an Esc-letter key operates on a word.

Table 5.4. Emacs editing commands.

Command	Action
^a	Move the cursor to the start of the current line.
[Esc *n*] ^b	Move the cursor left (backward) one character.
[Esc *n*] Esc b	Move the cursor back to the beginning of the current word.
[Esc *n*] ^c	Change the character(s) at the current cursor location to uppercase and move right.
[Esc *n*] Esc c	Change the remainder of the word at the current cursor location to uppercase and move to the beginning of the next word.
[Esc *n*] ^d	Delete the (*n*) character(s) underneath the cursor.
[Esc *n*] Esc d	Delete from the cursor position through the end of the word. (If Esc *n* is specified, deletes *n* words.)
^e	Move the cursor to the end of the current line.
[Esc *n*] ^f	Move the cursor right (forward) one character.
[Esc *n*] Esc f	Move the cursor forward to the next character following the current word.
Esc ^h	Delete the previous word.
Esc *n* Esc ^h	Delete the *n* previous words.
Esc ^?	Delete the previous word.
Esc *n* Esc ^?	Delete the *n* previous words.
Esc h	Delete the previous word.

Command	Action
Esc *n* Esc h	Delete the *n* previous words.
[Esc *n*] ^h	Delete backward to the beginning of the current word. (The terminal Backspace key usually generates ^h.)
^j	Execute the current line. Same as ^m.
[Esc *n*] ^k	Delete text from the current cursor position up to column *n* (when column *n* is to the right of the cursor), or from column *n* up to the cursor position (when column *n* is to the left of the cursor). If Esc *n* is omitted, this command deletes from the cursor through end of line.
^l	Move to the next screen line and display the current line. This command is used to restore a garbled screen image.
[Esc *n*] Esc l	Change the remainder of the word at the current cursor location to lowercase and move to the beginning of the next word.
^m	Execute the current line. Same as ^j.
[Esc *n*] ^n	Move to the next line of history (toward the most recently entered command). If Esc *n* is specified, skip forward *n* lines in the history file.
^o	Execute the current line, then fetch the next line of command history.
Esc p	Push the characters from the cursor to the mark into a save buffer. (The characters are not deleted.)
[Esc *n*] ^p	Make the previous command history line the current line and display it. If Esc *n* is specified, skip backwards *n* lines in the history file.
[Esc 0] ^r [*string*] Return	Search back through the history file for a line containing *string*, or forward if Esc 0 specified. If *string* is omitted, repeat the last search.
[Esc 0] ^r ^ *string* Return	Same as ^r*string* except that *string* must occur at the beginning of the line.
^t	In Emacs mode, exchange the current and next character; in Gmacs, mode exchange the two previous characters.

continues

ksh

Table 5.4. continued

Command	Action
^u	Repeat the next operation four times. Same as [Esc 4].
^v	Display the version of the Korn shell. The line is temporarily replaced by the version information, and is redrawn on the next keystroke.
^w	Used with mark (see Esc space). Deletes characters to the left of or to the right of the cursor up through the marked character.
^x ^x	Exchange the mark and the cursor. The cursor moves to the marked location, and the previous cursor position becomes the new marked location.
^y	Insert the contents of the save buffer (from the previous *push* or delete operation) in front of the cursor position.
Esc space	Mark the current character. Marking a character doesn't change its appearance, but the editor remembers the location of the marked character for future reference.
[Esc *n*] Esc .	Insert the last word (*n*th word from the beginning) of the previous line of command history at the cursor position.
Esc =	List all files that start with the same characters as the current word. The current line is redisplayed after the list is printed.
Esc *	Replace the current word with a list of all matching path names, as if the word ended with *; if no matching path names can be found, sound the bell.
Esc _	Same as Esc .
Esc <	Back up to the oldest command history line.
Esc >	Advance to the most recent command history line.
\	Escape the next keystroke, and enter the key as data into the line at the cursor position. The Ctrl keys are entered as the equivalent letter preceded by a caret (^).
^]*c*	Move forward to the next occurrence of the character *c* in the current line.
[Esc *n*] ^?	Same as ^h. (The terminal Del key, on some keyboards, generates the ^? code automatically.)

Command	Action
EOF	Exit the shell. The EOF key has this meaning only when pressed at the beginning of the line; otherwise it is treated as data and inserted into the line at the current cursor position. (You can disable the EOF function by setting the ignoreeof option.)
[Esc *n*] ERASE	Delete the character to the left of the cursor and move the cursor left one position (destructive backspace). The ERASE key can be set with the stty system command.
KILL	Delete the entire line. The KILL key can be set with the stty system command.
Esc Esc	If the current word matches any front part of the name of an existing file, extend the word with the remaining unmatched characters of the file name; that is, complete the word so that it is the name of an existing file. If the file name is the name of a directory, append / to the name; otherwise append a space.
Esc *letter*	If an alias exists with the name _*letter*, execute its value as a string of Emacs commands.

5

Summary

This chapter examined the most important additional features of the Korn shell. These include the shell options you can set when invoking the shell or the set command; command aliases; command history; and command editing.

These features were added to the shell to help users work more efficiently. If you don't like one of these facilities, that's fine. It is reasonable to expect that your preferences are quite different from others. Most important is that you not avoid these productivity features simply because they seem complex. Even occasional attempts to use the features help you slowly develop a full command of them.

The Korn shell has been available for a number of years unofficially, and was officially released with System V Release 4. If you have a version of the Korn shell that is not part of the System V Release 4 package, your version might have different features and might implement them differently as well. As time goes by, these earlier variants of the Korn shell will probably disappear. If your version of the Korn shell differs from the description in this book, you should avoid becoming dependent on the features unique to your version. Better yet, try to acquire the official version of the Korn shell.

This chapter completes the description of shell facilities used primarily at the keyboard. The next chapter begins Part II, "Shell Programming." Whether or not you plan to use shell programming, you should practice the material you've learned in the past chapters because the following chapters build heavily on that material. If you don't plan to program with the shell, be advised that you don't have to be a full-fledged shell programmer to prosper from the shell's programming features. Depriving yourself of that knowledge will hinder you, not help you.

5

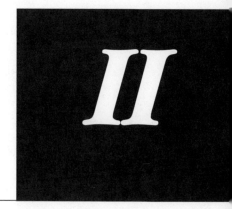

Part II

Shell Programming

Introduction to

Shell Programming

The Bourne and Korn shells are much more than command processors; they are full-fledged programming languages. In fact, the shells are technically classed as interpreters because they execute statements of the language immediately after reading them. The shells do not generate object code that must be linked, and, therefore, are much easier to use than compilers.

Many compiled programming languages and most interpreters suffer from an inherently limited range of capabilities that restricts their usefulness; COBOL, for example, is a poor choice for implementing a new device driver, and FORTRAN is ill-suited to compiler writing. To get around this problem, most compiled languages and some interpreters allow programs to be combined with routines written in other languages, even assembly language.

The shell is uniquely rich compared to other programming languages because, aside from its structured control directives (if, while, case, and so on) its basic operations are whole programs: the commands of the UNIX operating system. More than 300 commands are supplied with standard UNIX and an untold number are available as public domain, shareware, or packaged software; in addition, if no command exactly meets a particular shell programming need, the user can create a new command in any convenient language, thereby expanding the command set available to the shell programmer.

Of course, if most shell programming required new support commands, the shell would rarely be used as a vehicle for applications and tools development. Such is not the case, however. UNIX commands include many highly generalized and widely applicable commands that are sufficient for most purposes. In fact, the shell and the standard UNIX commands provide an application development and prototyping tool of great power.

Programming with the shell can be as simple or as complicated as you make it. Shell programming is somewhat like cooking: if you have the patience and skill, you can concoct extravagant dishes. But just as most people can fry an egg, so too most people can write a simple shell program. The reward for your efforts will be a new command that saves you time and effort every time you use it.

In this chapter, you will begin to study shell programming by looking at the basic mechanics of creating and using shell programs, called *scripts*.

Creating Shell Scripts

Creating a shell script is easy. There are only two steps:

1. Create a file with the text editor of your choice that contains the shell commands to implement the function of the script.

2. Using the chmod command, make your new file executable. The following command is all that's necessary, but you must replace the word *filename* with the name of your file:

```
$ chmod +x filename
```

Having completed these two steps, you should now be able to type the word *filename* as if it were a command. In fact, *filename* is a command because the file it names is marked executable. UNIX automatically arranges to have the shell process the commands that are stored in the file, so your new shell script (it also can be called a *program*) is just as executable as any program written in C that has been compiled and linked for execution.

Command Search Order

After you've created a new shell script and marked it executable, you might want to consider in which directory the file will be permanently stored.

You can always execute a command by entering the full path name of the command file. For example, if you called your shell script `sample` and stored it in the `misc` subdirectory of your home directory, you could execute the `sample` command by entering the following:

```
$ /u/home/louise/misc/sample
```

However, if you enter the file name, like this:

```
$ sample
```

the shell has to search for the file because you have not specified the directory.

The shell locates command files by using a directory search order. The directories the shell searches are listed as the value of the PATH environment variable (see the section "Shell Variables" in Chapter 3, "Shell Basics"). For example, you could check which directories are currently in your search order like this:

```
$ echo $PATH
/bin:/usr/bin:/usr/local/bin:.
$
```

The colons in the value of PATH separate the directory path names from each other. The value of PATH shown earlier instructs the shell to look first in the `/bin` directory for commands. If the command is not found there, then the shell must search the `/usr/bin` directory. The shell continues to search the directories listed, in the same order they are listed, until either the command file is found or there are no more directories to search.

In the value of PATH shown previously, the last directory that was searched is your current directory (the *dot* directory). No matter what your current directory happens to be, the shell finds command files located there. If you change to another directory with the `cd` command, the shell still finds commands located in your current directory, but that directory is different from the one you were in before you executed the `cd` command; command files located in your previous directory are now inaccessible.

There are two ways around this problem:

1. List all the directories where you might store command files in PATH.

2. Store all your executable files in one directory and put the path name of that directory in PATH.

6

The second is the better alternative because you end up with a shorter directory list in PATH. A long directory list in PATH forces the shell to search many directories. Command files in directories near the end of PATH take noticeably longer to find and execute than command files in directories near the front of PATH.

By tradition, UNIX users who write their own commands (whether shell scripts or compiled programs) store the executable files in a subdirectory named bin of their home directory. (The term *bin* is short for *binary*, referring to the fact that compiled programs are stored in a binary rather than an ASCII format.)

To add your own personal bin directory to the search order, use the following command:

```
$ PATH=$PATH:$HOME/bin
$
```

Now peek at the PATH directory list again:

```
$ echo $PATH
/bin:/usr/bin:/usr/local/bin:.:/u/home/louise/bin
$
```

Notice that the command PATH=$PATH:$HOME/bin tacked the path name of your new bin directory onto the end of PATH, properly prefixed with a colon. Do you really want your bin directory searched *after* rather than *before* your current directory? Probably not. For various reasons—one of which is to ensure that the system behaves predictably—you should always have your current directory searched *last*, after all the standard places. A better search order would be:

```
PATH=/bin:/usr/bin:/usr/local/bin:/u/home/louise/bin:.
```

If you add this one line to your profile (file name .profile in your home directory), then PATH will be set automatically to include your bin directory every time you log in.

With this search order, command files in the official program directories (your bin directory can now be considered an official directory) are always used in preference to commands of the same name in your current directory. Therefore, this search order prevents you from accidentally overriding or replacing a standard command with one of your own.

But what do you do if you *want* to replace a system command with a shell script of your own? No problem. Change your command search order to look in your own bin directory first, like this:

```
PATH=/u/home/louise/bin:/bin:/usr/bin:/usr/local/bin:.
```

There is nothing sacred about the value of PATH; you can adjust its value at any time to suit your needs and preferences.

A Simple Shell Script

Now that you have seen *how* to create a shell script, take a brief look at *what* a shell script might do. In the following example, you see the complete process of entering a shell script, storing it, and executing it. You should try this example at your own terminal; type it exactly as shown in Listing 6.1, and see what happens.

Listing 6.1. A sample shell script.

```
$ cd
$ cd bin
$ ed info
?info
0a
:
# @(#) info 1.0 - A sample shell script
echo "
Today is..................... `date`
Your system identification is... `id`
Your terminal address is........ `tty`
Your current directory is....... `pwd`
Your file-creation mask is...... `umask`

The following people are logged in:"
who | sort -u +0 -1
.
w
165
q
$ chmod +x info
$ info

Today is..................... Thu Jun 20 12:22:41 EDT 1991
Your system identification is... uid=100(louise) gid=7(user)
Your terminal address is........ /dev/cons1
Your current directory is....... /u/home/louise/bin
Your file-creation mask is...... 0022

The following people are logged in:
barb        tty1        Jun 20 08:36
jjv         cons1       Jun 20 08:57
root        console     Jun 20 12:21
herb        tty42       Jun 20 09:12
$
```

This shell script implements a new command: info. When entered, it lists some important information about you and your environment. Because the info file is located in your bin directory and bin is included in your search path, you can execute the info command any time. You could even use the info command in another shell script, building on your previous work to create ever more sophisticated tools.

You might be wondering about the first of the shell script, which contains just :. You usually should include this as the first line of any Bourne or Korn shell script that someone might try to execute with the C shell. (Remember, the C shell is another kind of shell available to users of the UCB variant of UNIX.) When the C shell begins to execute a shell script, it first checks whether the script begins with :. If it does, the C shell calls the Bourne shell to execute the script. The : line therefore enables C shell users to use the script just as easily as Bourne and Korn shell users.

Unlike most other programming languages, the shell provides no input /output commands. The UNIX commands provide input/output capability, and the I/O redirection and pipe features of the shell provide all the remaining support that is needed.

The sample shell script called info used only the shell facilities you learned in Part I, "Using the UNIX Shell." In the rest of Part II, "Shell Programming," you will look at the additional facilities of the shell that exclusively support shell programming. Among these are a full complement of structured control directives including an if-then-else construct, while and until loops, the for loop, and subroutine structures called functions, which you already reviewed in Chapter 4, "Compound Commands." Among these are a full complement of structured control directives including an if-then-else construct, while and until loops, the for loop (each discussed in Chapter 8, "Conditional Execution"), and subroutine structures called functions (which you already reviewed in Chapter 4, "Compound Commands").

Using Variables

Using variables properly is an essential part of shell programming. Without variables, it would be impossible to write useful shell scripts; with them, you can write commands that are modified at execution time to suit the needs of the moment. In effect, when you write commands that use variables, you are actually writing *model* commands. The actual command that your shell script will execute is determined by replacing each variable name with its current value.

A variable is a symbol that stands for something else. In shell programming, all variables represent *strings*. A string is nothing more than a series of characters, varying in length, that are treated as a unit. You can do three things with a variable:

- *Set* its value; this is an operation where you specify the actual character string the variable represents

- *Reference* its value, which causes the shell to replace the reference with the actual character string that is the current value of the variable

- *Unset* the variable, which removes the variable as if it had never existed

You can repeatedly set a variable to different strings, thus changing the variable's value each time. It does not matter how often you change a variable's value, or whether you ever reference its value. A variable can have only one string value at a time, however. (The Korn Shell supports variable *arrays*, a feature that allows a variable to have multiple values.)

A variable can have the *null string* as its value. A null string is a string containing zero characters. It is distinct from a completely undefined variable because a variable with the null string as its value is still set.

You can reference a variable's value any number of times between successive settings. Each reference is replaced with the same character string until you assign a new string to the variable.

An Overview of Shell Variables

The shell supports a bewildering variety of variables and ways to reference them. Before delving into the details, let's briefly overview the general nature of variables.

Types of Variables

Shell variables come in two main varieties: *regular* and *special*. (The Korn shell also supports *array* variables. Array variables are discussed in Chapter 12, "Advanced Shell Features.")

The regular variables are named according to certain well-defined spelling rules. Most variables fall into this category. Examples of regular variables are PATH, opt1, or user_name.

Variable Names

The following are rules for choosing a variable name:

- A variable name must begin with an upper- or lowercase letter (a through z or A through Z), or the underscore (_).

- The initial letter or underscore can be followed by any number of additional upper- or lowercase letters, the decimal digits 0 through 9, or the underscore (_).

- Any other character marks the end of the variable name, except for the special variables $@, $#, $$, $*, $-, $?, and $0 through $9.

The leading dollar sign ($) marks a variable reference and is *not* part of the variable's name.

7

Special variables use special characters as their name. You cannot invent special variables; they are defined and their values are assigned by the shell. The special variables provide scripts to your shell. These scripts often have access to information that is otherwise difficult or impossible to acquire. Examples of special variables are $*, $#, $?, and $0 through $9.

Regular variables can be *local* or *global*. A local variable is known only to the shell that defined it. A global variable, also called an *exported* or *environment* variable, is one where the value is known to the shell that defined it and to all commands invoked by that shell. Environment variables provide a convenient way to pass information to commands. Examples of environment variables are PATH, HOME, and LOGNAME.

You can turn any regular variable into an environment variable simply by naming it on the export command. From that time forward, the variable is passed to every command called by the shell. Although commands you call can change the value of an environment variable, the change is visible only to commands it calls. A called command cannot change the value of an environment variable or add or delete a variable from the environment of its calling command or shell.

Special variables are always local to the current shell. They cannot be unset or exported.

Assigning a Value to a Variable

To assign a value to a regular variable, use the special command format *name=value*.

Format of a Variable Assignment

name=value [name=value ...]

Be careful you do not insert any white space before or after the = (equal sign), otherwise the shell attempts to execute the command called *name* (whatever you wrote as the variable's name). Also notice that you do not write a $ in front of the variable's name on the left side of the = sign; the $ sign denotes a variable *reference*, and you are attempting to *assign* the variable.

In response to the *name=value* command, the shell creates the variable if it does not already exist and assigns the string *value* to the variable called *name*. If the variable exists, the shell does not have to create it and merely assigns the new value to the variable.

On the command line, a variable assignment looks like this:

```
$ EDITOR=vi
$
```

Notice that there is no output from this command. The shell internally stores both the name of the variable (EDITOR) and its new value (vi).

You write a variable assignment in a shell script similarly, the only difference being the absence of a prompt in front of the command. Inside a shell script, the assignment of EDITOR looks like this:

```
EDITOR=vi
```

You can write several variable assignments in the same command by separating each assignment from the next with white space (one or more blanks or tabs), as is done in the following shell statement:

```
EDITOR=vi COUNTRY=USA TERM=vt100-nl
```

To assign the null string to a variable, simply omit the *value* part of the assignment:

```
EDITOR= COUNTRY=USA TERM=vt100-nl
```

This command sets the COUNTRY and TERM variables to non-null strings. The EDITOR variable has a null value but is still considered defined. If you used the value of EDITOR in a string, as in "-$EDITOR-", the resulting string, after substitution of the value of EDITOR, would be --.

One final caution: You must not follow a variable assignment with any other command on the same line, otherwise the shell construes it as a temporary environment override for that command. That is, the command

```
EDITOR=vi mailx
```

adds the variable EDITOR to the environment of the mailx command, and mailx can refer to the EDITOR variable, but the variable is not added to the variable definitions of the current shell. You can see the effect of this by executing the following series of commands at your terminal:

```
$ EDITOR=emacs
$ EDITOR=vi echo $EDITOR
emacs
$
```

You get quite a different result by inserting a semicolon (;) after the assignment:

```
$ EDITOR=emacs
$ EDITOR=vi; echo $EDITOR
vi
$
```

The shell always treats a semicolon as equivalent to a newline character, so the shell sees EDITOR=vi as a command rather than as an environment override. (For a deeper discussion about variables, see the section "Environment Variables" in this chapter, and the section "Shell Variables" in Chapter 3, "Shell Basics.")

Variable References

A reference to a shell variable can be a *simple reference* or an *expression reference*. You form a simple reference by prefixing the metacharacter $ to the name of the variable. When the shell encounters the dollar sign, it makes the following characters the name of the variable, and replaces the $ and variable name with the value of the variable.

An example of the use of a simple reference occurs in the simple command echo $HOME. The reference is the word $HOME. It starts with the special character $ that informs the shell: "Here is a variable reference." The following characters are the name of the variable, HOME. When the shell sees this command, it looks up the current value of the HOME variable, and substitutes the value for both the $ and the variable name.

The result of this substitution is a customized echo command: for example, echo /u/barb. The echo command never sees the word $HOME; the shell replaces the variable reference with the *value* of HOME (in this case, /u/ barb) before executing the echo command.

You can write the command echo $HOME in a shell script and achieve the same effect as if you had written a different echo command for each user's home directory. This is the big advantage of variables.

When writing a variable reference, carefully consider the characters that follow the variable's name. Illegal characters included in a variable name stop the shell's scan for the variable name. The shell uses the longest possible name it can recognize.

The reference $HOME/lib is substituted as /u/barb/lib because the slash is not legal in a variable name. On the other hand, if you write $HOME_ECONOMICS, the shell attempts to substitute the value of the variable HOME_ECONOMICS.

The shell provides a way to run a variable name and alphabetic text together, which brings you to the subject of variable *expressions*.

Variable Expressions

Use a variable expression to explicitly delimit a variable name or to control variable substitution.

Variable Expression

${name}

or

${name op word}

where
- *name* is the name of the variable
- *op* is one of these operators: -, +,=, ?, : -, :+, :=, :?
- *word* is any ASCII text

Table 7.1 lists the specific expression types that are supported.

Table 7.1. Types of variable expressions.

Type	Result
${name}	Replaced with the value of *name*
${name-word}	Replaced with the value of *name* if the variable is defined, otherwise with *word*
${name+word}	Replaced with *word* if the variable is defined, otherwise with nothing
${name?word}	Replaced with the value of *name* if the variable is defined; otherwise the shell issues the error message *name*: *word* and exits
${name=word}	If the variable *name* is not set, the shell assigns *word* as its value. The expression is then replaced with the value of *name*

The colon operators (: -, :+, :?, and :=) test whether the variable is set or null; without the colon the shell merely tests whether the variable is set.

You should try the following experiments at your terminal to better understand variable expressions:

- Assign some values to work with:

```
$ object=car
$ object1=feather
```

- Use simple reference to display the variable values:

```
$ echo $object
car
```

```
$ echo $object1
feather
```

- Try a variable expression without operators:

```
$ echo ${object}
car
$ echo ${object}mine
carmine
```

- Now try an undefined variable name:

```
$ echo ${obj}ect
ect
```

- Use ${*x-y*} to provide a default value:

```
$ echo ${obj-perf}ect
perfect
```

- Use ${*x+y*} to print *y* if *x* is defined:

```
$ echo ${object+perf}ect
perfect
$ echo ${obj+perf}ect
ect
```

- Use ${*x?y*} to cancel with message *y* if *x* is undefined:

```
$ echo ${obj?missing}
obj: missing
```

- Use ${*x=y*} to provide a default value for *x*:

```
$ echo ${obj=sample}
sample
```

- Check the value of *obj* now:

```
$ echo $object
car
$ echo $obj
sample
```

There is more to using variable expressions than simply being familiar with the syntax definition. The rest of this section covers some of the shell programming problems that variables solve, and some problems they cause.

Using ${x}

Each of the variable expression formats was added to the shell to help solve a particular problem. The simple expression ${*x*} was intended to simplify the concatenation of a variable with a string that starts with a letter or digit.

For many uses of shell variables, this problem does not arise. For example, the following code fragment uses the variable tmp to hold the path name of a work directory:

```
$ tmp=/usr/tmp
$ mkdir $tmp/workarea
$ cp *.c $tmp/workarea
```

Usually a variable containing a path name string is followed by white space or the / path delimiter. If you want to embed text values in a text string, you might write something like this:

```
$ cs='$'
$ echo "Earnings to date: $cs105.29"                #wrong
$ echo "Earnings to date: ${cs}105.29"              #right
```

Without the braces to mark the variable name, the shell would have taken the variable name to be cs105. You can always avoid this kind of ambiguity by using double quotation marks, as in the following examples:

```
$ echo "Earnings to date: "$cs"105.29"
```

```
$ echo Earnings to date: "$cs"105.29
```

However, the quotation marks are more awkward to use than the ${x} expression.

Specifying *word*

All variable expression formats allow an optional *word* following the -, +, ?, or = operator. The shell actually allows any kind of string expression for *word*.

Nesting one variable reference inside another is permitted, as in the following command:

```
$ echo ${file-${TMPDIR-/usr/spool/uucppublic}/receive/$LOGNAMEnixric/}
```

If the file variable is defined, then its value is the value of the expression passed to echo; otherwise the shell evaluates

```
${TMPDIR-/usr/spool/uucppublic}/receive/$LOGNAME/nixric/
```

to form the value of the expression. Note that this expression contains a variable expression. No problem. The shell checks whether TMPDIR is currently assigned a value, and, if so, it substitutes that value for the entire ${...} term; otherwise it substitutes the string /usr/spool/uucppublic for the ${...} term. The shell then appends the string /receive/$LOGNAME/nixric/ to the intermediate result, substituting the value of LOGNAME as it does so.

You also can use command substitution as all or part of *word*. The following command uses the cwd variable, but if cwd is not set it calls the pwd command to get the path name of the current directory:

```
$ echo ${cwd-`pwd`}
```

Anything normally permitted between back quotations is permitted inside a variable expression also. The following command extracts the user's home directory path name from the /etc/passwd file when the variable dir is undefined:

```
$ echo ${dir:-`awk -F: '$1 == "'$LOGNAME'" {print $6}'`}
```

The following is a shorter way to enter the same thing:

```
$ echo ${dir:-$HOME}
```

When you want to specify a string as the value of *word*, you can either enclose *word* in double quotation marks or enclose the entire variable expression in double quotation marks. Thus, the command

```
$ cd ${wdir?"wdir: undefined."}
```

is equivalent to

```
$ cd "${wdir?wdir: undefined.}"
```

Using ${x-y}

The expression forms ${x-y} and ${x:-y} simplify the use of default values for *x*.

For example, suppose you want to write a shell script to collect and print all the parts of a document. If all the document parts are stored in files ending in .txt, the essential command in the script would be

```
$ cat *.txt | pr | lp
```

With this method, users can use only the shell script when their document files end in .txt. To avoid this limitation, you can use a variable to hold the suffix of the file names. Assuming you knew how to do so, you probably would want to change the essential command in the script to

```
$ cat *.$sufx | pr | lp
```

Unfortunately, this solution also has its drawbacks. What if the user has provided no file name suffix to the shell script? If you leave the command as written, it either produces the wrong result or fails altogether. Providing a default value for sufx, as follows, is a better method:

```
cat *${sufx-.txt} | pr | lp
```

In this final form, the default value for the sufx variable is the string .txt, so whenever users follow the standard naming convention, they do not have to provide any file name suffix to the shell script.

Using ${x:-y}

The expression form ${*x*:-*y*} is similar to ${*x*-*y*}, the only difference being that the value of the expression is *y* when the variable *x* is not set or is the null string.

You should use the colon form whenever the expression must have a non-null value. In the following example, the variable *TMPDIR* must designate a directory, so the command employs : - to ensure a directory is specified:

```
$ cat *.txt >${TMPDIR:-/usr/tmp}/workarea
```

Using ${x+y} and ${x:+y}

The expression form ${*x+y*} enables you to substitute the specific string *y* when the variable *x* has been set to anything; when *x* is undefined, the effective value of the expression is null. The expression ${*x*:+*y*} tests whether *x* is undefined or the null string; the expression ${*x+y*} tests only whether *x* is undefined.

These expression types are particularly useful when you construct a command with arguments that might be omitted. For example, suppose the variable HDG indicates whether the user wants a special heading on a printed listing. The value of HDG is either a text string or undefined. You can easily write an lp command with or without the heading option, as follows:

```
$ lp ${HDG+"-h$HDG"} *.txt
```

If the value of HDG is Monthly Accounts Summary, the command actually executed is

```
$ lp "-hMonthly Accounts Summary" *.txt
```

but if HDG is undefined (implying the user has supplied no special heading) then the command executed is

```
$ lp *.txt
```

By the way, note that using : + in the lp command would be incorrect. If HDG were defined and null, the lp command would see lp -h *.txt and take *.txt as the heading!

The appropriate use of ${*x+y*} expressions makes for simpler, easier-to-read code than would an equivalent if statement (the shell if statement is described in Chapter 8, "Conditional Execution").

Notice that the expression ${HDG+"-h$HDG"} uses nested variables. The shell fully supports variable references (including variable expressions) inside the *word* part of an expression.

Use :+ when you want to treat a variable with a null value the same as if it were not set. Actually, :+ is more commonly used in shell programs than +. In the following code, the programmer must use :+ because the variable DIR always has a value:

```
$ echo "Specify headers directory: \c"
$ read DIR
$ cc -c ${DIR:+"-I$DIR"} prog.c
```

Using ${x?y} and ${x:?y}

The ? operator tests whether the variable *x* is undefined. The ?: operator tests whether *x* is undefined or null. If a value exists, the value of the expression is also the value of the variable. If the value does not exist, the shell writes an error message and terminates.

If the expression ${HOME:?pathname} failed, the message produced by the shell is HOME: pathname. In other words, the shell first notes the name of the variable that was undefined, then writes the word *y* in the expression ${x?y} as the message text. Because the message text you write as *y* is the only hint the user has as to what went wrong, you should try to make the *y* text as informative as possible. A good explanation of the error usually requires more than one word (see the section "Specifying *word*" earlier in this chapter).

If used at the keyboard, the shell stops processing the current statement and issues a prompt after writing the error message. If ? or :? fails inside a shell script, the entire shell script is abandoned; the effect is equivalent to issuing the exit command within the script.

The ? operator is used to simplify error checking inside shell scripts. To find out whether a given variable is defined (or defined and non-null), you only have to use the variable expression in a command; the shell checks and, if the variable has no value, automatically writes an error message and performs exit (see the exit command description in Chapter 10, "Built-In Commands").

Here's an example of the ? expression used on the first line of a shell script:

```
: ${HOME?"home directory"} ${EDITOR:?"editor command"}
```

The : simply returns a zero exit value (see Chapter 10, "Built-In Commands"). Its arguments are evaluated, but the command ignores the results of the evaluation. The net effect is that the : command either does nothing or cancels the shell script due to undefined variables.

The ? expression also is useful anywhere in a shell script, especially when a variable value is set later in the execution of the script. The following command, for example, does not make a default value for the `tmp` variable; if no directory path is defined, the shell script is simply canceled:

```
cat *.txt >${tmp?work-directory}/combined.txt
```

If this command were embedded in a shell script named `docprint` and the ? test failed, the terminal dialog would look like this:

```
$ docprint
tmp: work-directory
$
```

Using ${x=y} and ${x:=y}

Use the expression formats $*{x=y}* and $*{x:=y}* to permanently assign a default value to *x* when it has none.

The = operator is much like the - operator because the text specified as *y* in the expression becomes the value of the expression when *x* is undefined. It differs in that the default value is permanently assigned to the variable *x* when you use =; the substitution is only temporary when you use -.

The = operator is most useful when your shell script refers repeatedly to a variable. You have used the expression $*{x=y}* only once to permanently assign a default value to *x*; in subsequent references you will not have to use a variable expression at all.

In the following command sequence, the programmer knew the `file` variable was undefined and proceeded to use the = operator:

```
cat *.txt >${file=/usr/tmp/combined.txt}
nroff $file ¦ lp
```

The `cat` command is designed not only to specify the path name of the output file as `/usr/tmp/combined.txt` but also to save that path name in the `file` variable. Subsequent commands, such as `nroff`, can then refer to the file using the symbolic name `$file` rather than the actual path name. If the path name ever has to be changed, changing the `cat` command automatically changes the path name also used in all subsequent commands.

Special Variables

In the beginning of this chapter, you learned that there are two general kinds of variables: regular and special. You have looked closely at the regular variety in the preceding pages; now it's time to expose the mysteries of special variables.

Special Variables

The shell automatically updates the following variables so they always contain the indicated value:

$0	The name of the current shell script
$1–$9	Command-line arguments 1 through 9
$*	All command-line arguments as the string "$1 $2 $3 ... "
$@	All command-line arguments as the list "$1" "$2" "$3"...
$#	The number of arguments
$?	The exit value of the previously executed command
$-	The shell options currently in force
$$	The process-ID of the shell

Of all the special variables, the most important are the argument variables $0 through $9. When the shell begins executing a shell script, it assigns the words of the command line to the argument variables $0 through $9. The $0 variable contains the command name by which the shell script was invoked (usually the same as its file name). The $1 variable contains the string value of the first argument, $2 contains the string value of the second argument, and so on.

If there are more than nine arguments on the command line, the remaining arguments are saved but cannot be directly referenced. That is, $10 is *not* the name of the tenth argument! The shell interprets $10 as $1 and tacks an ASCII zero onto the end of the string value of $1. If the first command argument is prog.c, for example, then the value of $10 is the string prog.c0. This is exactly the same effect you get with the expression $HOME/bin, where the shell replaces $HOME with the value of the HOME variable and appends /bin to form the result string /u/barb/bin (assuming the value of HOME is /u/barb). The point is that the shell recognizes $n where *n* is a single digit, and double digits cannot be read.

ksh
Using the Korn shell, you can reference variables beyond the ninth one by using the syntax ${*nn*} where *nn* can be any number of digits. For compatibility with shell scripts written for the Bourne shell, however, the Korn shell still does not recognize $10 as a reference to the tenth variable; you must write ${10} to get the value of the tenth variable.

You can become familiar with this feature in practice by trying to write a simple command as a shell script. The name of the command is ap and its function is to append a file to an existing file, inserting a divider line between the two files, and to delete the original files that were appended. Think of the large file as a notebook, and the file to be added to it as an individual entry, which you now want to add to the end of the notebook.

The ap command could be invoked like this:

```
$ ap contacts comtech.nb
```

where contacts is the name of the notebook file and comtech.nb is an individual note file to be added to the end of contacts.

Listing 7.1 shows a basic implementation of the ap command as a shell script.

Listing 7.1. The ap command shell script.

```
# @(#) ap 1.0 - append files to a notebook
nbfile=$1
echo "\nCONTACT: $2 **********" >> $nbfile
cat $2 >> $nbfile && rm $2
```

The ap script contains only three operative commands; the first line is only a comment used as a title for the file.

The first command (nbfile=$1) saves the file name of the notebook file in the variable nbfile. It is good technique to save the command arguments in named variables at the beginning of the program, and useful here because the variable name nbfile is more meaningful than $1 is.

The second command uses echo with output redirection to write a divider line at the current end of the notebook. The line separates previous entries in the notebook from the new entry that is about to be appended.

The final command, cat, copies the file that is the second argument of the command to standard output, and the use of output redirection causes the copied text to be added to the end of nbfile. If the cat command finishes without error, the rm command is executed to remove the note file that was just added—because it was safely added, you don't need to retain the note in two places.

Shell Arguments: $* and $@

The special variable $* refers to the entire collection of arguments on the command line, except for the command name. The shell does not force the value of $*$ to be a single string; if you want it to be treated as such, you must enclose the variable in double quotations (`"$*"`). If not enclosed in quotations, the value is subject to tokenization, using white space as separators and again using the IFS characters.

For an example of the effect of tokenization, use the set command to assign a list of values to the arguments:

```
$ set one two three "buckle
> my
> shoe" four five six
$ echo "$1"
one
$ echo "$4"
buckle
my
shoe
$ echo $*
one two three buckle my shoe four five six
```

(Note that because the third line contained no unmatched delimiters, the shell kept looking for a closing `"`; therefore, the shell did not give the secondary prompt again.)

Although the value of argument 4 contains the newline characters that separate buckle from my and my from shoe, as the command echo `"$4"` demonstrates, the newline character is one of the field separators in the default IFS character set (see the section "Shell Variables" in Chapter 3, "Shell Basics," for more about the IFS shell predefined variable). The shell always discards IFS characters from the command line, unless they are enclosed in quotations, and replaces them with a single space. Thus, after tokenization, the original value of $4 became the three words buckle, my, and shoe.

The point of all this discussion is that, due to tokenization, the value of $* is not necessarily identical to the original list of arguments on the command line. A single argument value might appear as two or more arguments after IFS tokenization.

On the other hand, enclosing $* in quotations does not yield the original list of command-line arguments either; the value of `"$*"` is a single string with one blank inserted between each of the original arguments. The quotes surround the expanded value of $* and force the expanded value to be a single string.

Once again, look at a concrete example of the problem. Suppose, to conserve disk space, your company stores all files of a particular type in packed format. You know the pack command is used to compress the files, and the pcat command can be used to convert a packed file into its original form on standard output. Your problem is to provide a shell script that works like the grep command but can be used on packed files.

You can easily accomplish this task at the keyboard by entering the following command:

```
$ pcat 0690.gl | grep restaurant
```

This should be easy enough to do in a shell script, except for one complication: the grep command supports a number of options as well as multiple file name arguments. You want to support the same options as grep, but you do not yet know how to separate the options from the file name arguments. As a compromise, you decide the pgrep command allows only one file name as the first argument, but any valid grep options can follow it.

A first attempt to write the shell script might look like this:

```
:
# pgrep 1.0 - search a packed file with grep
filename=$1
shift 1
pcat $filename | grep $*
```

After saving the name of the file in *file name*, the shift built-in command (described in detail in Chapter 10, "Built-In Commands") can be used to discard the first argument, leaving only those that should be grep options. The $* special variable passes the options to grep, as shown on the last line.

If you think this version of pgrep works, you might type it and try it, remembering to create a sample packed file first. To create a packed file, first create a regular text file containing the sample text, then pack the file by using the command pack *file name*. (If you get the message no savings, file not packed you must add more text to the file.)

Now try the following command after creating the pgrep shell script:

```
$ pgrep sample "data processing"
grep: can't open processing
$
```

What went wrong? After substitution, the last line of the shell script was executed as if

```
pcat sample | grep data processing
```

had been typed. Due to tokenization, the single argument "data processing" became two arguments, and the grep command took data as the search string and processing as the file name to be searched. Finding no file named processing, the grep command then issued the error message processing not found and canceled.

You might change the pgrep script to this:

```
:
# pgrep 1.1 - search a packed file with grep
filename=$1
shift 1
pcat $filename ¦ grep "$*"
```

The change (enclosing $* in quotes) will make the shell script work correctly. But test the shell script with this command:

```
$ pgrep sample -i data
grep: illegal option --
grep: illegal option -- d
grep: illegal option -- a
grep: illegal option -- t
grep: illegal option -- a
Usage: grep -blcnsvi pattern file . . .
$
```

This time you are searching the file sample for the string data but ignoring case distinctions. Due to the double quotation marks, "$*" in the grep command was replaced with the single string "-i data", which grep misunderstood as a string of option letters.

The point of this discussion is that there are times when you want to substitute the exact values of the command arguments. When at least one of the arguments contains white space or IFS characters, the $* variable cannot do the job.

To substitute the exact list of arguments written on the command line, you must use the special variable $@ and enclose it in double quotation marks. The quotations protect the value of $@, which is already properly tokenized from further tokenization. (Interestingly, the string "$@" is one of few cases where a quoted string results in more than one word.)

Now change the grep command in the last line of the pgrep file to read pgrep "$@" and try it again with both tests. This produces the correct results.

The Number of Arguments: $#

Whereas the $* and $@ special variables provide access to the actual values of the command arguments, the value of $# provides the number of arguments. If the number of arguments is changed (for example, see the set or shift command in Chapter 10, "Built-In Commands"), the shell automatically updates the value of $# to reflect the new number of arguments.

You can use the $# variable in many different ways, but the most common way is to check that the right number of arguments are provided on the command line. For example, the following modification of the pgrep command you looked at earlier ensures that at least two arguments have been provided: one to specify the name of the file to search, and at least one more to provide the search string. If the script finds fewer than two arguments, it exits after printing an error message.

```
:
# pgrep 1.3 - search a packed file with grep
test $# -lt 2 && {
    echo "Usage: pgrep filename grep-args" >&2
    exit 1
}
filename=$1
shift 1
pcat $filename ¦ grep "$@"
```

The method used to perform the test uses only the UNIX test command as well as techniques you learned in Part I. See the shell if statement in Chapter 8, "Conditional Execution," which provides a more natural way to perform the test.

The Last Exit Value: $?

The special variable $? always contains the exit value returned by the most recent command executed in the shell script. If no previous command was executed, its value is 0; otherwise its value is an integer in the range 0 to 255. The value of $? is changed by each command executed in a shell script.

Current Shell Options: $ -

The special variable $ - contains the shell options currently in effect as a string of characters. The hyphen (-), which usually begins an option string, is not included in the value of $-.

Use $- to test whether a given shell option is in effect, or to save and restore the current options across a dot command or function call. The following command uses $- to invoke another shell that is using the same options currently in force:

```
$ sh -$- setup
```

Current Process-ID: $$

The special variable $$ displays the process-ID of the current shell. When used with a command typed at the terminal, the value of $$ is the process-ID of your login shell. When used in a shell script, the value of $$ is the process-ID of the shell executing the command script (usually not the login shell).

The $$ variable is most often used for forming unique, temporary file names because UNIX guarantees that no two active processes have the same process-ID. The following commands, for example, safely write a temporary file in /tmp even though many users might be using the /tmp work directory at the same time:

```
$ grep "meeting" mbox >/tmp/grep-$$
$ pg /tmp/grep-$$   # Look at the result
$ rm /tmp/grep-$$   # Discard the workfile
```

Changing the Shell Arguments

Newcomers to shell programming often think of the shell arguments $0 through $9 as permanent values that never change throughout the execution of a shell script. However, there are many useful commands and shell programming techniques that do change the set of arguments. For this reason, it is good practice as well as good documentation to save the arguments in named variables early in a shell script.

The set command changes all the arguments (and the $# variable) at once. The following samples use this fact to extract selected pieces of information from the output of the date and who commands:

```
$ set `date`       # Format: Wed June 22 09:23:51 1991 EDT
$ echo "Time is $4 $6"
Time is 09:23:51 EDT
$

$ set `who am i`   # Format: jjv cons1 08:23
$ echo "Login name is $1"
Login name is jjv
$
```

The shift command also changes the argument list by "rotating" the argument list left one or more positions. The effect of shifting is illustrated by the following dialog:

```
$ set bill john ted
$ echo $# $*
3 bill john ted
$ shift
$ echo $# $*
2 john ted
$ shift
```

```
$ echo $# $*
ted
$
```

Shifting the argument list is the only way you can access arguments beyond $9.

Environment Variables

From the standpoint of writing shell scripts, an environment variable is simply a variable that is defined and has a value without any action on your part. From the standpoint of the shell, an environment variable is a regular variable that is included in the argument list of export, and is therefore global. The shell takes special measures to pass a variable that has been exported to all commands called by the shell script.

To access an environment variable in a shell script, you must reference the variable in the same manner as any other variable. Environment variables also can be referenced by commands written in other languages so their use is not limited to shell scripts.

Some environment variables are automatically defined when you log in. They are described in the section "Shell Variables" in Chapter 3, "Shell Basics." You can create other environment variables for your own use. Shell programmers typically create new environment variables when a shell program is implemented as two or more script files, with one serving as the main program and the others called on when needed. Environment variables are as a convenient way to pass data and control information from the main shell script to a called shell script.

Another common use of environment variables is to let the user specify a choice once, often by setting an environment variable in the login profile. Without environment variables, the user would have to specify the choice on each invocation of the command.

The following simple shell script implements a command called spk that displays a packed file. Its use of the original environment variables TMPDIR and PAGER enables the user to customize the behavior of spk merely by setting the variables to a preferred value.

```
:
# @(#) spk 1.0 - shell program to show packed file

[ $# -eq 1 ] || {
    echo "Usage: $0 filename"
    exit 1
```

```
    }
tmpfile=${TMPDIR:-/tmp}/spaAA0$$

pcat $1 >$tmpfile
eval ${PAGER:-pg} $tmpfile
rm $tmpfile
```

Users specify their preferred display utility by using the commands

```
$ PAGER=view
$ export PAGER
$
```

To use any display utility for one specific invocation of spk, the user can use an environment variable, as follows:

```
$ PAGER=more spk anyfile
```

If the shell option -k is in effect, the PAGER=more can appear anywhere on the command line:

```
$ set -k
$ spk anyfile PAGER=emacs
$
```

Summary

This chapter does not present all there is to know about shell variables.

Chapter 3, "Shell Basics," in Part I, explained in detail the variables used by the shell itself, which you can use in your shell scripts as a source of information or to control the behavior of the shell. Chapter 11, "Shell Arithmetic," provides more information about doing arithmetic with values stored in shell variables. And Chapter 12, "Advanced Shell Facilities," presents array variables and shows how to use them.

There are certainly features more essential to the shell than variables, but none that you will use as often nor find as useful. It is almost impossible to write a shell script without using them, and at the keyboard you will often concern yourself with the current setting of shell environment variables such as PATH and CDPATH.

The overview section described the basics of shell variables and introduced the fundamentals of assigning a value to a variable and later retrieving the value with a reference. The overview section is critical to the chapter, and essential to the remainder of the book. You must understand the variable assignment statement (for example, pubdir=/usr/spool/uucppublic), and how to call up the value of a variable (for example, $pubdir) to make any sense of shell programming.

The section "Special Variables" introduced the shell arguments $0 through $9 and the special variables $*, $@, $#, $?, $-, and $$. The variables $0 through $9 receive their values automatically from the command line that executes a shell script. The shell sets the special variables to provide useful information to your shell script. Once again, these subjects are basic techniques for shell programming.

The section "Changing the Shell Arguments" described ways to change the values of the $0 through $9 variables, and suggested some reasons why you might want to do so. In fact, manipulating the shell arguments with set and shift often provides the only means of solving a great many shell programming problems. As an example, successively using shift to access the arguments is the oldest and still the best way of processing an arbitrary number of command-line arguments.

In Part I, you learned about the environment variables defined and used by the shell. In this chapter you learned that you can create new environment variables and use them to pass data between the user and a shell script, or from a calling script to a called shell script. The techniques described in the section "Environment Variables" are used in many professional-quality shell scripts to simplify the user interface while still providing a lot of functionality.

If you don't feel that you've mastered shell variables at this point, don't stop here; you may get stuck forever. The following chapters contain many examples of using shell variables, and may serve as a guide to how they work.

Shell variables provide one way of varying the commands executed in a script according to context; for example, by taking into account the arguments provided by the user on the command line.

The next chapter, "Conditional Execution," shows another way to vary the processing performed by a shell script.

## Chapter 8

Conditional Execution

he shell provides two statements for decision making: the if statement and the case statement. With them you can create shell programs of great flexibility. The if statement tests the exit value of a command and chooses one of two alternative continuations based on the outcome. The case statement evaluates a string expression and chooses one of many alternatives based on the result.

The shell programming language also includes loop control statements (for, while, and until). The looping statements are examined in the next chapter.

The if, case, for, while, and until statements support structured programming techniques. A program can be more easily written, more readily understood, and more quickly corrected when it is well structured. The shell programming language not only encourages good structure but also makes it difficult to write a poorly structured program in the shell language because there is no goto statement to be misused. If you are not accustomed to writing well-structured programs, you might find shell programming slightly awkward at first.

The if statement is a principal element of program structure, so you should begin there.

Using Control Statements

The `if`, `case`, `for`, `while`, and `until` statements are not *commands* in the usual sense; you find no program file in the UNIX libraries called by any of these names. Changing your `PATH` value has no effect on the shell's ability to locate and perform an `if`, `case`, `for`, `while`, or `until` operation.

Neither are the control statements functions or built-in commands. They are *primitives*, meaning they cannot be defined in terms of any other operations. Their implementation is internal to the shell and cannot be changed, redefined, or removed.

If you write a program, shell function, or alias called `if`, for example, the only way to execute that command is to hide the name inside quotation marks so the shell will not recognize it. The shell recognizes control statements early in the processing cycle so the shell can analyze the statement's syntax. You must not attempt to generate the name of a control statement with variable substitution, with the output of a backquoted string (``` `` ```), or by any other means, because the shell cannot recognize a *generated* control statement.

The names of the control statements, and the words that introduce sub-parts of a control statement, such as `then` or `else`, work properly only when you write the word in lowercase letters without quotation marks or backslashes, and put it in the actual text of your shell script.

Control statement names are not reserved words, however. That is, you can use words like `if` or `then` as variable names as long as you and the shell do not get confused about the role played by the word. If a control statement name is the first word of a line or immediately follows a semicolon, the shell interprets the word as the control statement name.

Consider the following command as an example of this process:

```
echo if in rome then eat candles
```

The `echo` command actually contains three shell keywords: `if`, `in`, and `then`. However, the words appear in the position of command arguments and could not possibly have their standard meaning. The shell treats this appearance of the words `if`, `in`, and `then` as ordinary words.

In the following example, however, the attempt to use `while` as a variable name leads to an error message:

```
while=5
sleep $while
```

Why does this happen? Because the word appears at the beginning of a line, exactly where the shell would expect to find the `while` statement.

8

As a general rule, you should use the shell keywords only for their intended purpose. Confusing the role of words that have a special meaning to the shell, such as if, then, else, case, while, and until, only leads to eventual errors.

The if Statement

The syntax of an if statement follows:

The if statement

```
if list [ ; ]
then list [ ; ]
[ elif list [ ; ] ] ...
[ else list [ ; ] ]
fi
```

The syntax is a little complicated. The best way to learn how it works is with small steps. The simplest if statement you can write is

```
if command1
then command2
fi
```

When it encounters this statement, the shell executes the following series of actions:

1. Execute *command1* and notice its exit value.

2. If the exit value was 0, indicating the command went to a normal or successful conclusion, execute *command2*.

3. Set the exit value of the if statement to the exit value of commands if commands was TRUE, otherwise to FALSE.

To paraphrase, the if statement says "If *command1* works okay, then execute *command2*; otherwise do nothing." The word fi, which looks like if spelled backwards, simply tells the shell where the if statement ends. The shell absolutely requires a fi for each if statement. The *fi-if* notation was chosen to imitate parentheses, where) looks like (spelled backwards!

To get a feel for the if statement, you might try a few exercises at your keyboard to display the result of a test command, like this:

8

```
$  if test -d $HOME
>  then echo $home is a directory
>  fi
   /u/home/louise is a directory
$
```

The test command is explained in the section, "Using if with test," later in this chapter.

You might wonder why the shell requires a special mark to end the if statement. The answer takes you to the next level of if-statement complexity.

Using Command Lists in if

You might have noticed that the syntax description for if used the term *list* rather than *command*. The reason for this discrepancy is that the shell accepts a command list following if, where a command list is one or more commands separated by semicolons or newlines. The then clause also accepts a command list.

The following code is a valid statement using lists rather than single commands:

```
if get -s -p s.$file >g.$file
   cmp -s g.$file $file
then
   rm g.$file
   delta "-y`cat reason`" s.$file
   echo $file: updated
fi
```

The meaning of these commands is not important; look at the overall structure of the if statement. It's the same as the basic if-then-fi in the preceding section. The only difference is that two commands follow if, and three commands follow then. The role of the then and fi keywords should now be clear: They mark the end of the preceding command lists.

When you give more than one command following if, the exit value of the last command in the list determines whether the statement as a whole is true or false. If the last exit value is 0, then the if statement is true and the then command list is executed. If the last exit value is nonzero, the if statement is false and the shell skips the then command list.

8

The else Clause

The next increment in complexity of the if statement is the process of adding an else clause. The general format of the if statement in this case is as follows:

```
if command1
then command2
else command3
fi
```

You already know *command2* is executed only if the exit value of *command1* is zero (when if is true). If the exit value of *command1* is nonzero (false), then *command2* is skipped and *command3* is executed instead. One final rule: Either *command2* or *command3* is executed, but not both. This means if the shell executes *command2*, it skips over *command3*.

Try typing the if-then-else-fi statement and see what happens:

```
$ if true
> then echo "TRUE: did then"
> else echo "FALSE: did else"
> fi
TRUE: did then
$
```

The true command always returns an exit value of 0, so you should have been surprised if the then clause was not executed. Notice also that the else clause was not executed; the shell skipped over it. Now try this experiment:

```
$ if false
> then echo "TRUE: did then"
> else echo "FALSE: did else"
> fi
FALSE: did else
$
```

This is exactly opposite to the former trial. The false command always returns a nonzero exit value, so the shell skipped over the then clause and executed the else clause.

Figure 8.1 diagrams the shell execution of the if-then-else-fi command. Obviously, *command1* must be executed first to determine its exit value; the shell then chooses one of two paths to continue along: either then if the exit value was 0, or else if the exit value was anything else. Finally, the two alternative paths come together again at fi and the shell resumes normal execution of commands.

8

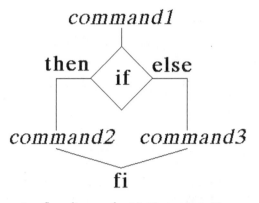

Figure 8.1. Execution flow diagram for if-then-else-fi.

The following code shows a practical example of the if-then-else-fi structure. The purpose of the code is to compare two files using the diff command. If the files are identical, the code removes one of them and reports the result; otherwise the code displays the list of differences.

```
if diff $fn1 $fn2 >/tmp/diff.out
then # the files are equal
   echo $fn1: $fn2: files are equal
   rm $fn2 /tmp/diff.out
else # the files are unequal
   pg /tmp/diff.out
   rm -i $fn1 $fn2 # let user choose now
   rm /tmp/diff.out
fi
```

Notice that, as *command1* and *command2* can be a command list, so too the else clause (*command3*) can be a command list.

The elif Clause

The if statement, as described so far, is sufficient for choosing between two alternatives. If the program must choose between three or more alternatives, and all are mutually exclusive, you must use the elif clause.

Real life is full of multiple-choice decisions. An example occurs in the process of maintaining computer programs. Assume you use SCCS to administrate the shell scripts you're responsible for. (SCCS is a standard— and important—component of UNIX System V.) The official text of your scripts is stored in files with names like s.payw, where the prefix s. indicates that the file is an SCCS file. To change the file, you must use the get command to retrieve the current version, an editor to modify the ASCII text, and the delta command to store the updated version back into the SCCS file. Listing 8.1, a command called update, automates this process for you.

Listing 8.1. The update command, which updates an SCCS file.

```
# @(#) update 1.0 - edit an SCCS file
if [ $# -ne 1 ]
then
    echo "Usage: update filename"
    exit 1
fi
filename=$1
edit=${VISUAL:-${EDITOR:-ed}}

# Update procedure
if [ -r p.$filename ]
    then eval $edit $filename
elif [ -r s.$filename ]
    then get -e s.$filename && eval $edit $filename
else # new filename - create an SCCS file
    admin -n s.$filename
    get -e s.$filename && eval $edit $filename
fi
```

The program in Listing 8.1 begins by checking that an argument is present on the update command. If so, the program saves the file name and chooses the command the user wants to use to edit the file.

The main procedure in Listing 8.1 is a single if statement. If the named file already exists, an update is also already in progress, so you can edit the file. If the named file does not exist but an SCCS file exists, extract the current version with get and edit it. If neither file exists, the else clause uses the admin command to create the file and calls the editor to create the text for it.

Although this example uses an SCCS application, it's not essential that you understand how SCCS works. The point is to show how the if, elif, and else clauses progressively test for and eliminate the various cases. The first test that succeeds is the one in which the then clause is executed. The else clause is executed only when neither the if test nor any of the elif tests is true.

The else clause is optional. If you do not provide it, the if statement does nothing when none of the tests succeeds. The shell encounters fi without having performed any of the then clauses and quits the if statement altogether.

The elif clause is simply a contraction for else if. Just as a then clause must be associated with an if statement, so too must a then clause follow every elif statement.

8

Nested if Statements

You could improve the sample program in Listing 8.1 by using a *nested* if statement—that is, an if within an if. The chief difficulty with the program, as written, is that it tests for the existence of the plain file first. According to the problem statement, the update program is intended to maintain files kept in SCCS format. Therefore, the file name should be considered new if the SCCS file does not exist; whether or not the plain file exists is immaterial.

Listing 8.2 modifies the update command so it tests for the existence or nonexistence of the s. file. The plain text file is updated only if both an s.*name* and a p.*name* file exist. (SCCS uses the p.*name* file to record any pending changes to the file.)

Listing 8.2. An improved update command.

```
# @(#) update 2.0 - edit an SCCS file

# Set the shell to exit immediately on any command error
set -e

# Make sure at least one argument was given on the command line
if [ $# -ne 1 ]
then
   echo "Usage: update filename"
   exit 1
fi
filename=$1
edit=${VISUAL:-${EDITOR:-ed}}

# Update procedure
if [ -r s.$filename ]
then # update an existing file...
   if [ -r p.$filename ]
   then # update in progress
      eval $edit $filename
   else # start a new update
      get -e s.$filename && eval $edit $filename
   fi
else # new filename - create an SCCS file
   if [ -f $filename ]
   then # an initial text is available
      admin -i$filename s.$filename
      rm $filename # Delete the original file
   else # completely new... create an empty file
      admin -n s.$filename
   fi
   get -e s.$filename      # Retrieve for edit
   eval $edit $filename    # Edit the file
fi
```

8

This revised `update` command contains no `elif` clause; instead, the command is divided into two main procedures: one for the case where an `s.name` file exists, and one for the case where it doesn't. In both cases, an additional `if` statement occurs inside the `then` or `else` clause.

The shell imposes no fixed maximum limit on the number of `if` statements you can nest one inside another. The limit that does exist is actually dependent on the amount of free memory available to the shell. The shell is dependent on the total amount of memory accessible to the shell, the amount already committed to holding variable values, and other parts of the statement currently being processed, among other things.

Using `if` as a Command

As the previous section stated, the shell treats the `if` statement as a command. In fact, the shell considers everything between the `if` and its matching `fi` part of the same command. This fact has a number of implications, which are now examined.

First, the `if` statement, being a command, returns an exit value. Its exit value is the last exit value generated while processing the `if` statement. Thus, if only the test on the `if` statement itself is performed, then that exit value becomes the exit value of `if`. If a `then` or `else` clause is executed, the exit value of the last command executed in that clause becomes the exit value of `if`.

Second, because the `if` statement is a command and has an exit value, an `if` statement itself can be the command following `if`. Consider the following statement as an example:

```
if if pcat $file >tmpaa$$
   then nroff tmpaa$$ >tmpab$$
   else rm tmpaa$$; nroff $file >tmpab$$
   fi
then col <tmpab$$ ¦ lp
else echo Errors in document - not printed.
fi
```

Here, the command tested by the first `if` is itself an `if` statement. The inner `if` statement formats a text document from either a compressed or plain ASCII file; the `then` clause prints the formatted document if `nroff` was successful, otherwise the `else` clause writes an error message. Although this type of structure is rarely used, it is valid.

8

Using I/O Redirection with `if`

A second important implication of the command nature of `if` is that, like any other command, `if` lets you redirect the input or output of the entire statement.

Because the `if` statement extends to the `fi`, the proper place to write the redirections is following `fi`. The following example shows the proper placement of redirections:

```
if pcat s.$filename
then :
else cat $filename
fi > file.out
```

This one statement copies either a packed or plain ASCII file into `file.out`. Because the redirection is placed on the `fi`, it applies to all commands included in the `if` statement, namely the `pcat` and `cat` commands in this example. This is because the shell executes an `if` statement by creating a subshell. Any redirections applied to `fi` apply to this subshell and any commands executed by it. Thus, when the `pcat`, `=` or `cat` commands are executed, they are already running in a redirected environment. (By the way, the `:` command in the `then` clause is the shell *no-operation* command; it does nothing. See Chapter 10, "Built-In Commands," for a full discussion of the `:` command.)

Writing `if` on a Single Line

Although the `if` command is normally spread over several lines, you can write it on a single line. The shell requires each clause of the command to be separated from the previous clause by a semicolon (;). The following code is an example of the technique:

```
if cmp -s $f1 $f2; then echo Same; else echo Different; fi
```

Any number of newlines are permitted before `then`, `else`, and `fi`, but the shell permits only one semicolon in these positions.

Many programmers like to use the semicolon to place the word `then` on the same line as `if` to enhance readability:

```
if cmp -s $f1 $f2; then
   echo Same;
else
   echo Different
fi
```

You *must* use semicolons rather than newlines to delimit the clauses of if in certain circumstances, usually when another program is passing the command to the shell. When writing commands in a makefile for the UNIX make command, for example, you must keep an if statement on one line.

Using if **with** test

The if command is often used with the test built-in command; you have seen a few examples in this chapter. The test command is explained in Chapter 10, "Built-In Commands." To enhance the readability of shell scripts, the shell lets you write the test command in the form [*exp*] rather than the more traditional command format test *exp*.

The test command provides a way to check for the existence of a file, to compare two strings or numbers, or to test the value of a variable. (Chapter 10, "Built-In Commands," describes the test command in detail.) Due to its great many uses, the test command is used frequently in shell scripts.

Here is an example of testing whether a file exists:

```
if [ -f $filename ]
then echo $filename: exists
else echo $filename: not found
fi >&2
```

The -f option tells test to check for the existence of the file named in the next argument and returns true if it exists, otherwise false.

To test whether a variable has a value, you can write

```
if [ -z "$filename" ]; then
    echo Filename must be specified; exit
fi
```

The -z option tells test to check whether the following argument is a zero-length string. This if statement checks for a null file name and issues an error message, "File name must be specified," when the value of *file name* is null.

To test whether a variable has a specific value, you can use the if statement with test as follows:

```
if [ "$user" = "fred" ]
then :
else
    echo $user: Illegal access >&2
    exit 38
fi
```

The test command supports a full set of numeric comparisons, including -eq (equal), -ne (not equal), -gt (greater than), -ge (greater than or equal to), -lt (less than), and -le (less than or equal to). These tests ignore leading zeroes so numeric values compare equally even if their string representations are not the same. You can try the following experiment as a demonstration:

```
$ if [ "002" -eq 2 ]
> then echo Same
> else echo Not the same
> fi
Same
$
```

In early versions of UNIX, test was a separate command that had to be loaded and executed like any other command. More recently, however, the test command has been added to the shell as a built-in command, considerably improving the overall performance of shell scripts. Because modern implementations of the shell include test as a built-in command, you should not hesitate to use test in your shell scripts as often as you like.

The case Statement

The case statement is a special shell command similar to if in many respects except for what it does.

Syntax of the case statement

```
case string-expression in
  [ pattern [ ¦ pattern ] ... ) command-list ;; ] ...
esac
```

The first line of the case statement must completely contain the command name case, *string expression*, and in. The *string-expression* can be any combination of literal text, quoted text, variable references, and command substitutions. You must enclose the entire expression in quotation marks if the string contains any white space or characters special to the shell. Notice that the shell does *not* rescan the string expression for IFS characters; the shell always treats the string expression as one word, even if variable or command substitution introduces white space into the value of *string-expression*.

8

The case line can be followed by any number of *pattern* clauses. A *pattern* clause consists of one or more string patterns. Multiple patterns must be separated by the *or-bar* (¦), which is a shell metacharacter and therefore cannot occur in a pattern except when quoted or backslashed. The list of patterns must be coded on one line, and must end with a right parenthesis.

A single pattern can contain ordinary characters and wild cards. If the pattern contains wild cards, the corresponding part of the string expression is ignored when determining whether a match has been found. The pattern y* matches any of the words *yes*, *yup*, *yeah*, and *y*, for example, but does not match *no* or *ok*. For more information about wild cards, see Chapter 3, "Shell Basics."

The shell tests whether the evaluated `string expression` matches any of the specified `pattern`s. If so, the `command list` following) is executed; otherwise the `command list` is skipped.

A `command list` can contain any number of commands (including zero). The last command in the list must be followed by a double semicolon. (Notice that no white space can appear between the two semicolons.) The shell uses the double semicolon to indicate where the command list ends.

If the case statement contains more than one pattern line, the shell executes the first pattern line that matches the evaluated string expression. If no pattern matches the string expression, then no pattern command-list is executed. At most, one pattern line can match the string expression, because the shell automatically skips the rest of the statement after executing the matched command list.

The esac command must be present and must follow the last pattern line of the case statement. Like fi, the esac command is not a valid command by itself; it can appear only after a case command and the list of patterns, if any exists.

The following sequence of commands reads a line from the terminal and then checks whether the line begins with the letter *y:*

```
read answer
case $answer in
    y*) ;;         # Okay, fall through to next command
    * )  exit 1 ;; # Terminate on anything else
esac
```

The pattern statement beginning with *) uses the * to match any value of $answer that no other pattern matched; it acts as a default case.

You can try the case statement at your keyboard:

```
$ read answer
yes
$ case $answer in
> y*) echo you said: "yes." ;;
> *) echo you said: "no" ;;
> esac
  you said yes
$
```

The following modified version of the previous example uses multiple patterns to recognize either an upper- or lowercase *y:*

```
read answer
case $answer in
    y* ¦ Y*) ;;   # Okay, fall through to next command
    *)  exit 1 ;; # Terminate on anything else
esac
```

The case statement provides more flexibility than if with test for identifying a string because the case statement matches a string against a string *pattern* and the test command checks only for an exact match.

When writing a case statement, you must consider the order in which the patterns are tested. The shell always performs the tests in the same order as you write them. If you write two patterns, one of which is a more general case of the other, the more general case should appear *after* the more specific case. In the example

```
case $filename in
    *.c)      cc -c $filename ;;
    s.*.c)    get s.$filename
              cc -c $filename
              rm $filename
              ;;
esac
```

the file name s.payroll.c would always match the first pattern (because s.payroll.c ends with .c) and the second pattern, even though it is a closer match, would never be checked. The command should actually be written as follows:

```
case $filename in
    s.*.c)    get s.$filename
              cc -c $filename
              rm $filename
              ;;
    *.c)      cc -c $filename ;;
esac
```

Just as Input/Output redirection is valid on the if statement, so too is redirection valid on the case statement. The case statement spans everything from case to esac; a redirection should therefore be appended to esac when it is intended to apply to all the commands in the statement:

```
case `file $filename ¦ cut -d: -f2` in
   *commands*)   pr -t -n $filename ;;
   *nroff*   )   nroff -mm $filename ;;
esac ¦ lp
```

In this last example, notice that the redirection of case takes the form of a pipe. All the output of either pr or nroff is piped to the lp command. The example also shows a complex *string expression*. The *pattern* statement that is executed is the first pattern that matches the second field of the output of the file command.

Like the if statement, the case statement can be infinitely complex. For each pattern, you can specify a (possibly null) list of commands. Because the if and case statements are commands as well, you can embed these statements inside each other to any extent (limited only by the amount of memory available to the shell).

In the following example, an if is embedded in a case which, in turn, appears in an if statement:

```
if [ ! -d $dir ]; then
   case $dir in
      . ¦ .. )
         echo Cannot create . or .. >&2 ;;
      *)
         if mkdir $dir; then
            chmod 0765 $dir
         else
            echo Cannot create $dir >&2
         fi ;;
   esac
fi
```

If you were to try this script at your keyboard (assuming you have entered it into a file called makedir), you would see the following kinds of output:

```
$ makedir
Cannot create . or ..
$ makedir trash
$ makedir /usr/bin
$
```

Notice that the command prints nothing when it is successful. This is typical of UNIX programs.

The shell provides a great deal of power to structure programs conveniently. You can abuse that power by writing statements so complex that other programmers cannot understand them. You should try to keep your programs as simple as your processing requirements allow.

8

A Sample Program

At this point you have already learned much about the shell, certainly enough to write a useful program. In this section you will build a sample application to show how the pieces you have studied can be tied together to make a real program.

Effective shell programming must be based on knowledge of the UNIX commands supplied with the system. The UNIX commands provide the basic instruction set of the shell language. If you are new to UNIX, you won't yet be familiar with the UNIX commands. As you work through this exercise, carefully note how the various UNIX commands work and combine to achieve a goal. If you have the patience, it would be helpful for you to look up each new command you encounter, and even to experiment with the command at your terminal. To help you out, the book briefly explains each command as the code is discussed.

Program Requirements

In any programming job, it is important to begin with a clear statement of the program's purpose. This statement is often called the *requirements* because it summarizes the key points of the program's behavior. You begin, therefore, by stating the program's requirements.

The overall purpose of the program is to maintain a name and address book; that is, a file containing the names, addresses, phone numbers, and other useful information about a person. The program must provide a way to add new entries to the book, to display the name and address information in the book, to change an entry, and to delete an entry.

To make the program easy to use, it prompts the user for all input. The user does not have to specify any command-line options, nor does the program support any. When invoked, the program displays a main menu from which users choose the function they want to perform. The menu looks roughly like this:

```
===== Name & Address File =====

1.   ADD    a new name & address entry
2.   LIST   all or selected entries
3.   CHANGE the information in an entry
4.   DELETE an entry

What function (1-4)?
```

8

The user should enter a number from one to four. An invalid entry receives an error message. When adding an entry, the user must enter a name, a one-line address, a city, state, and ZIP code, and a telephone number. For each entry the user also can record one line of remarks containing anything the user wants.

Step 1: Display the Menu

The program overview from the previous section describes the program's *external interface;* its appearance from the end user's point of view. The overview tells you nothing about how to actually implement the program. The next step is to invent the step-by-step procedure the program must follow.

The program overview has at least described the program's operation in the schematic form shown in Listing 8.3.

Listing 8.3. Design of the book command.

```
# book - maintain a name & address book
display menu
ask what choice
if choice 1
then
    add a new entry
if choice 2
then
    list all or selected entries
if choice 3
then
    change an entry
if choice 4
then
    delete an entry
otherwise
    incorrect choice!
end
```

Actually, this is quite a bit of code to infer from a brief program overview. The code formulates the program's behavior as a series of steps, each of which is simpler than the program as a whole. This method of analyzing the program's function is called *stepwise refinement*. By repeatedly applying the method first to the program as a whole, then to each step and substep, you eventually obtain a series of statements the shell can actually execute.

The first step in the program is display menu. Can it be refined further? You know how to display information on the screen; the echo command

8

writes whatever text you desire to the terminal. With the echo command, you can translate display menu directly into the following shell statement:

```
echo "===== Name & Address File =====

1.   ADD     a new name & address entry
2.   LIST    all or selected entries
3.   CHANGE the information in an entry
4.   DELETE an entry

What function (1-4)? \c"
```

Notice that the entire menu has been written as a single string. The shell preserves newline characters inside a quoted string (see the section "Quoting with "" in Chapter 3, "Shell Basics"). You can do the same job using an echo command for each line, but this way is easier to type, and easier to change later if the menu text has to be revised.

\c is used in the string argument of echo to tell the echo command not to output a newline character when it's finished. As a result, the screen cursor is left at the end of the last output line—the most natural position for users to enter their responses.

There is one other thing you might like to do before displaying the menu: clear the screen. The tput command can do that, if you specify the right argument. Most terminals can perform a variety of control functions in addition to displaying text; clearing the screen is one such function.

You can now rewrite the first part of your program as shown in Listing 8.4.

Listing 8.4. The book command—display menu.

```
# book - maintain a name & address book

# Display function menu

tput clear
echo "===== Name & Address File =====

1.   ADD     a new name & address entry
2.   LIST    all or selected entries
3.   CHANGE the information in an entry
4.   DELETE an entry

What function (1-4)? \c"
```

Step 2: Read the Menu Choice

Going back to your program design in Listing 8.3, the next step in the program is to read the user's reply to the question "What function?" The shell provides a built-in command, read, to help with this task. (See Chapter 10, "Built-In Commands," for a full description of the read command.)

The syntax of the read command is

```
read varname1 varname2 ...
```

Each argument of read must be a variable name (without the leading $). The command reads a line of input from the keyboard and separates the line into individual words using the IFS characters. Notice that read does *not* automatically recognize white space as a word separator; only the characters in the IFS shell variable are used to break the line into words. Each word in the line is stored in one of the named variables, moving from left to right; that is, the first word in the line is stored in *varname1*, the second in *varname2*, and so on. If there are fewer variable names than words in the line, then all remaining words are stored as a single string into the last named variable. If there are more variable names than words, the excess variables are set to the null string.

Experiment with the read command to get a better idea how it works:

```
$ read name age other
bill 29
$ echo $name
bill
$ echo $age
29
$ echo $other

$
```

Notice that the first word, bill, became the value of the name variable, and the second word, 29, became the value of the age variable. The third variable, other, has no value because only two words were present in the input line. Now try entering some extra words:

```
$ read LastName FirstName
Smith, Joe E.
$ echo $LastName
Smith,
$ echo $FirstName
Joe E.
$
```

8

The value of `LastName` is `Smith` because by default the `IFS` variable includes only white space characters. The shell does not recognize the comma as a separator, so it is taken as part of the first word. The value of `FirstName` contains the rest of the input line because it is the last variable named on the `read` command.

Generally, if you want to read three words, you should name four variables on the `read` command; if you want to read four words, you should name five variables, and so on. The extra variable is null if the user enters the right number of words; otherwise it contains the extra input.

To read the user's reply to the menu of your sample program, you could write the following command:

```
read choice etc
```

If the user enters two or more words, the variable `etc` contains the extra words. You can disregard the extra input or consider it an error. If you want to consider it an error, however, you have to check `etc` for a non-null value.

Step 3: Analyze the User's Input

You now come to the most forbidding part of the program: identifying the user's input and directing the shell to execute the group of statements appropriate to that input.

The program design in Listing 8.3 used a series of `if` statements followed by an `otherwise`, but the shell doesn't have such a command. How do you translate these statements into shell language?

Remember that the `case` statement allows a multiple-choice matching between a string and a list of patterns. Certainly your program has to make a multiple-choice decision at this point. The user's reply, held in the variable `choice`, is also a string, to be sure. What patterns might you want to match against the value of `choice`? Patterns don't have to contain wild cards; they also can be strings of specific characters. The following `case` statement does the job nicely:

```
case $choice in
    1) add new entry ;;
    2) list entries ;;
    3) change an entry ;;
    4) remove an entry ;;
    *) improper choice? ;;
esac
```

When the user provides incorrect, unusable, or inappropriate input (meaning the program cannot handle the input), often the best thing to do is to issue a well-chosen error message and stop. Sometimes it might be more reasonable to ignore the erroneous input. As the programmer, you must decide what action is best. For *improper choice?*, use echo to display an error message, and exit to halt the shell's execution of the program.

What should you do about the other actions: *add*, *list*, *change*, and *remove*? Clearly you have more work to do. You must refine each of these generalized actions into specific commands the shell can execute. Before you tackle that job, though, take a look at your program at this stage. You have finished the first stage of refinement, and your program now looks like Listing 8.5.

Listing 8.5. The book command—first refinement.

```
# book - maintain a name & address book

# Display function menu

tput clear
echo "===== Name & Address File =====

1.   ADD     a new name & address entry
2.   LIST    all or selected entries
3.   CHANGE the information in an entry
4.   DELETE an entry

What function (1-4)? \c"
read choice
case $choice in
```

If you do a trial run at this point, you will see the following:

```
$ book
====== Name & Address File ======

1.   ADD     a new name & address entry
2.   LIST    all or selected entries
3.   CHANGE the information in an entry
4.   DELETE an entry

What function (1-4)? \c" 4
remove an entry
$
    1) add new entry ;;
    2) list entries ;;
    3) change an entry ;;
    4) remove an entry ;;
    *) echo Invalid choice; exit 1 ;;
esac
```

8

It's a good idea to actually enter this program and run it, if you first substitute dummy commands for the *add*, *list*, *change*, and *remove* statements. Such a test can prove that the overall program design is sound. After all, the details of the add, list, change, and remove operations do not affect the high-level code already present. A dummy command could be something as simple as echo add new entry.

Step 4: Second Refinement

As was previously stated, to finish the book sample program, you only have to add, list, change, and remove name and address entries from the file. Granted, these operations are the heart of the program and account for most of the code, but do not discount the progress already made. You can now consider each of the four operations independently because the program skeleton you have binds the four operations into a framework and at the same time isolates each from the other.

To show how the process of stepwise refinement furthers program design, analyze the procedure for adding a new name and address entry.

To begin with, you know you need a file somewhere to hold the information. To avoid complications, assume the file is kept in the user's home directory and is named names.db; in other words, its full path name is $HOME/names.db.

Because the choice of a path name is an arbitrary decision, you should keep the path name of the file in a shell variable and use the variable rather than the actual path name in your commands. It is then easier to change the path name later. A simple statement like the following suffices when added near the top of the program:

dbname=$HOME/names.db

Referring to the original program requirements, you find you have already been told what information must be kept in the file. You decide immediately that the file contains lines in the following format:

name:address:city:state:ZIP:phone:remarks

where the colons are used to separate individual fields. (Using white space as field separators is a poor choice because a name like Smith, Elgin would be taken as two fields, not one.)

To add a new entry to the file, you clearly have to do the following:

```
read name, address, city, state, ZIP, phone, remarks
if name is already in the file
then
    echo name: already on file
else
    write entry to the end of the file
    sort the file by name
fi
```

Not that complicated, is it? The read statement is almost usable as written, and the if-then-else-fi structure is pure shell language. Unfortunately, the procedure does not tell the user what information to enter; the read statement simply waits for input without telling the user that the program is waiting for input. To give the user a little assistance, prompt the user for each value and read the fields one at a time. The resulting code looks like this:

```
echo "Name     : \c"; read Name
echo "Address : \c"; read Address
echo "City     : \c"; read City
echo "State    : \c"; read State
echo "ZIP code: \c"; read ZIP
echo "Phone    : \c"; read Phone
echo "Remarks : \c"; read Remarks
```

This sequence of commands results in setting the value of each of the variables Name, Address, City, State, ZIP, Phone, and Remarks to the specific values the user wants to keep in the file. By combining this input procedure with the previous procedure outline, and substituting actual UNIX commands, you obtain the final implementation of the add function:

```
# Add a new entry to the name-address file
echo "Name     : \c"; read Name
if grep -i "^$Name" $dbname        # Already on file?
then
    echo $Name: already on file >&2
else
    echo "Address : \c"; read Address
    echo "City     : \c"; read City
    echo "State    : \c"; read State
    echo "ZIP code: \c"; read ZIP
    echo "Phone    : \c"; read Phone
    echo "Remarks : \c"; read Remarks
    {
        echo "$Name:$Address:$City:$State:$ZIP:$Phone:$Remarks"
        cat $dbname
    } ¦ sort -t: +0 -1 >/tmp/DBNEW.$$
    mv /tmp/DBNEW.$$ $dbname
fi
```

8

The grep command uses the -i option to ignore the case when searching for a person's name. This is a courtesy for the user, because she can enter either "smith" or "Smith" when updating an address book entry.

This implementation uses the grep command to search the name-address file; if the grep command finds such a line in the file, it executes a then clause and prints an error message. If the grep command fails, it's safe to add the name. The else clause proceeds to read the rest of the information, then create a new temporary file containing the added line. The final step is to replace the real file with the temporary file; then you are done.

Notice the use of the {} operators to generate a single standard output file that contains both the newline and the current contents of the name-address file. The redirection of standard output implied by the pipe operator (¦) applies to the commands inside the {} group. Unfortunately, you cannot safely use the sort command to store the information into the real name-address file; remember, all the commands in a pipeline run at the same time. If you wrote the output of sort into the name-name address file, you would be reading from and writing to the same file at the same time. The result probably would be the total loss of all the name and address information. The sort command provides an -o option to safely allow output to one of its input files, but most commands do not. The code above shows how to update an input file safely in any situation.

Finishing

The definition of the list, change, and remove operations proceeds similarly. To save time, Listing 8.6 presents one possible implementation of the program. There are many ways to solve the problem, and the methods shown here are not necessarily the best. Try to develop your own implementations of list, change, and remove. If you do, you will discover another truth about shell programming: no two programmers do things the same way.

Listing 8.6. The book command—a sample implementation.

```
# book - maintain a name & address book

# Display function menu

tput clear
echo "===== Name & Address File =====

1.  ADD    a new name & address entry
2.  LIST   all or selected entries
3.  CHANGE the information in an entry
```

```
    4.  DELETE an entry

What function (1-4)? \c"
read choice
case $choice in
    1) # Add a new entry to the name-address file
        echo "Name     : \c"; read Name
        if grep -i "^$Name" $dbname        # Already on file?
        then
            echo $Name: already on file >&2
        else
            echo "Address : \c"; read Address
            echo "City    : \c"; read City
            echo "State   : \c"; read State
            echo "ZIP code: \c"; read ZIP
            echo "Phone   : \c"; read Phone
            echo "Remarks : \c"; read Remarks
            {
              echo "$Name:$Address:$City:$State:$ZIP:$Phone:$Remarks"
              cat $dbname
            } | sort -t: +0 -1 >/tmp/DBNEW.$$
            mv /tmp/DBNEW.$$ $dbname
        fi
        ;;
    2) # LIST entries
        echo "Name (ALL to list all entries): \c"
        read name
        case $name in
            ALL | all) cat $dbname ;;
            *)   fgrep -i "$name" $dbname ;;
        esac | awk -F: '{
                print ""
                print $1
                print $2
                print $3 ", " $4 "  " $5
                print $6
                print $7
                }' | more
        ;;
    3) # CHANGE an entry
        echo "Name? \c"; read Name
        OLD_IFS="$IFS"
        IFS=:
        if set 0 `grep -i "^$Name[,:]" $dbname`
        then :
        else
            echo "$Name: " not found
            exit 3
        fi
        IFS="$OLD_IFS"
        shift 1
        if [ $# -lt 1 ]
```

continues

Listing 8.6. continued

```
    then echo $Name: not found
    else
        Name="$1" Address="$2" City="$3" State="$4" ZIP="$5"
        Phone="$6" Remarks="$7"
        eval echo "$display"
        echo "What do you want to change? \c"; read field
        echo "New value: \c"; read value
        case $field in
            [aA]ddress)   Address="$value";;
            [cC]ity)      City="$value";;
            [sS]tate)     State="$value" ;;
            [zZ]ip)       ZIP="$value" ;;
            [pP]hone)     Phone="$value" ;;
            [rR]emarks)   Remarks="$value" ;;
            *)            echo "Invalid field name" >&2
                          exit 3
                          ;;
        esac
        { sed "/^$Name:/d" $dbname
          echo "$Name:$Address:$City:$State:$ZIP:$Phone:$Remarks"
        } ¦ sort -t: +0 -1 >NEW.book && mv NEW.book $dbname
    fi
    grep "^$Name:" $dbname ¦ awk -F: '{
                print ""
                print $1
                print $2
                print $3 ", " $4 "  " $5
                print $6
                print $7
                }'
    ;;
4) # DELETE an entry
    echo "Name: \c"; read Name
    IFS=:
    if set `grep -i "^$Name[,:]" $dbname`
    then
        eval echo "$display"
        echo "\nDelete this entry? \c"
        read answer
        case $answer in
            y* ¦ Y*)
                sed "/^$1:/d" $dbname > NEW.book
                mv NEW.book $dbname
                ;;
            *)  echo Entry not deleted. ;;
        esac
    else
        echo $Name: not on file
    fi
    ;;
*) echo Invalid choice; exit 1 ;;
esac
```

Summary

This chapter has examined the shell control statements for conditional execution. Conditional execution statements let you make a decision: to choose one list of commands to be executed rather than another based on the outcome of a test. This lets your shell script react differently to different situations. For example, you might choose to create a directory if it doesn't already exist, thereby relieving your users of the need to create the directory "by hand." The ability to make decisions, such as to react intelligently to the nonexistence of a file, is a fundamental property of modern computer programming, and is the primary distinction between computers and calculators.

The `if` statement provides a simple two-way choice mechanism. The operand of the `if` statement must be a UNIX command, shell built-in command, function, or another shell statement. The `if` statement chooses between two alternative lists of commands to be executed based on the outcome of executing the command given as its operand. If the command executes without error (its exit value is zero), the `then` clause is executed. But if the command indicates that it found an error by returning an exit value other than zero, the `else` clause is executed.

The exit value of a command does not necessarily indicate that an error occurred; sometimes a command sets its exit value as a means of passing information back to your shell script. The `test` command is an example of this. You describe the condition you want to test with the arguments of the `test` command. If the condition your test describes is true, the `test` command returns an exit value of 0, causing the `if` statement to execute the `then` clause. But if the outcome of the test is *not* true (for example, you tested a file name to see whether it exists, and in fact it does not), the `test` command returns a nonzero exit value to indicate that the condition is false.

You can write any command you want as the operand of the `if` statement. When you do this, you are testing whether the command worked. Or you can write the `test` command as the operand of `if`. When you use `test` with `if`, you're actually testing an external factor of your environment and deciding how to proceed based on what you find.

The shell provides one other conditional execution statement: the `case` statement. For the operand of the `case` statement, you provide a string expression. The shell evaluates the string expression to get an actual character string, then chooses one of several command lists to execute by matching the actual character string with a string-matching pattern associated with each command list. Although this sounds complicated, what actually happens can

8

be as simple as checking whether the user responded "yes" or "no" to a prompt.

With older versions of the shell, any command you might execute as the operand of `if` required loading and executing a program—a time-consuming operation at best. But the `case` statement used only facilities built into the shell. Thus it used to be that decisions made with `case` would run much faster than the same decision made with `if`. Today, with many commands including the `test` command built into the shell, decisions made with `if` run as fast as those made with `case`, so there is no longer any reason to prefer the one statement over the other for making decisions. When you want to compare a string against several possible values, use `case`; when you want to use the `test` command, or check that a UNIX command executed without error, use `if`.

The Korn shell has a new statement, `select`, which is a combination of conditional execution and looping functions. The `select` statement is examined in Chapter 12, "Advanced Shell Facilities," because it doesn't exactly fit in either this chapter or the next, and because you should concentrate on learning the basics of shell programming before experimenting with more advanced features.

The next chapter, "Looping," examines another basic programming method: repeatedly executing a list of commands. After you study Chapter 9, you will have mastered all the basics of shell programming.

8

Loops

o programming language would be complete
without loop control statements. Loop control
statements are essential for repeatedly executing a set of
commands; the repetition might continue for a predetermined number of times, or might be terminated when a
conditional test is satisfied.

The Bourne and Korn shells provide the for, while, and
until statements as the basic tools for loop control:

- The for statement repeats a set of statements a
  predetermined number of times, setting a *control*
  variable to the next word in a list of words for each
  iteration.

- The while statement repeats a set of statements as
  long as a specified command does not fail (returns an
  exit value of zero).

- The until statement repeats a set of statements as
  long as a specified command does not succeed
  (returns a nonzero exit value).

The while and until statements are similar enough that
they can be covered in one section. The for statement is the
most interesting of the three, so we'll examine it first.

The for **Statement**

The following box lists the syntax of the for statement.

Syntax of the for Statement

```
for var [ in words ]
do
   list
done
```

Semicolons can be used in place of newlines, as follows:

```
for var [ in words ; ] do list ; done
```

The essential part of the for statement is the list of *words*. You can specify a series of literal words, variable references, command substitutions, and wild-card file names for *words*; in fact, any shell expression that reduces to a list of strings can be validly specified as the value of *words*.

If you omit *words*, you also must omit the keyword in. The default list of words is the set of arguments $*; that is, for *var* in $* means the same thing as for *var*. Notice that the value of $* is the list of all shell arguments, not just those having a name ($1 through $9).

You must specify a variable name for *var*. Omit the leading $ because the shell requires the name of a variable here, not its value. The statements in *list* are executed once for each word occurring in *words*, with the control variable *var* adopting the value of each word in turn. The list of words in *words* is processed in left-to-right order.

The following trivial example shows how you can use the echo command to print the value of the control variable on each execution of the loop:

```
$ for fruit in apple peach pear
> do
> echo fruit is $fruit
> done
fruit is apple
fruit is peach
fruit is pear
$
```

9

The result would be the same if you stored the list of words in a shell variable:

```
$ read fruits
apple peach pear
$ for fruit in $fruits
> do
> echo fruit is $fruit
> done
fruit is apple
fruit is peach
fruit is pear
$
```

The latter example works because the shell automatically scans the *words* expression for word delimiters after performing any variable or command substitutions. Of course, enclosing the variable reference in quotation marks prevents the shell from identifying the individual words in the variable value:

```
$ read fruits
apple peach pear
$ for fruit in "$fruits"
> do
> echo fruit is $fruit
> done
fruit is apple peach pear
$
```

A more interesting example uses wild card substitution to step the control variable through a list of file names:

```
$ set -x       # Display executed commands
$ for FILE in *.c
> do
> cb -s $FILE > ${FILE}b
> done
+ cb -s main.c > main.cb
+ cb -s term.c > term.cb
+ cb -s report.c > report.cb
$
```

The expression *.c of the for statement is expanded into a list of file names (main.c, term.c, and report.c). Finding three values for the control variable, the for statement executes the lines between do and done for each value, and changes the value of FILE each time. The first time FILE has the value main.c, so the cb command becomes:

```
cb   -s   main.c   > main.cb
```

9

On the second and third iterations, FILE takes on the second and third values of the file name list, thereby generating the other two cb commands.

A Sample Shell Script

The for statement is often essential in building useful shell scripts because it provides a basic mechanism for repeating an operation on each word in a list of words, whether the words are file names, user names, or others. The following script implements a command, called tell, that sends a message to each user named in a list. The list of users might have the same format as the /etc/passwd system file; in fact, if no list is specified on the command, tell uses /etc/passwd as the default list:

```
# tell - send a message to a list of users
#    Set 'list' to $1 or, if omitted, '/etc/passwd'
list=${1:-/etc/passwd}
#    copy message to temporary holding file
cat > ${msgfile=${TMPDIR:-/tmp}/msg.$$}
#    extract user names and loop for each user
for USER in `cut -d: -f1 < ${list} ¦ sort -u`
do
   mail $USER < $msgfile && echo Notified $USER >&2
done
rm $msgfile
```

You could make up any number of user lists to use with the tell command. For example, a list named team might name all the users in your department, and look like this:

```
bill
sally
ted
fran
oscar
winnie
```

This list assumes that log-in names on your system are the first name of each user. If your installation uses more formal log-in names, the list might not be so readable:

```
d51u0409
d51u0420
d51u0435
d51u0716
```

The result of executing tell with this list would be equally cryptic:

9

```
$ tell team
Meeting at 4PM today in conference room 371-B.
Pizza will be served after, bring your own drink.
^d
Notified d51u0409
Notified d51u0420
Notified d51u0435
Notified d51u0716
$
```

When user names are this cryptic, you might want to store the user's real name in the name list file, and print the real name rather than the log-in name. The for command is not the best tool to use for this chore. To implement the improved form of tell, you should use the while command, which the next section covers.

More about Tokenization

The beginning of the for statement discussion noted that the *words* expression is separated into its component words before beginning the loop. The specific procedure the shell uses bears closer examination.

As with any shell input, the for statement is split into words and special characters when it is first read. For this first scan, the shell looks only for white space characters in the line (quoted strings receive special treatment so the string remains intact). Any white space you write in *words* always forces word separation. For example, the shell input

```
for x in a $mod plane
```

always results in at least three words: a, the value of variable mod, and plane. Subsequently, when the shell executes the statement, it further processes the $mod variable reference.

When retrieving the current value of the mod variable, the shell might find, for example, that it consists of the string really fast. The shell checks this value for characters that occur in the IFS variable. (See the section "Shell Variables" in Chapter 3, "Shell Basics," for a detailed description of the IFS variable.) Each character occurring in the value of IFS, if also present in really fast, causes the string to be split into separate words at that point. If the value of IFS contains the letter *a*, then the string is broken into the words re, lly, f, and st.

Notice that the shell automatically assumes white space separates words only when the shell first reads the for statement. Thereafter, any substituted values are separated into words only where the substituted value contains one of the IFS characters.

9

By default, the IFS variable contains only the white space characters as its value, namely the blank, tab, and newline characters. You can change the value of IFS with a simple assignment, but if the value you assign does not contain the white space characters, then white space in substituted text does not cause word breaks.

You will understand this behavior better with some examples. First, here is an example you can type at your terminal that uses the default IFS values:

```
$ mod="big red-and-white"
$ for word in a $mod plane
> do
> echo $word
> done
a
big
red-and-white
plane
$
```

Now change the value of IFS and try the same exercise:

```
$ IFS="-"
$ for word in a $mod plane
> do
> echo $word
> done
a
big red
and
white
plane
$
```

Notice that the words a and plane that appear in the original for statement are still treated as separate words. The value of mod treats white space differently; it no longer forces word splitting (big and red make one word), but the hyphen does split words, causing breaks after red and and.

To break words at both white space and hyphens, you must include both in the value of IFS:

```
$ IFS="$IFS-"
$ for word in a $mod plane
> do
> echo $word
> done
a
big
red
```

```
and
white
plane
$
```

The assignment statement IFS="$IFS-" sets IFS to its current value—the white space characters—followed by a hyphen. Later, when the shell expands $mod, it breaks the string at both the blank and hyphen characters.

If you never modify the value of IFS, then tokenization of *words* always is performed in the usual way—using white space to break substituted strings into words. You should not make a personal rule to avoid changing IFS, because you then miss out on some of the power of the shell.

The while and until Statements

The syntax of the while and until statements is the same except for the command name itself, as shown in the following box.

Syntax of the while and until Commands

```
while list1
do
    list2
done

until list1
do
    list2
done
```

Each statement also can be written on one line:

```
while list1 ; do list2 ; done
until list1 ; do list2 ; done
```

The operand of while or until is a command *list* (*list1* in the syntax description). That means you must provide at least one command following while or until, and you can provide more than one command.

The while command first executes the statements in *list1*. If the exit value of the last command executed is zero, then the while command executes the statements in *list2* next. This process is repeated until the last

9

exit value of *list1* is nonzero, at which point the while command stops looping. Notice that, due to this definition, the commands in *list1* is always executed one time more than the commands in *list2*.

The while command lends itself nicely to an implementation of an improved version of tell. This improved version sends a message to each member of a list of log-in names, but logs the real name of each user notified. The following example shows the result of this version of tell:

```
# tell - send a message to a list of users
# --    list format is 'logname:realname'

#    Set 'list' to $1
list=$1

#    copy message to temporary holding file
cat > ${msgfile=${TMPDIR:-/tmp}/msg.$$}

#    extract user names and loop for each user
IFS=:
if [ "$list" = "" ]
then cut -di -f1,5 /etc/passwd
else cat $list
fi ¦ sort -u ¦
while read log-in uname etc
do
    mail $log-in < $msgfile && echo "Notified $uname ($log-in)" >&2
done
rm $msgfile
```

The contents of your team file should look like this:

```
d51u0409:Marshall Dillon
d51u0420:Fred Flintstone
d51u0435:Archie Bunker
d51u0716:George Jefferson
```

If you execute the tell command, you will see the following output:

```
$ tell team
Meeting at 4PM today in conference room 371-B.
Pizza will be served after, bring your own drink.
^d
Notified Marshall Dillon (d51u0409)
Notified Fred Flintstone (d51u0420)
Notofied Archie Bunker (d51u0435)
Notofied George Jefferson (d51u0716)
$
```

This implementation of tell demonstrates a number of useful techniques:

9

- The while or until statement is treated like a command and its input and output can be redirected or piped as with any other command. When using redirection, the redirection operator must be placed on the done clause, like this:

```
while read log-in uname etc
do
    mail $log-in < $msgfile
    echo Notified $uname
done > $HOME/.tell
```

This form of the while command logs the list of notified users in the file .tell in your home directory rather than on your terminal. The redirection appearing on done applies to all statements inside the do...done list, except where explicitly overridden with another redirection.

- The read built-in command is often useful with while because together they provide a way to step through the lines of a file, processing each line in turn. The IFS special variable can be used to specify the character that separates the individual fields of each line. (For more information about the IFS special variable, see the "Shell Variables" section in Chapter 3, "Shell Basics"; the description of the read command in Chapter 10, "Built-In Commands"; and the section "More about Tokenization" earlier in this chapter.)

The until command is basically the opposite of while; it executes statements in *list2* as long as the commands in *list1* fail. The following example shows how you can use until to indicate when a user has logged in:

```
until who ¦ grep abigail >/dev/null
do
    sleep 60 # wait 1 minute then try again
done
echo Abigail has logged in.
```

If you are alert, you noticed that the command following until is not a single command; it is a pipeline. The legality of its construction is implied by the syntax definition, which calls for a command *list* following while or until. As defined in Chapter 4, "Compound Commands," a command list is a sequence of one or more simple commands, and a simple command can be a series of pipelines joined by && or ¦¦.

In other words, the command following while or until can in fact be an entire self-contained shell program. The following shell code implements a driver for balancing a batch of daily transactions; it continues to loop until a zero exit value from payw indicates that the batch balances:

9

```
until
    sort +0 -1n daily.batch >daily.tmp
    sort +0 -1n control.batch >control.tmp
    diff daily.tmp control.tmp >diff.tmp
do
    vi diff.tmp daily.batch
done
```

Although this example is hypothetical, the principle still applies; any number of shell commands can appear following while or until, and the last exit value determines whether or not the loop continues.

Using break

The break command causes the shell to immediately exit from the current for, while, or until loop and resume execution at the statement following the next done command. Statements that fall between the break command and the next done are skipped.

Syntax of the break Command

```
break [ n ]
```

The break command allows one optional argument that, if specified, must be an integer (or a shell expression that evaluates to an integer). The value of the integer indicates the number of nested loops that should be terminated. By default, *n* is assumed to be 1; thus, break and break 1 have an identical meaning.

In the following example, break is used to terminate the while loop when the user enters a satisfactory reply to a prompt; an unrecognized reply results in an error message and another iteration around the loop. Notice, in this example, nothing convenient could be tested on while to stop the loop; break is the easiest way to stop this loop:

```
while :
do
    echo "OK to delete the $dir directory? \c"
    read answer
    case $answer in
        y*)  rmdir $dir ; break ;;
        n*)  echo $dir kept; break ;;
        *)   echo Please answer y or n ;;
    esac
done
```

9

For comparison, look at an implementation of this loop that doesn't use `break`. The implementation uses a flag to indicate when the loop should be stopped, which is a typical technique used with other programming languages.

```
NeedReply=true
while $NeedReply
do
    echo "OK to delete the $dir directory? \c"
    read answer
    case $answer in
      y*)  rmdir $dir ; NeedReply=false ;;
      n*)  echo $dir kept; NeedReply=false ;;
      *)   echo Please answer y or n ;;
    esac
done
```

The introduction of the extra variable `NeedReply` complicates the program and increases the probability of making a programming mistake.

You can use the `break` command inside a `for`, `while`, or `until` loop because all three indicate the end of the loop with `done`. The `break` command simply skips ahead until it finds the number of `done` commands specified by the argument of `break`.

The following example shows how you can use `break` to exit from a `for` loop inside a `while` loop:

```
while :
do
    for dev in /dev/lp1 /dev/lp2 /dev/lp3
    do
        if [ -w $dev ]; then
            break 2 # available printer found
        fi
    done
    echo Waiting for printer >&2
    sleep 60 # Wait 1 minute before trying again
done
```

This `while` statement loops until one of the printers /dev/lp1, /dev/lp2, or /dev/lp3 becomes available to the user. If none are available, the `sleep` command waits one minute before trying again. Some action must be performed outside this program to make a printer available; otherwise the program waits forever.

9

Using `continue`

The `continue` command causes the shell to abandon the rest of the current `for`, `while`, or `until` loop and to immediately begin the next iteration of the loop. Statements that fall between the `continue` command and the corresponding `done` are skipped.

Syntax of the `continue` Command

`continue [ n ]`

The `continue` command allows one optional argument that, if specified, must be an integer (or a shell expression that evaluates to an integer). The value of the integer indicates which loop should be restarted when `continue` is embedded inside nested loops. By default, *n* is assumed to be 1; thus, `continue` and `continue 1` have identical meaning.

When *n* is greater than 1, *n*-1 loops are terminated as if `break` (*n*-1) had been issued. Only the outermost loop designated by *n* is restarted at the next iteration. The following example shows a procedure that might be useful to a system administrator because it initializes the home directories of users listed in /etc/passwd who do not already have a home directory:

```
IFS=:
while read log-in pass uid gid name home shell etc
do
    mkdir $home || continue
    for FILE in .profile .exrc .mailrc
    do
        if cp /usr/std/$FILE $home
        then :
        else
            echo cannot create $home/$FILE ($log-in) >&2
            continue 2
    done
done < /etc/passwd
```

If the user's home directory already exists, the `mkdir` command fails and the `continue` command is executed, causing the shell to execute the next iteration of the active loop. All statements to and including the next `done` are skipped. The final `done` is executed normally, causing the `while` statement to go on to the next line in the /etc/passwd file. The shell must skip the first `done` it finds because it matches a `do` statement that is not active.

9

If the `cp` command fails, however, the shell also skips the next `done` it finds because, although its corresponding `for` loop is active, the `continue` command specifies a count of two.

This example demonstrates that the shell does not literally count `done` statements when processing a `continue` count. When developing the count for the operand of `continue`, you count the loop containing the `continue` statement as 1, and add one to the count for each outer loop until you reach the `for`, `while`, or `until` statement you want to resume.

Looping with Recursion

Besides the `for`, `while`, and `until` commands, there is another way to repeatedly execute a series of statements: by using *recursion*.

Recursion calls a procedure that is already active. For example, if you are executing a shell script called `generate` and within itself it executes the `generate` command, then the shell script is being invoked *recursively*. Recursion is a powerful concept, but dangerous. Whenever you invoke a procedure recursively, you must provide a way to stop the recursion, otherwise the procedure continues to call itself over and over until the system runs out of memory.

Shell functions also can call themselves recursively, because a function can contain any command including its own function name. A command alias, however, cannot cause recursion due to the way the Korn shell treats the first word of the alias value. (Command aliases are a feature of the Korn shell.)

To show how simple it can be to use recursion, here is a sample shell script that displays its arguments by using recursion:

```
# showargs - display command arguments using recursion
echo $1
if [ $# -gt 1 ]; then
    shift 1
    showargs $*
fi
```

When called with none or only one argument, this script simply prints the argument (or a blank line if it has no argument) and exits. Otherwise it prints its first argument, discards the argument with `shift`, and calls itself with all the remaining arguments.

9

This script is guaranteed to terminate because on each call the `shift` command reduces the number of arguments by one, eventually reaching zero, after which it does not call itself again.

You also can implement the `showargs` command without using recursion, as in the following example:

```
# showargs - list command arguments
for ARG
do
    echo $ARG
done
```

In this particular case, the nonrecursive implementation is easier to write than the recursive version; however, this is not always true. In the next section, you will consider a real-life application of recursion that for all practical purposes can be written no other way.

A Recursive Application

The purpose of this application is to create a path. This differs from the function of `mkdir`, which creates only a single directory because the command you are about to write creates all the missing directories in a path name.

Suppose you want to create a directory called `/tmp/payroll/checks`. Because the system boot procedure cleans out the `/tmp` directory daily, the odds are that not only the `/tmp/payroll/checks` directory is missing but that `/tmp/payroll` does not exist either. Using only `mkdir`, you would have to issue the following command to create two directories:

```
$ mkdir /tmp/payroll /tmp/payroll/checks
```

The `pave` command that you are about to write creates the desired directory and all missing parent directories with one invocation. In other words, the command

```
$ pave /tmp/payroll/checks
```

creates both `/tmp/payroll` and `/tmp/payroll/checks`. The command is called pave because its action is like laying down the successive flagstones of a path, starting from an existing point and proceeding until the destination is reached.

At first you probably think of paving a path as a loop, creating one directory after another until the last directory in the path has been created. There is an easy way to do the job, though, using recursion.

9

The secret of the recursive programming technique is to think of a basic operation that yields a result and that can be repeated, operating on the former result, to yield a new result closer to the desired end.

For the job at hand, the simplest situation arises when the desired path name already exists; in this case, the pave command does nothing. Considering this simple and obvious fact, you already can write the basic outline of the pave command as shown in Listing 9.1.

Listing 9.1. Outline of the pave command.

```
# pave - create a directory path
#   Make sure the command has a path name argument:
if [ $# -ne 1 ]
then
    echo "Usage: pave pathname" >&2
    exit 1
fi
#   If the path already exists, do nothing.
if [ -d $1 ]
then exit 0
else # create the missing directories
fi
```

The program begins by checking that the user supplied a path name on the command. If the value of $# is not 1, then no argument was supplied at all or you supplied too many arguments; in either case, you obviously do not know the proper command format. The simplest way to get past this hurdle is to learn straight out how to code the command line. The echo statement does this by writing a command usage (that is, syntax) description to the standard-error file. (If you forget the significance of the expression >&2, refer to the section "Input/Output Redirection" in Chapter 3, "Shell Basics.")

If the program has exactly one argument, you can assume it is a proper path name. If it is not, the shell script fails naturally when it tries to use the path name. To attempt to syntax-check the path name at this point would be a waste of time because you would be duplicating the error-checking code already present in the system.

As coded in Listing 9.1, the shell script next performs its mainline procedure, although it is only skeletal at this point. Based on your earlier observation that the shell script did nothing when the path name already exists, the main step here is to use the test command (written [...]) to check whether the directory exists. (The test command and the equivalent shell notation [...] are fully described in Chapter 10, "Built-In Commands.")

9

If the directory exists, then the script exits with an exit value of 0 to indicate success. Otherwise, it performs the as-yet-undefined procedure to create the missing directories.

To complete the `pave` command implementation, you only have to convert the final comment into suitable commands. Doing so does not alter the basic shape of this shell script. Its mainline code is already complete. The design method of *stepwise refinement*, which was alluded to in Chapter 8, "Conditional Execution," has already taken you through a portion of the coding on the strength of one simple and obvious observation.

So how do you complete the implementation of this command? You have already looked at the simplest case, where the path already exists. Consider the next simplest case, where all the parent directories exist and only the final directory has to be created. For the path name `/tmp/payroll/checks`, this is equivalent to an example where the directory `/tmp/payroll` already exists and only `checks` in `/tmp/payroll` must be created.

Looking now only at the remaining block of code, you can write the simplest creation procedure as follows:

```
if parent of $1 does not exist
then create parent directory
fi
mkdir $1     # Create the final path
```

Fortunately, a standard UNIX command can remove the last part of a path name, giving the parent path: the `dirname` command.

Before proceeding, you might want to experiment with the `dirname` command at your terminal. Because `dirname` only works on path name strings and doesn't actually reference the named directories, you can experiment with its effect on any path name, as in the following sample terminal session:

```
$ dirname /tmp/payroll/checks
/tmp/payroll
$ dirname /tmp/payroll
/tmp
$ dirname /tmp
/
$ dirname /
/
```

Notice that `dirname` always drops the last part of a path name. When it reaches the root directory, it can go no farther. In fact, the parent of `/` is considered to be `/`, so that's what it returns. The point is that `dirname` always returns a result. (Whether or not the result is useful is another question.)

9

Using the `dirname` command, you could rewrite the creation procedure as follows:

```
if [ ! -d `dirname $1` ]
then mkdir `dirname $1`
fi
mkdir $1     # Create the final path
```

Before actually putting this code into `pave`, consider the problem in creating the parent directory of `checks`. If that directory doesn't exist, then it also must be created. This is the same problem you had when trying to create the `checks` directory in one step.

In fact, you began writing the `pave` command to get around that problem. You can make an intuitive leap (doing recursive programming often requires an *aha!* insight into the problem) and proceed as if you already have a working implementation of `pave`. Of course you don't yet, but have a little confidence in yourself.

In that case, you should be able to use `pave` to create the parent directory of the path name. After all, `pave` should work on any path name. With this thought in mind, you can rewrite the creation procedure like this:

```
if [ ! -d `dirname $1` ]
then pave `dirname $1`
fi
mkdir $1     # Create the final path
```

By calling `pave` rather than `mkdir`, you handle with one stroke the problem that the parent directory or any of its parents might not exist.

Can you get away with this? Sure you can. Remember that the shell allows recursion. Each call of a command gets its own copy of shell variables, and called commands cannot modify the variables used in the calling shell script. Although this often seems like a disadvantage, in the case of recursive programming, you are guaranteed that a command cannot disturb its own variables by calling itself. The only other requirement for successful recursive programming is that the recursion eventually stop.

The recursive calls to `pave` eventually stop because the `dirname` command, if called enough times, finally reaches one of two directories, / in the case of an absolute path, and . in the case of a relative path. Both / and . are guaranteed to exist. Thus, eventually you find that the parent directory exists and skips the call to `pave`.

The final implementation of `pave` is shown in Listing 9.2.

9

Listing 9.2. Final implementation of the `pave` command.

```
# pave - create a directory path
#   Make sure the command has a path name argument:
if [ $# -ne 1 ]
then
    echo "Usage: pave path name" >&2
    exit 1
fi
#   If the path already exists, do nothing.
if [ -d $1 ]
then exit 0
else # create the missing directories
    pave `dirname $1`
    mkdir $1
fi
```

The final implementation omits the test to check whether the parent directory exists; rather, the script calls pave directly. This does not matter due to the basic design of pave; if the path name to be paved already exists, the command does nothing. In other words, the pave command already contains the test to determine whether the directory exists; there is no need to embed a second test in front of the call to pave.

If you still want some reassurance that pave works, store Listing 9.2 into a file, make the file executable, and try it. Test it with a long path name such as /tmp/this/is/a/test/of/the/pave/command, then use the ls -R command to display the result:

```
$ pave /tmp/this/is/a/test
$ ls -R /tmp/this
/tmp/this:
is

/tmp/this/is:
a

/tmp/this/is/a:
test

/tmp/this/is/a/test:
$
```

If you could watch the pave command execute the test, you would see the following commands executed:

```
$ pave /tmp/this/is/a/test
+ pave /tmp/this/is/a
+ pave /tmp/this/is
+ pave /tmp/this
```

9

```
+ pave /tmp
+ mkdir /tmp/this
+ mkdir /tmp/this/is
+ mkdir /tmp/this/is/a
+ mkdir /tmp/this/is/a/test
$
```

The calls to pave eventually stopped because the /tmp directory exists (it is a standard directory in every UNIX system). When pave /tmp exited without doing anything, control returned to the previous call of pave, which then executed the mkdir for /tmp/this. That call of pave exited, returning to the call for /tmp/this/is. Thus the mkdir commands were actually executed in the reverse order when the pave commands were called. Recursive commands always work like a push-down stack.

A Recursive Programming Exercise

If you would like to try your own hand at writing a recursive procedure, then try to write a shell script to solve this problem:

One day, while Sam is chatting with Betty, the system administrator, Betty comments that she has to set up a group account for each possible combination of users on the system. She says it's all part of an improved security plan to permit flexible sharing of files among users, yet maintain adequate protection. The problem is that Betty has been unable to come up with an exhaustive list of user groups, and she wants to have a program to do the job for her. Of course Sam volunteers to write the program, and asks her what she means by "combinations of users."

"Suppose we have four users: Alice, Bill, Joe, and Mary," she begins. "Well, that's a group right there. You also can have groups of three users each, and groups of two users each. Here, I'll show you," she says, and begins to write on the blackboard. When she's finished, Sam sees the following list:

Group	Members
1	alice bill joe mary
2	alice bill joe
3	alice bill mary
4	alice joe mary
5	bill joe mary
6	alice bill
7	alice joe
8	alice mary
9	bill joe
10	bill mary
11	joe mary

9

"You see, there's one group containing all four users. Then there are four groups of three users each. Finally, there are six groups of two users each. Now, what I need is a program that will automatically list all the possible groups for any number of users." Sam nods, noticing a pattern to the list of names. "No problem," he says confidently, and goes off to write a shell script.

After chewing on the end of his pencil for a while and doodling on a note pad, Sam notices that the solution is trivial for two users and very simple for three users. Finally he notices a recursive procedure that grinds out the list of groups for any number of users, and he begins to work on the shell script at once.

With a little thought, you should be able to write a shell script for Betty that will work as well as Sam's, and that uses recursion to derive the names in each group.

Summary

This chapter presented all but one of the shell loop control statements. Chapter 12, "Advanced Shell Facilities," describes the select statement, a unique feature of the Korn shell, that assists with writing menu-style user prompts.

The for statement provides a capability that is crucial in enabling you to write powerful shell scripts: that of selecting successive words from a string for individual analysis and processing. The words in the string might be a list of file names to be processed, or a list of users to whom a message should be sent. The only other ways available to handle lists in the shell are the use of argument variables together with the shift command, and array variables (presented in Chapter 12). Because lists often arise in programming, the for statement provides a service you will depend on heavily.

The while and until statements provide a way to execute a list of commands an arbitrary number of times, stopping only when some condition arises such as end of file. Although the for statement provides a valuable capability, it is more appropriate to perform an action a set number of times. You need to use the while or until statement whenever the situation calls for repeating a series of commands an indefinite number of times.

The break and continue statements are not strictly necessary to the shell language; anything you can do with break and continue you can also do using variables and if statements. However, the break and continue statements are a great convenience whenever you want to alter the normal repetition of program loops.

The last section of this chapter presents the topic of recursion. No single specific feature of the shell supports recursion in the way that for, while, and until support looping. Many programmers do not use recursion often because many programmers feel suspicious of the technique or feel that they don't understand it. Yet for many problems recursion provides the simplest solution. I encourage you to study the examples in the test and to seriously consider the use of recursion to solve your own programming problems; you will find that recursion makes your code simpler, yet more powerful.

You've now completed all the basics of shell programming. But there is still more for you to learn. The shell provides many features in the form of built-in commands (the subject of the next chapter), and the UNIX commands themselves provide many prepackaged solutions you can use to implement useful shell scripts. In fact, you can't write shell scripts at all without using UNIX and built-in commands. So read on. The next chapter will begin to build your repertoire of tools to use with the shell.

9

Built-In Commands

S ome of the commands you think of as basic to the UNIX environment are not actually commands in the usual sense. These pseudo-commands are built into the shell, and executing them does not require loading and executing a program as is normally the case.

Originally, the shell provided only those built-in commands that were absolutely required—those for which no other implementation was possible. A primary example is the cd command. If the cd command were implemented in the usual way, it would be completely ineffective; it would change the current directory for the duration of the execution of the cd command itself, but the current directory would revert to its original value when the command finished—not a desirable result.

Commands such as cd invoke operating system services that define the execution environment for a single process; when that process exits, any changes it made to its own execution environment are lost. As a result, the only practical way to implement the cd command and others like it is to get the shell to change its own environment; then all processes created by the shell inherit that environment. Built-in commands such as cd are really commands issued to the shell.

Because a built-in command can be executed without the time-consuming overhead of loading a program, built-in commands tend to execute quickly; they are faster than an equivalent implementation of a command program. For this reason,

10

a number of other commands have been added to the shell over the years due to the better performance that follows. Built-in commands in this category include test, pwd, alias, echo, and several others.

It is sometimes useful to know whether a command is built in because there are situations where a built-in command executes slightly differently from a regular command.

This chapter describes all the built-in commands of the Bourne and Korn shells. Differences between the two shells are carefully noted in the text. The Korn shell features described in this chapter are implemented in UNIX System V Release 4.0.

:   **Null Operation**

Syntax of the : Command
`: [ arg ... ]`

The null operation performs no action. The exit value is always zero.

The null operation has three principal uses: to force a shell script to be interpreted by the Bourne shell (regardless of the shell executing it); as a fast-executing true command; and to force the evaluation of its argument list.

UNIX commands implemented as Bourne shell scripts usually begin with the : command as the first line because the C shell calls the Bourne shell to execute the script when it sees : as the first command in the file. All shell scripts written for the Bourne shell should begin with the null command as the first line of the file.

As an alternative to writing while true in a shell script, the form while : executes faster because the : command is a built-in command, and true is not a built-in command in earlier System V Releases.

The shell evaluates the arguments of the null command even though the command does nothing. This command provides a useful way to assign a default value to a variable, as in the following example:

`: ${TMPDIR:=/tmp}`

This command sets the variable TMPDIR to the value /tmp only if TMPDIR is not already set. If you cannot supply a default value, use the following form:

```
: ${TMPDIR:?undefined}
```

If either of these lines were executed without the : command, the shell would try to execute the value of TMPDIR as a command; this would not be desirable unless the value of TMPDIR was actually a command name.

Because the arguments of : are evaluated by the shell, do not use the : command as a substitute for the # comment.

10

- **Execute the Statements in a File**

> **Syntax of the . Command**
>
> `. file name`
>
> `. file name [arg...]`

---

ksh

The dot command (.) causes the shell to read the file named *file name* and to execute its contents as commands. You can specify an absolute or relative path name for *file name*; the PATH directory list is used to locate the file if a relative path name is given.

One or more arguments may be specified and passed to file name as the variables $1, $2, $3, and so on. If you specify no arguments, the current values of $1, $2, $3, and so on, are passed to file name. Any arg values specified permanently replace the current shell arguments.

No subshell is invoked to process the *file name* command script; therefore, any variables set in the script, even if not exported, remain set after the script ends. An exit command issued in the file causes the current shell to exit; it cannot be used to halt execution of the script. Any commands that modify the process environment, such as cd or umask, have a lasting effect because the commands in the script are executed by the current (shell) process.

The .profile file in your home directory is automatically executed by the shell when you log in, as if you had manually entered the following command:

$ . .profile

You can issue this command explicitly yourself at any time to immediately activate any changes you make to your profile; this not only avoids

10

having to log in and out, it also allows you to detect any errors that you might have introduced into your profile.

The dot command also can be a useful way to break a large shell script into smaller parts (called *modules*). You do this by putting each smaller part into a separate file, and calling each file from your main shell script with the dot command.

alias   Define an Abbreviation for a Command

> **Syntax of the alias Command**
>
> ```
> alias [ -x ] [ name[=value] ... ]
> alias -t [ name ... ]
> ```

When issued without arguments, the alias command displays all the aliases currently defined. Use alias -t to display only tracked aliases. Use alias -x to display only exported aliases.

Each *name* specified as an argument of the alias command becomes a new command name or a new definition of an existing command. Thereafter, when you enter *name* as a command, the shell replaces the word *name* with *value* and executes the resulting command as if *value* had been entered instead. The number of aliases you can define is limited only by the amount of memory available to the shell.

It is usually immaterial whether *name* duplicates the name of another function, built-in command, or system command; the first word of an alias *value* is not checked further for aliasing. This enables you to invoke the function or command in the alias value. You could redefine the ls command to automatically use the -FC options, as in the following example:

```
$ alias ls='ls -FC'
```

To invoke the ls command without the -FC automatic options, you could either invoke the ls command with its full path name (/bin/ls ...) or set up another alias:

```
$ alias list='ls'
```

The list command now invokes the /bin/ls command because, after substituting ls for list, the shell does not notice that an alias named ls also exists; the shell simply looks for the ls command as usual.

Normally, the shell stops looking for alias names in the command input once it has checked the first word. However, if the value of an alias ends with a white space character, the shell checks the next word of input for aliasing as well. Using this facility, you can alias options as well as command names. The following command is understood by the shell if you first define the desired aliases:

```
$ list all

$ alias list='ls '
$ alias all='-aFC'
```

Now, entering the command `list all` is the same as entering the command `ls -aFC`.

The `-t` option defines the specified alias names as *tracked*; the shell automatically assigns the full path name of the command file as the value of the alias. You cannot assign a value to a tracked alias.

The `-x` option defines the alias names as *exported*; that is, the names are recognized as aliases, not only when entered at the keyboard, but also within called shell scripts. For example, if you define an exported alias for the `rm` command and invoke a system command that is implemented as a shell script, any `rm` commands in that shell script are aliased also. This can have an unexpected effect, as in the following dialog:

```
$ alias -x rm='rm -i'
$ lint foo.c
rm: remove /tmp/aaaAB10351: (y/n)?
```

The `lint` command is one of the UNIX commands implemented as a shell script, and it contains several `rm` commands. Because the alias for `rm` is exported, every invocation of `rm` from the `lint` command prompts you to respond whether or not you want to delete the file (due to the option `-i` provided by the alias). You must now respond y or n to the prompt issued for every temporary file the `lint` command creates and tries to delete before exiting. To avoid this undesired side effect, don't use the `-x` option with system command names:

```
$ alias rm='rm -i'
$ lint foo.c
$
```

Note: When a shell is invoked as a command, even exported aliases are not propagated to the subshell. The following sequence fails:

```
$ alias -x peek='vi -r'
$ ksh
$ peek memo
peek not found
$
```

10

ksh because the alias peek cannot be propagated across the explicit call of ksh.
Similarly, if you call the shell in another command—such as entering the :sh
command in the vi editor—the peek alias is undefined because a new shell
is loaded.

bg   Run the Current Job in the Background

ksh

> **Syntax of the bg Command**
>
> bg [*job*]

Use the bg command to restart the execution of a command you previously
stopped. Execution is resumed in the background. If no argument is supplied, the job most recently stopped is resumed. For *job* specify one of the
following values listed in Table 10.1.

Table 10.1. Values for job in the bg command.

Values	Meaning
num	Process number
%*num*	Job number
%*string*	Command name
%?*string*	Command name containing string
%+ or %%	Current job
%-	Previous job

The bg command is available only on versions of UNIX that provide the
job control feature.

The bg command can be used only with jobs that are stopped (see the
jobs command). You cannot stop a command you initiated in the background
with &; however, you can move such a job into the foreground with the
fg command and then stop it. When you resume a stopped job with the
bg command, it behaves in the same way as if you had issued the original
command with the & shell operator.

To stop an executing command, press the SUSPEND key. The SUSPEND key is settable with the stty command, as in the example stty susp ´^z´. If the key is already defined, stty -a shows susp = ^x, where x is the name of the assigned key. If no key is defined, stty -a shows susp = <undef>; if the facility is not available, stty -a does not list a susp value.

You can stop an interactive job such as a vi edit session with the SUSPEND key, but if you then use bg to resume the job in the background, the job is stopped again as soon as it tries to read or write to your terminal. All background jobs are stopped when they attempt to read from the terminal. Those that wrote to the terminal are stopped if tostp is set by stty.

break
Escape from a Loop or case Statement

Syntax of the break Command

break [*n*]

Use the break statement to skip over the remaining statements in a loop and to cancel any remaining iterations of the loop. The next statement executed after break is the statement following the for, while, until or select statement in which the break occurs.

The break statement is valid also in the do...done range of a select statement. It causes the select loop to terminate at once.

If the *n* argument is present, the break statement breaks out of *n* nested loop structures. It is an error for the value of *n* to be greater than the number of nested loops in which the break is embedded.

Here, the break statement is used to halt a loop when the user responds satisfactorily to a prompt:

```
while true
do
    echo "Use $tmp directory? \c"; read answer
    case $answer in
        y*)  break ;;    # Yes, stop looping
        n*)  echo "Enter directory name: \c"; read $tmp ;;
        q*)  echo Aborted; exit 2 ;;
    esac
done
sort -t: +0n -1 paydata >$tmp/paydata
```

10

Notice the distinction between a statement that occurs *within* a loop (such as the previous case statement), and the next statement that occurs *after* a loop (such as the sort statement). The break statement always transfers control to the next statement after the loop.

cd   Change the Current Directory

Syntax of the cd Command:

cd [*dirname*]

cd *old new*

Syntax of the cd Command:

cd -

The cd command changes your working directory to the path specified by *dirname*. If *dirname* does not begin with /, ./, or ../, the list of directories specified by CDPATH is searched for *dirname*.

You should change your working directory when you are planning a series of commands that work with files in another directory; changing to that directory enables you to type the file names on the commands rather than repeatedly typing the full path name.

The following techniques are useful with the cd command:

- To change to another directory, supply the path name of that directory as the one argument of the cd command:

  ```
  $ cd /usr/fred/payroll/register
  ```

- To change from anywhere to your home directory, issue the cd command with no arguments:

  ```
  $ cd
  ```

- Set up shell variables (See Chapter 7, "Using Variables") for path names you frequently have to reference:

```
$ pubdir=/usr/spool/uucppublic
$ inbox=$pubdir/receive/jjv/nixjjv
$ cd $pubdir
$ pwd
/usr/spool/uucppublic
$ cd $inbox
$ pwd
/usr/spool/uucppublic/receive/jjv/nixjjv
$
```

- Install the pushd and popd functions. (The source for the pushd and popd functions is given in Chapter 4, "Compound Commands," in the section "Functions." You can add these functions to your .profile so they are defined every time you log in and use them to maintain a directory stack. (For more information about .profile, see the section "Shell Invocation" in Chapter 5, "Special Features.")

```
$ pwd
/u/jjv/src/ksh
$ pushd /usr/spool/uucppublic/receive/jjv/nixjjv
$ pwd
/usr/spool/uucppublic/receive/jjv/nixjjv
$ pushd /usr/include
$ pwd
/usr/include
$ popd
/usr/spool/uucppublic/receive/jjv/nixjjv
$ popd
/u/jjv/src/ksh
$
```

The form cd - changes your current directory back to the previous current directory. You can use cd - to easily switch between two directories.

The form cd *old new* substitutes the string *new* for the first occurrence of the string *old* in the current directory path name. For example, if your current directory is /usr/src/payroll, you can change to the directory /usr/src/orders with the command

```
$ cd payroll orders
```

Because the Korn shell recognizes tilde wild cards (see the section "Using Wild Cards" in Chapter 3, "Shell Basics") you can use the tilde to shorten long path names:

```
$ cd ~/lib/payroll
```

rather than

```
$ cd /usr/home/nancy/lib/payroll
```

continue

Start the Next Iteration of a Loop

10

Syntax of the `continue` Command

```
continue [ n ]
```

Use the `continue` statement to skip the remaining statements in a loop and to start the next iteration of the loop at once. The next statement executed after `continue` is the first statement in the `for`, `while`, or `until` statement containing the `continue` statement.

The `continue` statement is valid also in the `do...done` range of a `select` statement. As always, it causes the next iteration of the `select` loop to start at once.

If the *n* argument is present, the `continue` statement terminates that number of nested loop structures. The next statement executed will be the beginning of the *n*th outer loop. If the value of *n* is greater than the number of nested loops in which the `continue` is embedded, an error occurs.

Here, the `continue` statement is used to skip an iteration of the loop for unprocessable values of FILE:

```
for FILE in *.c
do
    if [ ! -r s.$FILE ]
    then
        echo $FILE: no SCCS master. >&2
        continue
    fi
    if get -p -s s.$FILE | cmp - $FILE
    then
        echo $FILE: no change
        rm $FILE
    else
        delta -yP14795 s.$FILE && echo $FILE: updated
    fi
done
```

When the `continue` statement is executed, the iteration test for `while` or `until` is executed, or the `for` control variable is set to the next value, before the body of the loop is executed again.

echo   Write Arguments to Standard Output

Syntax of the echo Command

```
echo [ arg ... ]
```

The echo shell built-in command operates identically to the echo system command. It is provided as a built-in command to enhance the performance of shell scripts.

---

eval   Evaluate the Arguments as a Shell Command

Syntax of the eval Command

```
eval arg ...
```

The arguments of eval are combined into a command line, reevaluated for wild-card file-name generation, variable substitution, command substitution, and backslash sequences. They are then executed.

Normally, the shell checks a command line for variable substitution and command substitution only once. Thus, if the value of a variable or the output of a command substitution in turn contains variables, they remain unexpanded. A variable value, or any other text, can be reprocessed with eval to expand such inner variables.

Suppose you have previously set a variable to the command you want to use to display text files, as follows:

```
$ ed="pg -cns -p´Page %d´"
```

To display a text file, you merely enter the command

```
$ $ed file name
```

If you try it, though, you will get the error message %d´ not found. The problem originates from the order in which the shell expands variables and processes quotation marks; after substituting the value of ed in the command

10

line, the shell is no longer sensitive to quotation marks; it sees -p´Page and %d´ as separate words.

To avoid this problem, you must ask the shell to go through its tokenization step again, using the eval command:

```
$ eval $ed payw.c
```

This time the shell properly recognizes all the quotation marks and the command works. Try the following exercise:

```
$ echo ´Page %d´
Page %d
$ temp="´Page %d´"
$ echo $temp
´Page %d´
$ eval echo $temp
Page %d
$
```

The output from the first echo command omits the apostrophes, as it should. The output from the second echo command shows the apostrophes because, after substituting the value of $temp, the shell did *not* recognize the single quotations in the value and did not remove them.

The eval command also can be used to implement a kind of associative memory feature, or subscripted variables, because you can use it to construct variable names during execution. The following example uses eval to convert a month number to a month name:

```
echo "Enter month number:\c"; read month
M1=January M2=February M3=March M4=April M5=May M6=June
M7=July M8=August M9=September M10=October M11=November
M12=December
eval echo \$M$month
```

Because the first $ is hidden by a backslash, the command actually seen by eval is eval echo $M3 (assuming the user entered 3 in response to the read command). The eval command then rescans the line and replaces $M3 with March. The command finally executed is echo March.

exec   Execute Another Program without Return

Syntax of the exec Command

exec *command*

Use exec to replace the shell with the program named by the first word of *command*. For *command*, specify a simple command. You can include options, arguments, and redirections on *command*. The invoked command does not return to the shell, so it is not useful to combine exec with other commands by using the && or ¦¦ operators.

The most common use of the exec command at the keyboard is to replace your current shell with another shell. Suppose you are currently using the Bourne shell and want to move to the Korn shell. To switch shells, enter the command exec ksh.

If you enter the command ksh, you also enter the Korn shell, but your current shell is still present, consuming system resources while it waits for the ksh command to finish. Using the exec command gets rid of the old shell and replaces it with the new.

The exec command also can be used within a shell script, with caution. If the purpose of the shell script is to prepare to execute a command, perhaps by collecting the command's arguments with user prompts, then the work of the shell script is done when it is ready to invoke the command. You can conserve system resources by invoking the command with exec, which replaces the shell that is executing the script with the command. You could create an interactive file deletion command by using the following script:

```
# interactive file delete
echo "Name of file: \c"; read filename
exec rm $filename
```

If you do *not* use the exec command, two processes are needed to remove the file: the one executing the shell script, and the process running the rm command itself. If you use the exec command, only one process is required.

exit **Exit from the Current Shell**

> **Syntax of the exit Command**
>
> exit [*n*]

Use the exit command to terminate the current shell process. If the current shell is your login shell, you return to the login display.

10

With the optional argument *n*, you can return a specific exit value. If *n* is omitted, the exit value from the previously executed command is returned.

The `exit` command is used most often to terminate execution of a shell script, either because an error was detected or because you want to end the script normally. The following example shows both usages:

```
# Remove a file or directory so it can be recovered
if [ $# -lt 1 ]
then
    echo "Usage: scrap filename ..."
    exit 1
fi
tar rf $HOME/.trashcan $* ¦¦ exit
rm -rf $*
echo "Trashcan now contains:"
tar tvf $HOME/.trashcan
exit 0
```

The script uses the first and second `exit` commands to abort the shell script in the event of an error. The last `exit` command ends the script and returns an explicit exit value of 0 to indicate that the script completed without errors.

export   Add Variables to the Environment

Syntax of the export Command

```
export name ...
```

Use the `export` command to make a variable available to called commands. When exported, a variable is included in the *environment* of called commands. An exported variable can be referenced by name in a shell script even though the value of the variable is not set in the script.

To test whether a variable is exported, issue the `env` command. If the variable is listed, then it is exported. The following terminal dialog shows the effect of `export` on the variable environment reported by `env`:

```
$ pubdir=/usr/spool/uucppublic
$ env
HOME=/u/matt
MAIL=/usr/mail/matt
PATH=/bin:/usr/bin:/usr/local/bin:/u/matt/bin:
```

```
SHELL=/bin/sh
$ export pubdir
$ env
HOME=/u/matt
MAIL=/usr/mail/matt
PATH=/bin:/usr/bin:/usr/local/bin:/u/matt/bin:
SHELL=/bin/sh
pubdir=/usr/spool/uucppublic
$
```

10

fc   Reexecute a Previously Entered Command

---

ksh

Syntax of the fc Command

```
fc [ -e editor ] [ -nlr ] [ first [ last ] ]
fc -e - [ old=new ] [ command ]
```

The fc command can retrieve previously executed commands, modify the retrieved commands, and resubmit them for execution.

When the -l option is present, the fc command displays selected lines from the command history file. The -n option suppresses the line number that ordinarily appears in front of each line. The -r option reverses the order of the listing, showing the most recent command first and the oldest last. The -n and -r options are meaningful only in combination with the -l option.

The optional *first* and *last* arguments select the line or lines of the history file to be listed (-1) or reexecuted (-1 not specified). Either argument can be specified in one of the following forms:

- A line number assigned to the line by the shell

- A negative number, designating a line by counting backwards: -1 is the most recently entered command, -2 is the command entered before that, and so on

- A string; you select the most recent command that starts with that string

If both *first* and *last* are specified, the operation (display or execute) is performed on the range of lines beginning with *first* and ending with *last*. If only *first* is specified, the selection depends on the operation to be performed: execute is performed on the first line and a list operation is performed on the range of lines from *first* to -1.

10

If neither *first* nor *last* is specified, a list operation lists the last 16 lines and an execute operation uses the most recent line.

When -1 is not specified, an execute operation is performed. The behavior of the fc command is determined by the command format, as indicated in Table 10.2.

Table 10.2. Command formats for the fc command.

Command Format	Result
fc [*first* [*last*]]	The selected lines are copied to a temporary file, then an editor is invoked. Using the edit commands of the editor, you can modify the selected commands as desired, then save your modifications or quit the editor. In either case, the shell executes the lines found in the temporary file and deletes the file. If the shell variable FCEDIT is set and non-null, its value is executed as a command to invoke the editor; otherwise the /bin/ed editor is invoked.
fc -e *editor* [*first* [*last*]]	The editor named *editor* is invoked; otherwise this form works the same as the previous form.
fc -e - [*old=new*] [*command*]	No editor is invoked. The single most recent line starting with *command* is selected. If the *old=new* argument is specified, the first occurrence of *old* in the command line is changed to *new*. The resulting command is then executed.

The alias history is preset to fc -1.

The alias r is preset to fc -e -.

---

fg   Bring a Background Job into the Foreground

ksh

Syntax of the fg Command

fg [*job*]

10

Use the fg command to restart a stopped job or to move a background job into the foreground. Execution is resumed in the foreground. If no argument is supplied, the job last stopped is resumed. For *job*, specify one of the following values listed in Table 10.3.

Table 10.3. Values for job in the bg command.

Values	Meaning
num	Process number
%num	Job number
%string	Command name
%?string	Command name containing string
%+ or *%%*	Current job
%-	Previous job

The fg command is available only on versions of UNIX that provide the job control feature.

You can move only one job at a time into the foreground because the shell does not accept terminal input while a foreground job is running. You do not receive a prompt from the shell after issuing the fg command until the foreground job completes, or until you stop or kill the job.

If a background job attempts to write to your terminal, it is placed in the Stopped state (see the jobs command in this chapter). You can use the fg command to bring the job into the foreground, respond interactively with the job, then use the bg command to return the job to background execution. Thus the job control feature lets you overlap the execution of commands that otherwise must be executed consecutively.

getopts   **Parse Command-Line Arguments**

ksh

Syntax of the getopts Command

```
getopts options name [ arg ... ]
```

10

The `getopts` built-in command assists in the identification and extraction of command-line options and arguments. It renders the `getopt` command obsolete. All new shell scripts should be written to use `getopts`.

For *options*, specify a string describing the valid command-line options to be parsed. A letter in the string represents an option letter; a letter followed by a colon represents an option that takes an argument. The *options* string `abf:h` would describe any of the following command-line options:

```
-a -b -fvalue -h
-ab -f value -h
-abf value -h
-abh -f value
```

The order that options actually appear in the command line is immaterial to `getopts`. Keyletter options can be individually coded or combined together; `getopts` recognizes and returns options individually even when combined.

If the *options* string begins with `:`, `getopts` lets you handle invalid options; *name* is set to `?` and the offending option letter is set in `OPTARG`. If *options* does not begin with `:`, `getopts` issues its own error message and sets *name* to `?` (`OPTARG` is unchanged).

For *name*, enter a shell variable name. If the variable does not exist, `getopts` creates it. The value of the variable is not used; `getopts` uses *name* to return the next command option to you.

For *arg*, enter the argument list that `getopts` is to parse. This argument usually is provided in the form `$*` or `"$@"` to pass all the command arguments to `getopts`.

The `getopts` command must be called once for each command-line option because `getopts` finds and extracts options one at a time. On each call, `getopts`:

- Assigns the next option letter to *name*. If the option letter was preceded by `-`, the leading dash is dropped; if the option letter was preceded by `+`, the value of *name* is `+`, followed by the option letter.

- Sets global variable `OPTIND` to the index of the next command-line argument to be processed.

- Sets the option value in the global variable `OPTARG` (only for options taking a value).

The exit value of `getopts` is 0 (true) if an option was found and set in *name*; otherwise the exit value is 1 (false).

The following script illustrates the operation of getopts when stored in a file called opts and executed:

```
# Display the results of executing getopts
while getopts :abf:h OPTION "$@"
do
    echo "OPTION=$OPTION (OPTIND=$OPTIND) OPTARG='$OPTARG'"
done
shift OPTIND-1
echo "Args are '$*'"
```

The following shows a sample execution:

```
$ opts -abc -f "Nothing here" junk args
OPTION=a (OPTIND=1) OPTARG=''
OPTION=b (OPTIND=1) OPTARG=''
OPTION=? (OPTIND=1) OPTARG='c'
OPTION=f (OPTIND=4) OPTARG='Nothing here'
Args are 'junk args'
```

A typical use of getopts to identify command-line options looks like this:

```
while getopts :abf:h OPTION "$@"
do
    case $OPTION in
        a) AOPT=1 ;;
        b) BOPT=1 ;;
        f) FOPT=$OPTARG ;;
        h) HOPT=1 ;;
        \?) echo "Invalid option -$OPTION" ;;
    esac
done
```

hash   Control Command Hashing

Syntax of the hash Command

hash [-r] *name* ...

When you enter the name of a command, the shell searches for a program having the same name as the command. If the name is a built-in command or a function, the shell finds it quickly because built-in commands and functions are kept in memory. Otherwise, the shell must search the list of directories specified as the value of the PATH shell variable; each directory searched requires at least one disk access. The more directories the shell must search

10

to find the command, the longer it takes to execute the command. It can require many disk accesses and considerable delay to find and load a program residing in a directory near the end of the PATH list.

To minimize the need for long directory searches, the shell tries to remember where it found each command name you previously executed so it does not have to repeat any long directory searches. To do so, the shell keeps a list of the full path names of each command you have entered. Users call this list the *hash table*.

Although the hash table enables the shell to improve its overall performance, it also can cause problems. In particular, if you change the list of directories in PATH, create a new executable program file in one of the directories listed in PATH, or change your current directory, the shell might find the wrong program due to the hash table.

Suppose, for example, you have set PATH to /bin:/usr/bin:.. The shell searches three directories to find a command name: /bin, /usr/bin, and . (dot). The dot refers to your current directory. If the shell finds a command (payw, for example) in your current directory, it makes a note in the hash table of the command name and identifies your current directory by its full path name as the location of payw.

If you change your current directory and enter the payw command again, the shell still looks in the old current directory because that is where the hash table says payw is located. If your new current directory does not contain the payw command, the shell finds the command when it should not because your old current directory is no longer in the search path. On the other hand, if your new current directory contains an executable file named payw, the shell seems to correctly locate the command, but it executes the wrong one, using the command in your old current directory rather than the new one.

You can reduce the likelihood of running into this problem by selectively purging entries from the hash table whenever you change the value of PATH or change your current directory. The shell has no way of knowing about changes to the location of program files you make with the rm, mv, cp, or ln commands, or changes you make by compiling a new program with the same name as one already in the hash table.

Consequently, when you change the location of a program file by removing a command from a directory in the search path or by creating a new program file in such a directory, you must tell the shell to discard the invalidated entries from the hash table.

The command hash *name* makes the shell remove the hash table entry for the command called *name*. The next time you execute the *name* command, the shell performs a full search and finds the right command.

Invoking the hash command without arguments causes the command to print a list of all the entries in the hash table. This list provides you with the number of *hits* on the table entry (the number of times the hash table entry has saved the shell from having to perform a full search for the command), and the *cost* of a full search for the command in terms of the number of directories the shell had to search to find it.

The Korn shell implements the hash command as an alias of the alias command itself: alias hash='alias -t -'. The tracked aliases feature provides the functionality of hash tables without actually providing the tables. For more information, see the alias command in this chapter.

jobs   List Active Background Jobs

Syntax of the jobs Command

```
jobs [ -lp ]
```

The jobs command is available only with versions of UNIX that provide the job control feature. Use the command to list the status of all stopped and background jobs you are currently running.

If you have no active jobs, the jobs command does nothing. Otherwise, it prints a listing of your current jobs like this:

```
$ jobs -l
[1] - 580      Stopped              vi payw.c
[2] + 592      Running              make paygl
[3]   570      Done                 awk -f progw pay.mast
```

Supported options are:

-l   Include the process-ID in the output

-p   Print process-ID numbers only.

The first column displays the job number in brackets [ ]. The current job (the most recently initiated background process or command) is marked with +, the previous job with -, and other jobs are unmarked. The job status can be Running, Stopped, or Done. The last column of the line shows the command being executed by the job.

kill

10

Signal a Process

| ksh |

Syntax of the `kill` Command

`kill [ -sig ] job ...`

Use the `kill` built-in command to send a signal to a process or job. The signal generates a request for an interruption in the signaled process. The signaled process can ignore the interruption, can be terminated by the interruption, or can handle the interruption in an application-defined manner. The default action is to terminate the signaled process.

For `job`, specify one of the following:

`num`	Process number
`%num`	Job number
`%string`	Command name
`%?string`	Command name containing string
`%+ or %%`	Current job
`%-`	Previous job

If the `-sig` option is specified, signal `sig` is sent to the process or process group; otherwise signal 15 (TERM) is sent. Signal 9 (KILL) forcibly terminates all addressed processes regardless of the signal-handling procedures in effect for the processes. You can specify either a signal number or a signal name for `sig`. Use `kill -l` to get a list of the supported signal numbers and names. Table 10.4 shows the minimum set of signal names and numbers that are recognized.

Table 10.4. Signal names for the `kill` command in UNIX System V.

Number	Name	Meaning
1	HUP	Hangup; the user has logged off
2	INT	Interrupt; user pressed INTR key
3	QUIT	Quit; user pressed QUIT key
9	KILL	Force termination of process

Number	Name	Meaning
10	BUS	Bus error, usually a program error
11	SEGV	Segmentation violation, a program error
14	ALRM	Alarm; time out.
15	TERM	Termination; user requested termination

10

The processes to which the signal is sent are determined by the value of the *job* arguments, as follows:

- If *job* is a job identifier, the signal is sent to all the processes encompassed by that job.

- If *job* is a positive integer value, the value is taken as a process-ID and the signal is sent to that process.

  Use this option to request the termination of a process you initiated under the control of your current login shell. If *pid* is the process-ID of a process that you started from a different terminal or from a different login session, or a process that you did not start, then the kill command is rejected with an error message.

- If *job* is zero, the signal is sent to all processes in your current process group.

  Use kill 0 to terminate all background jobs that you started from your current login shell. Processes that you started from a different terminal or from a different login session, or which you did not start, are unaffected. Your login shell and all of its interactive subshells are unaffected by kill 0.

  It is not an error to issue kill 0 when no background processes are running.

- If *job* is equal to –1, then the signal is sent to all processes having the same user-ID as the process issuing kill (if you are the superuser, the signal is sent to all processes).

  Use kill -1 to terminate all processes, other than login and interactive shells, that you started. This command signals every process having your user-ID, regardless of the terminal or login shell you used to start it.

10

ksh

When issued by the superuser, `kill -1` sends the signal to all active processes other than *swap* and *init*.

• If *job* is negative but not –1, the signal is sent to all processes having a process-group ID equal to the absolute value of *job*.

Use `kill -n` to send the signal to process-ID *n* and to all processes started by process *n*. This command fails unless you are the superuser or you own the process-group.

Most processes terminate in response to signal TERM (15), and all terminate in response to signal KILL (9). The effect of other signals is dependent on the programming of the signaled process. Generally, you should use the default signal to terminate in an orderly, controlled termination of a process; use signal KILL only when you cannot kill the process any other way.

Do not send signal numbers other than KILL and TERM unless you know what program is being executed by the process and are aware of the effect the signal has. Used incautiously, `kill` can cause unexpected and undesirable results; for example, the `kill` command can produce incorrect output without providing any warning.

let   Evaluate an Arithmetic Expression

ksh

> **Syntax of the `let` Command**
>
> `let expr ...`

Use the `let` command to evaluate one or more arithmetic expressions. The `((expression))` command is equivalent to `let "expression"`.

Each argument of the `let` command is evaluated in turn, from left to right. Each evaluation either has no effect or assigns a value to a variable, depending on the expression itself. If an expression contains white space or characters special to the shell, the expression argument must be quoted.

See Chapter 11, "Shell Arithmetic," for a description of expression syntax.

newgrp   **Change the Current Group-ID**

10

Syntax of the newgrp Command

```
newgrp [ - ] [ group ]
```

The newgrp built-in command operates as if the command exec newgrp had been issued.

The current real and effective group-IDs are changed to those of the specified user group. If no *group* argument is supplied, the real and effective group-ID reverts to your default group as specified in the /etc/passwd system file. If *group* is not a defined group name, or you are not listed as a valid member of the group, your group affiliation remains unchanged but all other effects of the newgrp command still occur.

The - option causes your shell environment to be reset to the same condition as would exist if you were to log in again: shell variables revert to their default values, and your .profile is reexecuted.

In any case, the current shell is replaced with a new shell. Only exported variables survive; all other variables become undefined.

The purpose of the newgrp command is to enable a user to switch from one group to another.

---

print   **Write Arguments to Standard Output**

ksh

Syntax of the print Command

```
print [ -Rnprsu[n] ] [ arg ... ]
```

The print command supersedes the echo command and adds additional functionality (the echo command is still supported). If invoked with no flags or with only the special flag - -, the print command behaves identically to the echo command. The options supported by the print command are as follows:

ksh

10

- R   *raw* mode. All *arg* values are printed as they appear, without regard to escape sequences; that is, the strings \t, \n, and \c are not recognized as special and appear in the output unchanged. The only command option recognized after -R is -n.

- n   Suppresses the addition of a newline character to the output.

- p   Command output is written to the &¦ pipe rather than standard output.

- r   Same as -R, except no subsequent command options are recognized. Any arguments appearing after -r are printed exactly as they appear.

- s   Command output is written to the history file rather than to standard output.

- u   Command output is written to the open file descriptor specified by the adjacent digit *n*. If no digit follows the option, file descriptor 1 is assumed by default.

The command arguments *arg* are printed left to right, separated by a single blank. If the -R or -r options are not present, the string \t generates a tab character and the string \n generates a newline character at the position where the \t or \n occurs. The \t or \n is then deleted. If the -n option is not present, a newline is appended to the output.

The special argument - or - - suppresses the interpretation of following arguments as command options. Thus the command print - -n prints the character string -n.

---

pwd   **Display the Current Directory**

Syntax of the pwd Command
pwd

The pwd command displays the full path name of your working directory. The command takes no arguments. Many examples of the pwd command are in the previous section.

Contrary to what you might expect, the pwd command is almost an impossibility in the UNIX environment. There are situations where the pwd command might fail. This is not necessarily a disaster condition; in fact, some

10

forms of system security can foil the pwd command. The superuser chooses the system security type. (Technically, you must have search permission for the current directory and read permission for all higher-level directories for the pwd command to work.)

If the pwd command does fail, you can continue to work in the current directory or you can use cd to switch to another directory. The cd command can fail for the same reasons as the pwd command unless you specify a full path name (a path name beginning with /).

read   Read a Line from Standard Input

Syntax of the read Command

```
read [ name ... ]
```

Syntax of the read Command

```
read [ -prsu[n] ] [ name?prompt ] [ name ... ]
```

Use the read command to read a line from a file, parse the line into words, and assign each word to the successive shell variables given as the arguments of read. Each variable name must be formed according to the shell rules for variable names (see the "Shell Variables" section in Chapter 3, "Shell Basics").

The input line is first separated into words using white space as delimiters. Each word is then further separated using the IFS characters. The resulting list of words are assigned to the *name* arguments in left-to-right order.

If you specify no *name* arguments, the contents of the input line are discarded.

The Korn shell supports a number of options on the read command to enhance its flexibility. These options are:

-p   Read from a pipe created with the &¦ operator.

-r   *raw* mode. A backslash (\) at the end of the input line is treated as data and does not signify continuation of the line.

10

ksh
|

-s   Save the input line as a command in the history file.

-u   Read from the file descriptor specified by the adjacent digit *n*.
      If the next character is not a digit, file descriptor 0 is used by
      default.

If no *name* arguments are supplied, the input is stored in the variable
REPLY.

The first argument can consist of two strings separated by ?. The string
to the right of ? is used as a prompt to warn the user of the pending terminal
read. The string to the left of ? is taken as the first variable name.

readonly   Prevent Alteration of Selected Variables

Syntax of the readonly Command

readonly [*name* ...]

The readonly command marks the named shell variables as unalterable by
explicit value assignment and nonremovable by the unset command. If no
name arguments are present, the command lists all the shell variables that are
currently marked readonly.

For *name*, supply the names of one or more shell variables (without the
leading $). If a named variable does not exist, the variable is not created but
the shell remembers the read-only status of the name; a subsequent attempt
to assign a value to the variable fails with the message *name*: is read only.

Once a variable is declared to be read-only, its read-only status cannot
be changed.

ksh

In the Korn shell, you can assign a value to a variable when declaring it
to be read-only as follows:

readonly DISPLAY=unix:0

You can use the typeset built-in command to declare a variable read-
only or to reset the read-only status of a variable. For example, typeset +r
DISPLAY returns the DISPLAY variable to normal so you can modify or unset it.

return   **Return from a Shell Function**

Syntax of the return Command

```
return [ n ]
```

Use the return command inside a function definition to exit the function and return to the point from which the function was called. If *n* is specified, the exit value of the function is *n*; otherwise the value equals the exit value of the last command executed in the function.

The return command is like exit except that return does not terminate the current shell.

---

set   **Set Shell Options and Arguments**

Syntax of the set Command

```
set [±]aefhkntuvx][arg...]
```

---

ksh

Syntax of the set Command

```
set [±aefhkmnpstuvx][±o option]...[±A name][arg...]
```

Use the set command to change the setting of selected shell options, to redefine the current list of shell arguments, or both. Table 10.5 lists the supported shell options.

To cancel the effect of an option, use + rather than -. For example, set +f turns on the wild card substitutions feature, and set +x disables command tracing.

10

Table 10.5. Bourne shell set options.

Option	Effect
-a	Setting a variable causes it to be exported
-e	A nonzero command exit value aborts the current shell
-f	Wild card expansion is suppressed
-h	Functions are remembered when first seen, regardless of whether the function definition has been executed
-k	Keyword arguments are stripped from the command line and added to the command environment as variables
-n	Flow control commands (., case, for, if, while, until) are executed, but other commands are ignored
-t	The current shell exits after executing the next command
-u	Reference to an unset variable is treated as an error
-v	Print shell input as it is read
-x	Print each command before executing it
--	Stop processing options and treat the remainder of the set command line as new shell argument values

Shell options can be grouped (in the format -aef) or individually listed (for example -a -e -f). The first argument not beginning with -, or the first argument following --, is assigned to the special variable $1. Successive arguments, if any, are assigned to the special variables $2 through $9; any additional arguments are retained but not directly accessible.

If no arguments appear after the shell options (or following the -- pseudo-option), the current set of shell arguments remains unaltered by the set command.

The Korn shell built-in set command supports the additional options listed in Table 10.6.

ksh

Table 10.6. Korn shell set options.

Option	Effect
-A *name*	The *args* operands are assigned as the successive values of the variable array *name*
-m	Run background jobs in a separate process group; same as -o monitor

Option	Effect
-o *opt*	Set one of the keyword options (see Table 5.2 in Chapter 5, "Special Features")
-p	Protected mode (see option *protected* in the "Named Options" section in Appendix C)
-s	Sort the *arg* list into alphabetical order

10

shift   Shift Arguments Left

> **Syntax of the shift Command**
>
> ```
> shift [ n ]
> ```

Use shift to shift the shell arguments left by *n* positions. If *n* is omitted it defaults to 1. Used with an argument of 1, shift discards the value of $1; the value of $2 is assigned to $1; the value of $3 is assigned to $2; and so on. The number of arguments $# is reduced by *n*.

Because the shell allows explicit reference to only the first nine arguments $1 through $9, the shift command is commonly used to access arguments beyond the ninth. The following shows the use of shift to display arguments 10, 11, and 12:

```
shift 9
echo "args 10-12 = '$1' '$2' '$3'"
```

test   Evaluate a Conditional Expression

> **Syntax of the test Command**
>
> ```
> test expr
> [ expr ]
> ```

10

The test command evaluates the conditional expression *expr* and sets the exit value to 0 if it is true or to a nonzero value if it is false. The exit value from test can be used for decision-making with the if, while, or until shell commands and with the && and ¦¦ operators.

The test command can be written as [*expr*] to enhance the readability of shell scripts. To support this notation, the shell treats [as a built-in command, and the test command itself ignores a final argument of].

For *expr* specify one of the expression formats shown in Table 10.7.

Table 10.7. Test expression formats.

Format	Condition Tested
-b *file*	File *file* exists and is a block-special file
-c *file*	File *file* exists and is a character-special file
-d *file*	File *file* exists and is a directory
-f *file*	File *file* exists and is a regular file
-g *file*	File *file* exists and its set-group-ID bit is set
-h *file*	File *file* exists and is a symbolic link
-k *file*	File *file* exists and its sticky bit is set
-n *string*	The string *string* is not null
-p *file*	File *file* exists and is a named pipe
-r *file*	File *file* exists and is readable
-s *file*	File *file* exists and its size is greater than 0
-t [*num*]	File descriptor *num* (default 1) is a terminal
-u *file*	File *file* exists and its set-user-ID bit is set
-w *file*	File *file* exists and is writable
-x *file*	File *file* exists and is executable (or is searchable if *file* is a directory)
-z *string*	The string *string* is null (zero length)
string	The string *string* is not null
a = *b*	The string *a* is equal to the string *b*
a != *b*	The string *a* is not equal to the string *b*
a -eq *b*	*a* is numerically equal to *b*
a -ne *b*	*a* is numerically unequal to *b*
a -gt *b*	*a* is numerically greater than *b*
a -ge *b*	*a* is numerically greater than or equal to *b*

ksh

10

Format	Condition Tested
a -lt *b*	*a* is numerically less than *b*
a -le *b*	*a* is numerically less than or equal to *b*
-L *file*	File *file* exists and is a symbolic link
-O *file*	File *file* exists and its user-ID matches the effective user-ID of the current process
-G *file*	File *file* exists and its group-ID matches the effective group-ID of the current process
-S *file*	True if *file* is a socket
file1 -nt *file2*	True if *file1* is newer than *file2*
file1 -ot *file2*	True if *file1* is older than *file2*
file1 -ef *file2*	True if *file1* and *file2* are the same file

The reader should be careful to note that the test command (written [...]) and the test command (written [[...]]), while similar, are not identical and might give different results for some expressions.

You can invert the sense of a test by writing ! as a separate argument in front of the test. For example, test ! -d /usr/bin tests for "not a directory," and indicates false (a nonzero exit value) because /usr/bin exists and is a directory.

Multiple conditions can be tested by combining tests with the -a (and) and -o (or) operators. The -a operator has higher priority than -o. You can use parentheses (written as separate arguments) to explicitly specify grouping, as shown in the following examples:

```
test $a -gt 5 -a $a -lt 10
```

Returns true only if the value of *a* is one of the numeric values 6, 7, 8, or 9.

```
test $a -gt 5 -a $b -gt 10 -o $b -lt 5
```

Returns true if *b* is less than 5. Also returns true when *a* is greater than 5 and *b* is greater than 10. If either side of -o is true, the expression is true. The left side of -o is $a -gt 5 -a $b -gt 10, and the right side is $b -lt 5.

```
test $a -gt 5 -a\( $b -gt 10 -o$b -lt 5 \)
```

Returns true if *a* is greater than 5 and the value of *b* is not in the range 5 through 10. The insertion of parentheses changed the meaning of the expression in the previous example. Notice that the parentheses are backslashed to prevent the shell from interpreting them as subshell grouping operators.

times

10

Report Execution Times

> **Syntax of the times Command**
>
> ```
> times
> ```

Use `times` to display the cumulative amount of computer time used by the login shell and all commands invoked by the shell. The output format of `times` is not strictly defined but looks similar to the following:

```
0m0.08s 0m1.46s
0m0.19s 0m1.55s
```

The first line reports the time in minutes and seconds used by the shell itself; the first number is the amount of time used by the shell program itself, and the second number is the amount of time expended by the system in support of the shell program.

The second line reports the time in minutes and seconds used by all commands run by the shell. The two numbers report the amount of time used by the command programs and by the system respectively.

---

trap

Specify Exceptional Condition Handling

> **Syntax of the trap Command**
>
> ```
> trap [ command ] [ signal ... ]
> ```

Use `trap` to protect the shell (and, when executing a shell script, the shell script) from termination by a signal, and to specify an action to be taken on receipt of a signal. The *command* argument specifies a command list that is executed when *signal* is received. Multiple signals can be listed.

If *command* contains any characters special to the shell, including white space, the entire command must be quoted. The command argument is scanned twice: once when the `trap` command is executed, and again when *command* itself is executed. You might have to protect substitutions within *command* by quoting or backslashing if you want the substitution to be performed when *command* is executed.

10

If *command* is omitted, all signal traps are reset to their default or original setting. Normally the receipt of a signal which is not trapped by the `trap` command results in immediate termination of the shell or shell script.

If *command* is the null string, the specified signals are ignored. Interactive shells automatically ignore the interrupt (2) and terminate (15) signals, so these signals can be used to terminate child processes created by the shell without terminating the shell itself.

For *signal* specify one or more signal numbers separated by white space. Table 10.4 provides a list of the standard UNIX System V signals. (For more information about signals, see the *UNIX System V Release 4 Programmer's Reference Manual*, Prentice-Hall 1990, ISBN 0-13-957549-9.)

If *signal* is 0, then *command* is executed when the shell exits for any reason, including normal exit.

If you provide no arguments to the `trap` command, it prints the command action in effect for each signal. Table 10.8 lists the signal numbers and their names.

Table 10.8. Signal numbers.

Signal	Name	Cause
1	SIGHUP	You logged off while a process was still running
2	SIGINT	You pressed the INTR key (usually ^c)
3	SIGQUIT	You pressed the QUIT key (see the `stty` command)
4	SIGILL	Program error occurred in a command
5	SIGTRAP	You use `sbd` to set a break point that was reached by a child of the process you are debugging
6	SIGIOT	A command issued the `abend()` call
7	SIGEMT	An unrecoverable hardware error occurred
8	SIGFPE	Overflow or division by zero occurred in floating-point calculations or divide by zero
9	SIGKILL	The command `kill -9` was issued
10	SIGBUS	A program error occurred in a command
11	SIGSEGV	A program error occurred in a command
12	SIGSYS	A command issued an invalid system call
13	SIGPIPE	A command wrote to a pipe with no one to read it
14	SIGALRM	A programmed timer expired
15	SIGTERM	The command `kill -15` was issued

10

When using the Korn shell, you can use symbolic names for *signal* (HUP, INT, QUIT, ILL, TRAP, IOT, EMT, FPE, KILL, BUS, SEGV, SYS, PIPE, ALRM, and TERM respectively for signals 1-15.)

You can explicitly signify an omitted *command* argument by writing -.

The special signal name EXIT is defined for signal 0. An EXIT trap set inside a function is taken immediately following the return from the function. An EXIT trap set outside a function is taken when the shell exits.

The special signal name ERR (there is no corresponding signal number) can be used to set up a trap for any command that returns a nonzero exit value.

The special signal name DEBUG can be used to set a trap to be taken after the execution of every command.

type   Identify a Command

Syntax of the type Command

```
type name
```

The type command reports whether *name* is a command and if so how the command is defined. The output of type is not suitable for input to other commands.

The type command reports that *name* is one of the following:

- A regular command, by giving its full path name:

```
$ type ls
ls is /bin/ls
$
```

- A regular command that is currently listed in the hash table:

```
$ type ls
ls is hashed (/bin/ls)
$
```

- A built-in command:

```
$ type cd
cd is a shell builtin
$
```

- A function, by giving its definition:

```
$ type man
man is a function
man(){
/usr/bin/man $* ¦ pg -cns
}
$
```

10

- Unknown to the shell:

```
$ type foo
foo not found
$
```

ksh

The type command is an alias for whence -v.

The Korn shell also can report that a name is one of the following:

- An alias, by giving the alias value:

```
$ type pwd
pwd is the alias 'print -r ${PWD}´
$
```

- An exported alias, as follows:

```
$ type integer
integer is an exported alias for "typeset  -i"
$
```

- An undefined function:

```
$ typeset -fu handle
$ type handle
handle is an undefined function
$
```

typeset   **Define Characteristics of a Variable**

ksh

Syntax of the typeset Command

```
typeset [ -FLRZefilprtux[n] ] [ name=value ... ]
typeset ±f[tux] [ name ... ]
```

10

ksh

Use the typeset built-in command to define variables of a special type or to request special handling of a variable. The typeset command is available only in the Korn shell. Table 10.9 describes the legal command options.

Table 10.9. Korn shell typeset options.

Option	Effect
-Ln	Left-justify the variable value in a field n characters wide
-LZn	Left-justify and strip any leading zeros from the variable value to a length of n characters
-Rn	Right-justify the variable value in a field n characters wide
-RZn	Right-justify and zero-fill the variable value to a length of n characters
-Zn	Same as -RZn
-i	Maintain the named variables internally in an integer format
-l	Convert uppercase letters to lowercase
-r	Define the variables named as readonly variables. To assign a value to a readonly variable, you must use the form name=value on the same typeset command
-t	User-defined tag
-u	Convert lowercase letters to uppercase
-x	Define the variables named as exported variables. If no initial value is provided, the variable is defined with a null value

When the -f option is specified, the typeset command manipulates function names and values. The options t, u, and x can be specified in any combination with f. Their significance is as follows:

Options	Action
t	Specify the xtrace option for the named functions
u	Specify the named functions as undefined
x	Export the named functions to shell scripts called by name

For additional information about typeset, see Chapter 11, "Arithmetic," and Chapter 12, "Advanced Shell Facilities."

ulimit
Set or Display Process Limits

10

Syntax of the `ulimit` Command

```
ulimit [ -[HS][a] ]
ulimit [ -[HS]cdfnstv ] [ limit ]
```

The UNIX system imposes a number of limits on the amount of resources a process can utilize. You can use the `ulimit` command to display or alter the limits in effect for the current process and for all child processes.

For each type of limit, there is a *soft* limit value and a *hard* limit value. The *soft* value is simply the current value of the limit; you can set the soft value up or down as long as it does not exceed the hard limit value. The *hard* limit specifies an upper limit that you can set to lower values but not raise (for the duration of the active process). The system contains built-in default values for all the hard limits.

Options and corresponding limits are described below. If you specify no options, the soft filesize limit is displayed or set. You can specify only one of the H or S options and one of the limit selector options in any given command.

Option	Meaning
-H	Selects the hard limit value
-S	Selects the soft limit value
-a	Displays all limit values
-c	Coredump limit: the maximum number of 512-byte blocks that can be written to a core file on abnormal termination of a program
-d	Data limit: the largest data or heap segment, measured in kilobytes, allowable in a program file
-f	Filesize limit: the maximum size to which an output file can grow, as a number of 512-byte blocks
-n	No files limit: the maximum number of file descriptors that can be opened at one time (highest file descriptor number plus one)

10

Option	Meaning
-s	Stack limit: the largest stack segment, measured in kilobytes, allowable in a program file
-t	Time limit: the maximum CPU time, in seconds, the process can live
-v	Virtual memory limit: the maximum size, in kilobytes, of virtual memory for the process

For *limit* specify the new limit value as an integer number, or the string unlimited to set the largest allowable value. Only one limit value can be specified; therefore only one limit option can be given on one command. A *limit* argument is invalid when the -a option is specified.

The following shows sample output from the ulimit -a command. These are the default hard limits on my system; your system might show different values or show ksh: ulimit : bad options.

```
$ ulimit -a
time(seconds)        unlimited
file(blocks)         4096
data(kbytes)         16384
stack(kbytes)        16384
coredump(blocks)     2048
nofiles(descriptors) 64
vmemory(kbytes)      16384
$
```

unalias   Drop an Alias

Syntax of the unalias Command

unalias *name* ...

Use the unalias command to remove one or more command aliases previously defined with the alias command. For *name* specify the names of the aliases to be removed.

umask

Set or Display the File-Creation Mask

10

Syntax of the umask Command

umask [*nnn*]

Use umask to display or to modify the process file-creation mask. Without an argument, the umask command displays the current value of the mask. To change the mask, specify the new mask value as an octal number in the range 000 to 7777.

The bits of the process file-creation mask correspond to the nine permission bits of a file's access mode. If a bit of the process file-creation mask is set to 1, then the corresponding permission bit is set to 0 whenever a new file is created. If a bit of the process file-creation mask is set to 0, then the program creating the file can set the file permission bit to either 1 or 0.

The net effect of a file-creation mask of all zeros is generally to permit all users both read and write access to a file. Setting bits of the file-creation mask to 1 denies the corresponding access for all newly created files.

Table 10.10. summarizes the effect of typical umask values.

Table 10.10. Typical umask settings.

This umask *Value*	*Allows These File Permissions*	*Meaning*
000	rwxrwxrwx	Any user can read or write the file
002	rwxrwxr-x	Only owner and group can write the file
022	rwxr-xr-x	Only owner can write the file
007	rwxrwx---	Others can neither read nor write
077	rwx------	Only owner can read or write the file

Data files are usually created with access permissions of 666 (rw-rw-rw-), and executable files are normally created with access permissions of 777. The file-creation mask set by umask provides a way to uniformly and consistently modify the default access permissions assigned by programs that create files.

10

unset

Drop a Shell Variable

Syntax of the unset Command

unset *name* ...

Syntax of the unset Command

unset [-f] *name* ...

Use the unset command to remove the definitions of one or more shell variables or functions. For *name* specify the name of a variable (without a leading $) or a function to be removed. If the variable is exported, it is removed from the current process environment as well.

You can unset the following variables: IFS, MAILCHECK, PATH, PS1, PS2.

The following shows the current value of variable PUBDIR and the usage of unset to delete the PUBDIR variable, and then demonstrates that the variable is undefined:

```
$ echo $PUBDIR
/usr/spool/uucppublic
$ unset PUBDIR
$ echo ${PUBDIR?}
PUBDIR: parameter null or not set
$
```

Use option -f to remove function definitions. If -f is specified, all *name* arguments must be function names and the command deletes only function definitions.

If -f is not specified, all *name* arguments must be variable names and the command deletes only shell variables.

wait

Wait for Background Jobs to Finish

Syntax of the wait Command

```
wait [ n ]
```

Use wait to force the shell to wait for the finish of background jobs that the shell previously started. The shell does not issue another prompt until all active background jobs have finished, but when the last active background job finishes, the shell issues a prompt immediately.

You can use the wait command when you have run out of other things to do, and now need the results of a background command before you can continue.

If you want only the results from one background process and several are active, use the form wait *pid*, specifying the process-ID of the process you want to wait for as the argument. The shell waits for that one specific process to finish; other processes, if any, continue to execute.

If you omit the *n* argument, the shell waits for all your background jobs to finish.

---

whence

Describe Interpretation of a Command

Syntax of the whence Command

```
whence [ -v ] name
```

The whence command reports whether *name* is a command, and if so, how the command is defined. If you specify the -v option, the report is verbose; it includes comments that help you interpret the output of whence. The output of whence can be used as the input to another command when the -v option is omitted, as in the following example:

```
$ file `whence fgrep`
```

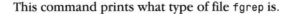

ksh

10

This command prints what type of file `fgrep` is.

The whence command is basically the same as the Bourne shell `type` command except the `type` command does not support the `-v` option; thus the output of `type` is not suitable for input to other commands.

The whence command reports that *name* is one of the following:

- A regular command, by giving its full path name:

```
$ whence ls
/bin/ls
$
```

- A built-in command, by giving its name:

```
$ whence cd
cd
$
```

- A function, by giving its name:

```
$ whence man
man
$
```

- An alias, by giving the alias value:

```
$ whence pwd
print -r ${PWD}
$
```

- Unknown to the shell, by printing nothing:

```
$ whence foo
$
```

Summary

This chapter contains a great mass of detail about shell built-in commands, without much in the way of underlying theory to tie the details together.

Probably you did not read the chapter straight through, but skimmed it to get an overview of the chapter's contents. Good for you. The best way to learn the material in this chapter is by repeated reference when you need to use specific built-in commands.

What do built-in commands mean to you?

Some commands are built into the shell because there is no other way to implement them. The cd, umask, and ulimit commands are examples of this kind of built-in command. The problem is that these commands change something about the current UNIX process, yet to execute a regular command UNIX has to create a new process. Unless these commands are built in, there's no way to make their effect last beyond the execution of the command itself. You will use the built-in commands in this category simply because you have no other choice; there is no regular command form for these commands.

Other built-in commands are provided as built-ins because they are used frequently, and they run faster when built into the shell—being built-in, there's no need to search program directories and read the program in before executing it. Whenever you have a choice between using a built-in and a regular form of a command, you should probably choose the built-in command. If you can achieve the same effect by using several built-in commands as using a regular command, then by all means consider doing a small amount of programming to avoid using the regular command; the run-time savings for your shell script will justify your efforts.

Unfortunately, the syntax and capabilities of some built-in commands do not exactly match that of the corresponding regular command. In such cases, you may sometimes prefer to use the regular command. To do so, you must make sure the shell doesn't execute the built-in version of the command instead.

To force the shell to use the regular command, write the full path name of the command rather than just its file name. Built-in commands have no path name, so the shell will not find the built-in command when the command you give starts with a slash. For example, to use the real echo command, write the command as /bin/echo.

To the best of my knowledge, the syntax and functionality of all built-in commands in the UNIX System V Release 4 Bourne and Korn shells exactly match that of the corresponding real command. For earlier versions of the shell and UNIX, differences do exist and you must take those differences into account when planning the commands to use in your shell scripts.

## Chapter 11

Shell Arithmetic

he Bourne shell provides no built-in arithmetic facilities, although calculations can still be done. The secret to this trick lies in the fact that several UNIX facilities provide computational facilities, and the results can be captured using command substitution.

The Korn shell, on the other hand, provides a rich calculation language that makes arithmetic much easier to do in the Korn shell, and much more efficient. Of course, because the Korn shell is compatible with the Bourne shell, you also can use the Bourne shell techniques for arithmetic purposes.

In this chapter, you will learn first about the techniques applicable to both the Bourne and Korn shells, then examine the Korn shell facilities for doing arithmetic.

Doing Arithmetic with expr

The expr command is the most commonly used command for simple arithmetic calculations. Each argument of the expr command must be a *term* or an *operator* in an expression. The expr command evaluates the expression and prints the result on standard output.

A *term* is a numeric value. The expr command cannot perform floating-point arithmetic; every number must be an integer value, although it can be signed. The following are valid numeric terms: 37, -5, 0, 20512. The largest positive number expr can work with is 2,147,483,647 and the largest negative is –2,147,483,648 (you must omit the commas in any actual number you give to expr).

An *operator* specifies an operation to be performed on two numbers. The operators supported by expr are shown in Table 11.1.

Table 11.1. Arithmetic operators for expr.

Operator	Meaning
+	Addition
-	Subtraction (also the *minus* sign)
*	Multiplication
/	Division
%	Modulus (also called *remainder*)
=	Equal
!=	Not equal
<	Less than
<=	Less than or equal
>	Greater than
>=	Greater than or equal

Use the standard arithmetic operators +, -, *, and / to perform integer addition, subtraction, multiplication, and division. Notice that the asterisk (*) must be quoted or backslashed to avoid confusion with the wild card character.

Use the modulus operator (%) to compute the remainder from a division. For example, 8 % 3 is 2 because three goes into eight twice, with two left over.

Use the comparison operators =, !=, <, <=, >, and >= to compare two integers. If the relationship holds, expr prints 1; otherwise it prints 0. For example, 5 = 5 prints 1 because the two numbers are equal, but 7 <= 6 prints 0 because seven is not less than or equal to six.

The following example shows how to use expr for simple counting. The example initializes a variable to 0 and performs a loop, adding 1 each time, until the variable reaches 10. (When typing this example, you key only the highlighted text.)

```
$ num=0
$ while [ $num -lt 10 ]
> do
> num=`expr $num + 1`
> echo $num
> done
1
2
3
4
5
6
7
8
9
10
$
```

Notice that the expr command is written inside backward quotation marks. This causes the shell to execute the command, then substitute the standard output of the command for the back-quoted expression. If you try the expr command by hand, as in the following example

```
$ expr 4 \* 7
28
$
```

you will see the expr command prints only the result. Thus the command substitution is equivalent to writing num=28, except the 28 is computed by expr.

When using operators that are special to the shell, such as * or <, you must ensure that the shell does not see these characters. You can use backslash (\) to hide one character, or single quotation marks to hide an entire string. The multiplication problem could have been written as expr 4 '*' 7.

Do not, however, enclose the entire expression in quotation marks. If you do, the expr command won't recognize the individual terms and operators of the expression. Each term or operator must be a whole argument. If you break this rule, you will not get the expected result, as the following example shows:

```
$ expr '4 * 7'
4 * 7
$
```

The expr command saw one argument that was neither a pure number nor an operator; it was a mixture of both, and therefore an arbitrary character string. The expr command also supports a few string operators, which explains why its reaction to a string argument is to print the string. For more information about manipulating strings with expr, refer to the user's reference manual for your version of UNIX.

You can use the expr command in back quotations to do arithmetic wherever a shell variable is valid. The following example shows the use of expr in an if statement to test for even numbers:

```
$ while :
> do
> echo "Enter a number: \c"; read num
> if [ `expr $num % 2` -eq 0 ]
> then echo $num is even
> else echo $num is odd
> fi
> done
Enter a number: 47
47 is odd
Enter a number: 38
38 is even
Enter a number: 202
202 is even
Enter a number: ^c
$
```

Doing Arithmetic with bc

The bc command is a much more powerful calculator than expr; it can work with floating-point numbers, with bases other than decimal, and with fixed scaling.

The trick to using bc is that the calculation to be evaluated must be piped to the command. The result appears on standard output. The following shell script, Listing 11.1, implements a utility to convert from decimal to hexadecimal.

Listing 11.1. A command to convert from decimal to hexadecimal.

```
# 2hex - a utility to convert from decimal to hex
( echo obase=16
echo $1) ¦ bc
```

Simple arithmetic also is possible with bc. Unlike expr, the bc command does not require terms and arguments to be separated by white space. The entire expression can be enclosed in quotations, simplifying your typing job.

The multiplication problem you worked earlier could be done with bc like this:

```
$ echo '4*7' | bc
28
$
```

If you have set scale to a positive value, bc also works with fractional digits:

```
$ (echo scale=10; echo '37/7') | bc
5.2857142857
$
```

For a last look at bc, convert the counting example from expr to bc:

```
$ num=0
$ while [ $num -lt 10 ]
> do
> num=`echo $num+1 | bc`
> echo $num
> done
1
2
3
4
5
6
7
8
9
10
$
```

Doing Arithmetic with the Korn Shell

Although you can do arithmetic with the Bourne shell, it runs slowly because, for each calculation, you have to load and execute a UNIX command program. The Korn shell provides built-in arithmetic facilities, making it much more practical to do arithmetic in shell scripts.

The Korn shell facilities for arithmetic include the typeset command, the let command, the ((expr)) and [[expr]] special commands, and the assignment statement.

Using Integer Variables

Use the `typeset` command to declare an integer variable. You also can use the alias `integer`, which the shell defines automatically. See the following example:

```
$ integer num
```

When you have declared a variable as integer, you can assign the results of calculations to the variable by using the simple assignment statement. You must use the `let` command to evaluate an expression and assign the result to any other type of variable.

To calculate the product of 4 and 27, use the following commands:

```
$ typeset -i num
$ num=4*27
$ print $num
108
$
```

If you had not defined the variable `num` to be an integer variable, the assignment `num=4*27` would give you quite a different result:

```
$ product=4*27
$ print $product
4*27
$
```

When a variable has not been declared to be an integer, the Korn shell assigns string values to the variable as the Bourne shell would. In the previous example, the variable `product` has not been declared an integer with `typeset` so the value it receives is the string on the right side.

Integer variables (and arithmetic expressions, discussed later) can be used in the following places:

- As an array subscript
- In the arguments of `let`
- Inside double parentheses (arithmetic evaluations)
- As the shift count in `shift`
- With the numeric comparison operators in `test`, `[`, and `[[`
- As resource limits in `ulimit`
- On the right side of an assignment statement

Whenever you reference an integer variable in one of the previously mentioned places, you omit the leading $ sign.

Forming Arithmetic Expressions

An arithmetic expression is formed by combining terms and variables. A *term* is a variable name or an integer constant. A variable name must *not* be prefixed with a dollar sign ($). An *integer constant* is a decimal number (10, for example) or a number in any base from 2 to 36. To specify a number in a base other than 10, write the number as *base#value*. For example, 2#101 is 5, 8#277 is 191, and 16#3ff is 1023. When *base* is greater than 10, the digits consist of 0 through 9 and as many letters starting with *a* as are needed. For base 12, the digits are 0123456789ab (uppercase letters can be used interchangeably); for base 16, the digits are 0123456789abcdef, and so on.

The Korn shell supports a large variety of arithmetic operators. Table 11.2 lists them all. The Result column shows the evaluation of the expression shown in the Example column, assuming x=2 and y=3, and r=Result.

Table 11.2. Korn shell binary arithmetic operators.

Operator	Operation	Example	Result
+	Add	r=x+y	5
-	Subtract	r=x-y	−1
*	Multiply	r=x*y	6
/	Divide	r=x/y	0
%	Remainder	r=x%y	2
&	And (bitwise)	r=x&y	2
¦	Or (")	r=x¦y	3
^	Exclusive or(")	r=x^y	1
<<	Shift left	r=x<<y	16
>>	Shift right	r=x>>y	0
==	Equal	r=x==y	0
!=	Not equal	r=x!=y	1
>	Greater than	r=x>y	0
>=	Greater than or equal to	r=x>=y	0
<	Less than	r=x<y	1
<=	Less than or equal to	r=x<=y	1

In addition, the shell also supports the assignment operators +=, -=, *=, /=, %=, &=, |=, ^=, <<=, and >>=. An expression of the form *var op = value* is defined to have the same meaning and effect as *var = var op value*. For example, you can write r+=x in place of r=r+x.

Integer variables play a primary role in Korn shell arithmetic, but ordinary (string) variables also play an interesting (if unusual) part. When the Korn shell encounters an ordinary variable in the right side of an assignment, it tries to evaluate the variable's value as if it were an expression.

Suppose the value of w, an ordinary variable, is the string x+2. When evaluating the assignment r=w*5, the shell first evaluates w by computing x+2. Finally, the shell multiples this result by 5 to obtain the final value assigned to r. Try the following experiment on your terminal to see how it works:

```
$ integer j k
$ k=7
$ m=k+2
$ print $m
k+2
$ j=m*5
$ print $j
45
$
```

Now figure the result by hand. The value of variable m is the string k+2, and the value of k is 7; therefore m is equivalent to 9. Finally, multiply that result by 5, getting 45. The value assigned to integer variable j is 45.

The original counting program you wrote can be modified to use Korn shell arithmetic, as follows:

```
$ integer num=0
$ while [ $num -lt 10 ]
> do
> num=num+1
> print $num
> done
1
2
3
4
5
6
7
8
9
10
$
```

Using the `let` Command

When the variable on the left side of an assignment statement is an integer variable, the Korn shell understands that the arithmetic value of the right side should be computed and assigned to the variable. When the variable is not an integer, the Korn shell performs string assignment to maintain compatibility with Bourne shell scripts.

There is no reason, however, that would prevent the shell from computing the value of the expression anyway and assigning the result to a string variable. The `let` command provides a way to tell the shell to arithmetically evaluate the right side of an assignment, even when the receiving variable is not type integer.

Each argument of the `let` command is separately evaluated. If an argument expression does not contain an assignment operator, no assignment is performed; the evaluated result is discarded.

For example, the following `let` command evaluates three expressions:

```
$ let x=2 y=3 r=x*6
$ print $x $y $r
2 3 6
$
```

Although, for this example, none of the variables x, y, or z are defined as integer, the `let` command forces evaluation to occur. The values of x, y, and z are still strings but they contain the expected results.

Usually you should enclose the arguments of `let` in quotation marks (either single or double quotation marks suffice), especially if the arguments include white space or shell special characters. For example, the following statement causes trouble:

```
$ let y=x<<2
```

The << operator is intended to produce a left shift operation, but the shell cannot distinguish the left shift operator from the << redirection operator. To ensure Bourne shell compatibility, the Korn shell must give priority of interpretation to the redirection operators. Thus, rather than performing a left shift, the shell tries to redirect standard input, leading to unexpected behavior of the command.

The following is a better way to write the same command:

```
$ let ´y=x<<2´
```

Even though the `let` command forces arithmetic evaluation of its arguments, the capability of using an expression as the value of a variable is still supported. For example, if the variable num has the value 11, and the variable x has the value num/3, then `let ´y=x+1´` sets y to 4 (11/3 + 1).

The `let` statement also can be used for decision making. Recall that the `if` statement executes the command given as its argument and selects either a `then` or `else` clause depending on the exit value of the command. The `if` statement considers an exit value of 0 to be the normal command return, and executes the `then` clause; any other nonzero value causes the `else` clause to be executed.

The `let` command returns an exit value because it is a command. When the last argument evaluates to zero, the `let` command returns an exit value of 1; in all other cases `let` returns 0. In other words, the `let` command effectively inverts a `true` result (such as `let "x>5"` when x is 6 or greater), so `if` executes the `then` clause.

The following example shows how this works in practice:

```
$ integer x=5
$ if let 'x > 4'
> then print $x is greater than 4
> else print $x is not greater than 4
> fi
5 is greater than 4
$
```

The use of `let` also provides a convenient way to set and test flags in a shell script. Here is a small shell script that either displays or prints a file depending on whether the `-p` flag appears in the command line:

```
# Display or print a file
PrintFlag=0    # Default to no print
case $1 in
   -p) PrintFlag=1; shift 1 ;;
esac
if let 'PrintFlag'
then pr $1 ¦ lp
else pg $1
fi
```

Note: `let` is slower than using integer typed variables, because the Korn Shell must first covert the values to integers when `let` is used with string values.

Using the ((. . .)) Statement

The command format `let "expr"` occurs so frequently that the Korn shell supports the syntax `((expr))` as an equivalent form; it can be used wherever the `let` command would be valid. Unlike `let`, which can have multiple arguments, the `((expr))` statement allows only one expression between the double parentheses.

Everything between the starting ((and the ending)) is processed as if quoted. You do not have to quote or backslash anything in the expression; if you do, the quotation marks or backslashes are retained and the shell tries to interpret them as part of an arithmetic expression. This gives you a syntax error.

In the sample `while` loop, the statement `num=num+1` was used to increment the value of `num`, even though the Korn shell supports the more succinct expression `num+=1`. Writing `num+=1` would generate only a syntax error, however, because only the basic assignment form is recognized by the shell at the start of a command; `num+=1` would be interpreted as a command name, leading to the message `not found`. You can now circumvent this problem by enclosing the expression `num+=1` inside ((...)) brackets, like this:

```
$ while ((num<10))
> do
> ((num+=1))
> print $num
> done
```

The syntax ((...)) is a *statement*, not an expression. You cannot use it as an argument of a command. If you do, you get a syntax error:

```
$ print ((num+=1))
ksh: syntax error: `((' unexpected
$
```

A Sample Program

The following sample program demonstrates many of the features of Korn shell arithmetic discussed in this chapter. The purpose of the program is to print the first 100 prime numbers. This is usually considered a computation-intensive task which, until the advent of the Korn shell, would be impractical to implement with a shell script. Listing 11.2 presents the text of the program.

Listing 11.2. Compute the first 100 prime numbers.

```
# Prime number calculation

integer n=3 ctr=0 prime primes=2
print 1
prime[1]=2; print 2
prime[2]=3; print 3

while (( primes < 99 ))
do
```

continues

Listing 11.2. continued

```
    n=n+2               # try only odd numbers
    ctr=0               # array index
    while (( ctr < primes ))
    do
        ctr=ctr+1
        if (( n % prime[ctr] == 0 ))
        then continue 2
        fi
    done
    primes=primes+1
    prime[primes]=n
    print $n
done
```

The program begins by declaring some variables to be integer. The *n* variable steps through the numbers to locate the primes; the *ctr* variable is an array index; the *prime* variable is an array holding all the prime numbers discovered; and *primes* is a count of the number of prime numbers in the *primes* array.

The first three prime numbers cannot be computed; they are considered primes by convention, so the program simply prints them. The array of known prime numbers is initialized with the values 2 and 3 to be used later.

The main program loop runs until the number of discovered primes reaches 99. Because the number 1 is not kept in the table, the program will stop when a total of 100 numbers have been discovered. Inside, the loop steps through the successive odd numbers. For each number, it tests whether the number can be evenly divided by one of the known primes. If so, the number is not prime, and the continue statement skips the rest of the loop and goes on to test the next number. If no primes evenly divide the number n, then it is a prime; the program stores the number in the primes array and prints it.

If you type the program in Listing 11.2 and try it, run the program at least once with the time command to measure how long it takes to run. On many systems, it takes only two to three seconds. Just for fun, try increasing the number 100 on the while loop to print more primes.

If you want to try your own hand at using Korn shell arithmetic, you might try modifying the primes program in Listing 11.2 to print 10 numbers across the line. You have to do some arithmetic to know when to print a line of numbers!

Summary

This chapter contains some hints on using arithmetic with the Bourne shell, and examines the much-improved capabilities of the Korn shell for calculation.

Because the Bourne shell contains no built-in support for arithmetic, there's no way to make arithmetic easy to learn or to do. However, the methods described for Bourne shell arithmetic work for the Korn shell, for all earlier versions of the Bourne shell, and even with some other shells, so they are good techniques to know.

The basic strategy for doing arithmetic with the Bourne shell centers around the fact that a number of UNIX commands support simple arithmetic. Given that, and the shell's ability to store the output of a command into a shell variable (using command substitution; see Chapter 3, "Shell Basics"), arithmetic is possible if not easy.

The primary tool is the `expr` command. The `expr` command prints the result of a calculation to standard output. A shell command substitution expression such as sum=`expr 4 + 7` will therefore capture the result of adding four and seven in the `sum` variable. Because you must write each term of an expression as a separate argument, it is not unusual to have to write such nonintuitive commands as result=`expr 4 \* \( 8 - 1 \)` to get the desired result.

Fortunately the Korn shell comes to the rescue with integer variables, arithmetic expressions in assignment statements, and the `let` command.

To set up a variable for doing arithmetic, use the `typeset` command. For example, `typeset -i sum=0` at once declares the variable `sum` to be used exclusively to hold numbers, and gives *sum* an initial value of zero. The Korn shell defines an alias called `integer` as a convenience; it means the same thing as `typeset -i`. To add a number to `sum`, just write a simple assignment: sum=sum+7. Even better, the arithmetic operators such as `*`, which ordinarily have another meaning to the shell, are automatically escaped inside an arithmetic expression so that you don't have to quote or backslash them.

If you haven't used `typeset` to declare a variable as an integer, you still can use the variable as the left side of an assignment by writing a `let` command. The `let` command acts as a global escape character, telling the shell that everything else in the command should be interpreted as arithmetic expressions. With `let`, you can write a calculation as `let sum='4*(7+1)'`.

The Korn shell also provides the special command ((...)) as an abbreviation for let. This abbreviation comes in handy on the if command, where you can write if ((sum<4)) and not be concerned with the shell mistaking < as the redirection operator; inside ((...)) the shell recognizes no redirection operators or wild cards.

The Korn shell even allows you to use numbers in bases other than 10.

For example, you can write 16#3c to mean hexadecimal 3C, and find that its value is 60:

```
$ let y=16#3c
$ print $y
60
$
```

Or you can add binary 101101 and 110110 to get 99:

```
$ let x=2#101101 y=2#110110 sum=x+y
$ print x=$x y=$y sum=$sum
x=45 y=54 sum=99
$
```

Unfortunately, you can't get the Korn shell to print numbers in any base other than 10.

If you have to write shell scripts that will work for the largest possible number of UNIX systems, you will have to forego Korn shell arithmetic; only the Bourne shell syntax is guaranteed to be available on any UNIX system.

## Chapter 12

Advanced Korn Shell Facilities

he primary purpose of the creation of the Korn shell was to enhance your productivity and the quality of your work. The Korn shell includes a number of new features that add to its power and flexibility considerably. Among these are an improved facility for managing background work (*job control*), the capability to "front-end" interactive programs (*coprocessing*), a menu-selection facility, and a more powerful `test` command.

For the most part, these facilities are intended to be used within shell scripts. The job control and command editing features actually are intended to assist with console work.

If you have mastered the material in the earlier parts of this book, get ready to turbocharge your applications with the new advanced facilities of the Korn shell.

Job Control

Some versions of UNIX System V Release 4 do not include support for job control. When the basic system omits job control support, the Korn shell disables or ignores the `bg` and `fg` commands.

ksh

The job control facility enhances your control over background jobs you start with the & operator (see Chapter 4, "Compound Commands") and enables you to switch a foreground command (one you started without &) into the background.

The job control facility uses the term *job* to refer to what previously has been called a command or a process. Specifically, a job is one or more programs executed as a unit. In the most prosaic terms, a job is what you create when you press the Return key after typing input to the shell (supposing you don't get the PS2 or > prompt; if you do, it means you haven't finished typing the commands for the job yet). A job can consist of a single command, several commands connected by pipelines, or an if-then-else-fi statement comprising a dozen or more pipelines.

A job can be executed in one of two ways: in the *foreground*, or in the *background*. A background job is a command list ending with the & operator. The shell does not wait for a background job to complete; it issues a prompt and lets you enter more commands while the background job continues to run unobtrusively and out of sight. Because you are not visibly reminded of background jobs, you could forget you have background jobs running, or what they are.

A foreground job, on the other hand, blocks terminal input. The shell waits for a foreground job to finish before sending you another prompt. If you enter a long-running command to run in the foreground (by not appending an & operator to the end of it), you have to wait for the command to finish unless you are willing to terminate the with commands execution with the kill or the INTR key.

The job control facility provides ways to relieve some of the traditional shortcomings of UNIX in managing your work. These improvements to your toolkit include four facilities: a SUSPEND keyboard function and the three new commands—jobs, bg, and fg.

The SUSPEND Keyboard Function

The job control facility depends on the support of a new keyboard function key called SUSPEND. By default, the SUSPEND function is assigned to the ^z (Ctrl + z) key. To determine the key currently assigned to SUSPEND, issue the command stty -a and look for the susp parameter; its value is the key on your keyboard to which the SUSPEND function is assigned. If no key is defined for this function, the entry susp = <undef> appears in the output of stty. You can assign any keyboard key to the SUSPEND function with the stty command like this:

```
$ stty susp ´^x´
```

12

Assigning Keyboard Function Keys

The standard terminal driver supports a number of control keys. These keys perform critical functions. You should know what these functions are and how to use stty to manage your terminal.

The following are the "normal" control key assignments:

Key	Function	Usage
^c	intr	Cancel all active processes
^d	eof	Send end-of-file on standard input
<undef>	quit	Cancel and dump core
^h	erase	Backspace one character
^q	start	Resume terminal output
^s	stop	Stop terminal output
^u	kill	Discard the current input line
^z	susp	Suspend the current job

Sometimes the system chooses other key values as the defaults for some keyboard functions. You can, for example, find ASCII DEL assigned for intr and @ for kill. You can easily set your own preferred values by using the stty command as follows:

```
$ stty intr '^c' kill '^u'
```

12

If you press the ^z key when nothing is running, nothing happens. If a command you've executed is running at the time, however, the command is stopped and placed in suspended animation. The program is unaffected by the suspension in any other way. The Korn shell tells you the job number of the halted job with a message that looks like this:

```
[2] + Stopped                 sort paydata
```

The number enclosed in brackets (here shown as [2]) is the *job number*. This is not the same as the process-ID. If a job consists of several commands, a whole family of processes might be associated with the job; figuring out which process-ID identifies the controlling process is not a trivial task. The job number eliminates that guesswork by associating one number with the entire group of processes.

When the currently running command is stopped with the SUSPEND key, your terminal is once again available as far as the shell is concerned, so it sends you a prompt. You can enter any command you like at this point, but you probably will want to run the bg command next. Regardless of what you do, the job you interrupted with the SUSPEND key is suspended and remains

ksh

suspended until you start it again. The only way to resume the execution of the suspended job is to execute either the bg or the fg command.

The bg Command

The bg command resumes the execution of a stopped job in the background. If you have only one stopped job at the moment, you don't have to provide any arguments to the bg command; by default it resumes the execution of the previous job you stopped.

If you've ever found yourself wishing you could cancel a running job and start it over with the & operator, or if you tell yourself you must get into the habit of using & because you spend too much time waiting for long-running jobs to finish when you don't have to, then the bg command is here to rescue you. Now, all you have to do when you find yourself twiddling your thumbs while that last job runs on and on is to press the SUSPEND key and type bg to move it into the background. The result is the same as if you had appended & to the job in the first place.

If you have more than one stopped job, you can tell the bg command which job should be moved to background execution by supplying the job's numeric process-ID as the bg command argument, if you know it, or supply the job's *job number*. You specify a process-ID as a simple number, such as bg 205. You must note a job number by prefixing it with a percent sign (%), as in bg %2. You also can use the command name associated with the job, such as bg %sort, as shown in the previous Stopped message.

Once you've stopped a foreground job and moved it into the background, your terminal is free. You can enter as many commands as you like. The shell informs you when your background job completes with a message like this:

```
[2] + Done                  sort paydata
```

The fg Command

The fg (*foreground*) command moves a stopped or background job into the foreground.

If you move a background job into the foreground, you do not receive a prompt after executing the `fg` command; you have to wait for the foreground job to complete before you can enter another shell command. Therefore, it's rather rare that someone uses the `fg` command to move a running background job into the foreground.

The `fg` command is used mostly to resume the execution of a foreground job you have stopped. With this facility, you can stop a full-screen editing session by using `emacs` or `vi` (the SUSPEND key function works just as well with a program that ties up your screen display as with batch-type commands), run a few other commands, then restart the interrupted edit session with the `fg` command.

By default, the `fg` command resumes the job you last stopped. If you want to resume another stopped job or a running background job, you must specify either the process-ID or the job number on the `fg` command, just as you would with `bg`. You specify a process-ID as a plain integer number—for example, `fg 1032` to resume process 1032. To specify a job, you must use the percent sign (%), such as in `fg %12` to resume job 12, or `fg %vi` to resume the job that is running the `vi` command.

The `kill` Command

The UNIX system has always provided a `kill` command. The job control facility of the shell provides a built-in version of the command that supports all the functionality of the `kill` system command and adds a couple of improvements.

The `kill` built-in command enables you to specify the signal number as a name rather than a number. To forcibly terminate a process, you must send it signal number 9. The `kill` built-in command enables you to specify this as `-KILL`. The entry for `kill` in Chapter 10, "Built-In Commands," lists the allowable signal names. You also can ask the `kill` built-in command to tell you the supported signal names, by entering `kill -l`.

The `kill` built-in command also enables you to specify a job number rather than a process-ID to designate the processes to be killed. No longer will you have to discover all the processes in a job with the `ps` command and then list them on the `kill` command. Simply enter the job number or command name; for example, `kill %2` or `kill %make`.

Coprocesses

ksh

The Korn shell augments the traditional pipe mechanism, which supports the passing of data in one direction only, with a new mechanism that allows your shell script to write to the standard input of another command and to read from its standard output. The invoked command, called a *coprocess*, is completely controlled by your shell script.

To initiate a coprocess, append the operator ¦& to the end of the command. Because coprocessing implies the redirection of both the standard input and standard output files of the called program, you should not use ordinary redirection on the command. The ¦& operator also implies a kind of detached execution similar to background mode, so you should not specify the & operator on the command line either. If you want, you can redirect the standard error file.

To send data or commands to the coprocess, use the print command with the -p option; this combination instructs the print command to write its arguments to the coprocess pipe rather than to standard output.

To read the output of the coprocess, use the read command with the -p option; this combination tells the read command to read from the coprocess pipe.

An Example

Listing 12.1 is a simple example of a coprocess in action. It prompts the user (presumably the system administrator) for a user-ID and, if the user-ID exists, allows individual fields of the password entry to be changed. The ed system utility is invoked as a coprocess to actually make the change.

Listing 12.1. A sample password file editor.

```
# chuser - change user information in /etc/passwd
tput clear                          # Clear the screen
while [ -z "$USER" ]
do
    print -n "User name? "; read USER etc
done

# Invoke the editor as a coprocess

ed - passwd ¦&
print -p "/^$USER"
IFS=":"
```

```
read -p name pwd uid gid info home shell etc
if [ "$name" = "?" ]
then
    print "No such user"
    print -p q
    exit 1
fi

print "Found $name:"
print

while :
do
    print "\nuid=$uid gid=$gid info='$info' home=$home shell=$shell"
    print -n "Change which field? "
    read ITEM etc
    case $ITEM in
        uid ) print -n "uid: "; read uid ;;
        gid ) print -n "gid: "; read gid ;;
        info) print -n "info: "; read info ;;
        home) print -n "home: "; read home ;;
        shell) print -n "shell: "; read shell ;;
        "")
            print -p c
            print -p "$name:$pwd:$uid:$gid:$info:$home:$shell"
            print -p .
            print -p w
            print -p q
            break ;;
    esac
done
```

If you would like to try this program, just copy the system password file to your own directory (cp/etc/passwd .).

You may notice that the cd command near the beginning of the program does not edit the system password file directly; it would be dangerous to do so even if you had the necessary permissions. If you don't have superuser permission, you must copy the edited passwd file back after you are done making changes.

The key elements of the program's operation center around its use of the ed command. The statement print -p "/^$USER" is sent to the standard input of ed due to the -p option; it instructs the editor to search for a line beginning with the string $USER. The shell then reads the editor's response: either the text of the password line or a question mark to indicate the name was not found.

If the name is not found, the shell sends the command q to the editor, telling it to quit. After printing an error message, the shell exits as well.

ksh

If the name is found, the shell enters a loop. On each iteration, the loop prints the current setting of each password field, then gives the user an opportunity to change one of the fields. If the user enters one of the field names, the shell prompts for the field value and stores the new value in the corresponding uid, gid, info, home, or shell variable. If the user hits return, the shell uses the editor to update the line:

- print -p c sends the command to change the current line.

- The next print -p command sends the new line image.

- The dot command (.) tells the editor to stop reading replacement lines.

- print -p w sends a write command to the editor.

- print -p q tells the editor to quit.

12

Running Multiple Coprocesses

To run a second coprocess, you first must free the special file descriptors the shell uses to communicate with the coprocess. You can reference these file descriptors only implicitly, by using the -p option on the print and read commands. Once you have transferred the input and output pipes to other file descriptors, you can use the |& command to start another coprocess.

You use the exec command to reassign file descriptors.

To reassign the coprocess input to a numbered file descriptor, use this command:

```
$ exec 3>&p
```

You must determine the proper file descriptor to use, of course. File descriptor 3 is usually available, unless you have used it for some other file earlier in your shell script. Notice the special notation for the coprocess pipe; the symbol p appears where a digit is usually expected.

After moving the coprocess input pipe to a numbered file descriptor, you can no longer use print -p to write to the program—you must print to the numbered file descriptor instead. Use the -u option of print to do so, as in print -u4.

To reassign the coprocess output to a numbered file descriptor, use output redirection:

```
$ exec 4<&p
```

To force the coprocess to terminate, you close its input file. You can do so using the `exec` command and the redirection operator signifying close:

```
$ exec 3>&-
```

Alternatively, you can write appropriate commands to the coprocessor to tell it to stop, if it supports such commands.

The `select` Statement

The `select` statement is an addition to the Korn shell that is not available in the Bourne shell. Its purpose is to simplify the generation of a menu screen from which the user selects. To facilitate this process, the `select` statement is a combination of the `while` and the `case` statements.

The basic structure of a `select` statement is similar to a loop:

```
select var in words
do
    ...actions...
done
```

The `select` statement continues to loop until you execute a `break` command or the user cancels the shell script.

For *words*, you list each of the choices you want to appear on the menu. The shell formats a menu display (without clearing the screen) by listing each word in *words*, preceded by a selection number running from 1 through the number of words listed. The shell then prompts the user to enter one of the numbers preceding a menu selection. The user's actual entry is stored in a shell variable called REPLY, and the word text the number selects is stored in the variable name you gave as *var*.

Listing 12.2 does nothing useful, but demonstrates the general behavior of the `select` command. You are encouraged to enter the example into a file and run it.

Listing 12.2. Building a menu with `select`.

```
# Sample execution of select

PS3="Enter the number of your choice: "
select choice in "Accounts file maintenance" \
        "Payee file maintenance" \
        "Write checks" \
        "Balance monthly statement" \
```

ksh

Listing 12.2. continued

```
        "Done"
do
    case $REPLY in
    1)    print -r . acctmenu ;;
    2)    print -r . paymenu  ;;
    3)    print -r . dochecks ;;
    4)    print -r . balance  ;;
    5)    exit 0 ;;
    esac
done
```

12

First, notice the assignment to variable PS3. The select statement uses this variable as the text to print at the bottom of the menu to prompt the user for input. If you do not supply a value, PS3 defaults to the string #?, not a very informative prompt.

The select statement demonstrates that you can use any text you want for each of the menu item selections. If the list of items is too long to fit on one line, append a backslash (\) to continue onto the next line.

The body of this do...done loop simply prints the name of another shell script that would be invoked to execute the user's selection in a full implementation. Of course, you can write any list of commands you want for each selection number.

If you run this shell script, you will see something like this:

```
$ menu
1) Accounts file maintenance
2) Payee file maintenance
3) Write checks
4) Balance monthly statement
5) Done
Enter number of choice: _
```

Notice that the shell has numbered each of your selection words. Due to this automatic numbering, you can easily construct a menu even when you don't know how many selections there are. For example, the statement select FILE in *.c would generate an unknown number of items.

If the user enters nothing at all, the body of the do loop is not executed; the select statement simply reprints the menu and prompts for input again. This is a feature for the user's benefit; most users will quickly learn how to get a fresh display of the selection menu.

If the user enters an invalid selection (a character other than a number, or a number that is larger than the number of items in the menu), the shell sets *var* to the null string and sets REPLY to the actual input. You can either test for an improper reply or ignore it.

The [[...]] Statement

ksh

The [[...]] command is similar to the [] command but offers improved readability and supports more kinds of tests. It is available only with the Korn shell.

The standard test command, which can be written also as [*expr*], allows the use of -a and -o (for and and or respectively) to combine tests. The [[...]] command provides the same capability, but allows the use of the operators && and ¦¦ to indicate and and or relationships. Because you probably are accustomed to reading && as and, and ¦¦ as or, a compound test written with the [[...]] command is easier to read.

The [...] command supports the same tests whether you use the Korn shell or Bourne shell. The [[...]] command supports many of the same test expressions, and adds some more. Table 12.1 lists all the test expressions supported by the [[...]] command.

12

Table 12.1. Conditional expressions used with [[...]].

Expression	Condition Tested
-b *file*	*file* is a block-special file
-c *file*	*file* is a character-special file
-d *file*	*file* is a directory
-f *file*	*file* is a regular file
-g *file*	*file* has the set-group-ID bit set
-k *file*	*file* has the sticky bit set
-n *string*	*string* has a non-zero length
-o *option*	Option name *option* (vi, noclobber, and so on) is set
-p *file*	*file* is a named pipe
-r *file*	*file* is readable
-s *file*	Size of *file* is greater than zero
-t [*num*]	File descriptor *num* (default 1) is open and is a terminal
-u *file*	*file* has the set-user-ID bit set
-w *file*	*file* is writable
-x *file*	*file* has execute permission

continues

ksh

Table 12.1. continued

Expression	Condition Tested
-z *string*	*string* has a length of zero
-G *file*	*file* group matches the effective group-ID
-L *file*	*file* is a symbolic link
-O *file*	*file* owner matches the effective user-ID
-S *file*	*file* is a socket
s1 = *s2*	String *s1* does not match pattern *s2*
s1 != *s2*	String *s1* matches pattern *s2*
s1 < *s2*	String *s1* sorts alphabetically before *s2*
s1 > *s2*	String *s1* sorts alphabetically after *s2*
file1 -nt *file2*	*file1* is newer than *file2*
file1 -ot *file2*	*file1* is older than *file2*
file1 -ef *file2*	*file1* and *file2* are the same file
e1 -eq *e2*	Expressions *e1, e2* evaluate to the same value
e1 -ne *e2*	Expressions *e1, e2* evaluate to unequal values
e1 -lt *e2*	Expression *e1* is less than *e2*
e1 -le *e2*	Expression *e1* is less than or equal to *e2*
e1 -gt *e2*	Expression *e1* is greater than *e2*
e1 -ge *e2*	Expression *e1* is greater than or equal to *e2*

The following are a few examples of the use of the [[...]] statement type:

- [[x+2 -gt y-3]] Evaluate the expressions x+2 and y-3 and compare the results. If the value of the first expression is greater than the second, set an exit value of 0 (true). The -gt operator implies numeric evaluation, so the variables x and y do not have to be declared integer with typeset.

- [[/bin/ksh -ef /usr/bin/ksh]] Test whether the path names /bin/ksh and /usr/bin/ksh are real or symbolic links to the same file. In UNIX System V Release 4, the result would be true (exit value is zero).

- [["x$PrintFlag" = "xP" ¦¦ "x$DebugFlag" = "xD"]] If the string value of PrintFlag is P, then the entire expression is true. Otherwise, if the string value of variable DebugFlag is D, the value of the entire expression is true. The expression is false only if both comparisons are unequal. Notice the technique used to support the case where either PrintFlag or DebugFlag is the null string.

- [[-t 0]] Test whether the standard input file is assigned to a terminal device.

- [[-x $FILE && ! -d $FILE]] Test whether the path name value of FILE is not a directory and has execute permission. Testing for -x alone is not sufficient to confirm that a file is executable, because directories often have execute permission. Notice the use of ! to invert the sense of a test.

Array Variables

12

ksh

This chapter introduces you to array variables. Array variables are a standard feature of the Korn shell, but are not supported at all by the Bourne shell. If you plan to implement a shell script so that it can be executed by either the Bourne or Korn shell, you must not use array variables in the script.

Introducing Array Variables

A variable with more than one value is called an *array* variable. The terminology is from mathematics, where a structured set of values sharing a common name is called an array. A single value in the array is called an *element*, and is referenced by giving the name of the array and a number (called an *index*) to identify the desired element.

In mathematics, array elements are counted starting at 1, and an array can have an arbitrarily large number of elements. In the Korn shell, array elements are counted starting at 0, and an array can have no more than 512 elements. (Some versions of the Korn shell allow more than 512 elements per array.) If an array has 12 elements, the indexes range from 0 to 11.

Each element of an array can be individually set or unset, null or non-null.

You do not have to assign values to the elements of an array in any particular order. That is, you can assign a value to elements 0 and 511 and leave the other elements unset if you want. Also, you can assign a value to element 511 before assigning a value to element 0.

Assigning Values to an Array

To assign a value to one element of an array, use the assignment statement.

ksh

The special notation [*index*] follows the variable name to specify the element to receive the value. The following example shows how to assign some values to an array:

```
$ fruits[0]=orange
$ fruits[1]="rome apple"
$ fruits[2]=grape
$ fruits[3]=banana
```

You do not have to use typeset to declare a variable name as an array; you can make any shell variable, of any type, an array variable simply by using array notation with the variable. You might want to use typeset to declare an array of integer variables, and specify the number of elements in the array at the same time:

```
$ typeset -i fruits[50]
```

By specifying -i you restrict the entire array to contain only integer values. By specifying [50] you do not, however, restrict the array to only 50 elements. The Korn shell treats the number of elements as a comment. You can later assign values to array elements greater than 49 if you want.

You can assign a value to all the elements of an array at once by using the set command. Use the -A *name* option, like this:

```
$ set -A fruits orange "rome apple" grape banana
```

The set statement discards any previously assigned elements of the array and sets the array to contain just the new values. After this set statement, the fruits array will contain just four elements, even if it previously contained more than four.

Beware of using the set command after you have already used typeset to associate attributes with the array: the set command destroys any attributes set with typeset. If you must use typeset with the array, execute typeset after the set command; the values assigned with set will be converted to the specified type.

For example, to set all the elements of fruits to uppercase, use these commands:

```
$ set -A fruits orange "rome apple" grape banana
$ typeset -u fruits
```

If you want an array element to be unset even if you have previously assigned a value to it, use the unset command and specify the index of the element to be unset:

```
$ unset fruits[3]
```

Referencing Elements of an Array

If you reference an array variable without specifying an element index, the Korn shell returns the value of element 0.

Using the example of fruits, you would get the following result:

```
$ print $fruits
ORANGE
$
```

To reference any other element of an array, you must specify an element index. But the obvious notation won't work:

```
$ print $fruits[3]
ORANGE[3]
$
```

The problem is that the Korn shell strives above all to maintain full compatibility with Bourne shell syntax. Compatibility is very important because it enables Korn shell users to use the many thousands of shell scripts already written for the Bourne shell without modifying the scripts.

Unfortunately, the expression $fruits[3] is valid Bourne shell syntax; it expands to the value of fruits followed by the string [3]. For the expression to be compatible, the Korn shell must do the same thing. To refer to a specific element in an array variable, you must use the general notation ${*varname*[*index*]}.

For example, you can display element 3 of fruits as follows:

```
$ print ${fruits[3]}
BANANA
$
```

To expand all the elements of an array, use the special index * or @. Elements of the array that are unset are just ignored; all other elements are listed in order of increasing index with a blank between each element.

For example, using the fruits array, you would get

```
$ print ${fruits[*]}
ORANGE ROME APPLE GRAPE BANANA
$
```

Notice that element 1, which was assigned the value "rome apple", appears as two words in the expansion of ${fruits[*]}. This might cause you a problem if you intended to use the expanded value in another command such as grep:

```
$ grep ${fruits[1]} farm.report
grep: can't open APPLE
$
```

Here, grep took the first word of the value of ${fruits[1]} (namely, ROME) as the search string, and the second word as the first of two files (APPLE and farm.report) to be searched. To avoid this problem, use ${fruits[@]} to expand the elements of fruits as if they were quoted strings.

The ls command shows the difference between * and @ more clearly:

```
$ ls ${fruits[*]}
ORANGE: No such file or directory
ROME: No such file or directory
APPLE: No such file or directory
GRAPE: No such file or directory
PAPAYA: No such file or directory
$ ls "${fruits[@]"
ORANGE: No such file or directory
ROME APPLE: No such file or directory
GRAPE: No such file or directory
PAPAYA: No such file or directory
$
```

> ***Note:*** the expression ${fruits[@]} must be enclosed in double quotes to avoid retokenization of the command line by the shell. The string substituted by [@] does not actually contain double quotes, so the shell still separates the substituted value into words at each blank without the explicit double quotes.

The Korn shell also lets you use an arithmetic expression as an array index. (Arithmetic expressions were explained in Chapter 11, "Shell Arithmetic.") Any variable names you use in the expression must either be integer variables (declared with typeset -i) or ordinary string variables with a numeric value. Here are a few examples:

```
$ typeset -i i=3 m=1
$ j=2
$ print ${fruits[i]}
PAPAYA
$ print ${fruits[i+1]}

$ print ${fruits[m+1]}
GRAPE
$ print ${fruits[j]}
GRAPE
$ print ${fruits[j+m]}
PAPAYA
$
```

Because you can use an arithmetic expression as an array index, you can easily write a loop to process elements of the array:

```
$ integer ctr=0
$ while ((ctr < 4))
> do
> print element $ctr contains "´${fruits[ctr]}´"
> let ctr=ctr+1
> done
element 0 contains ´ORANGE´
element 1 contains ´ROME APPLE´
element 2 contains ´GRAPE´
element 3 contains ´PAPAYA´
$
```

Determining the Number of Elements in an Array

In the previous example, you knew that the fruits array contained only four elements. But using a literal number is not possible when you don't know how many elements an array contains. The Korn shell provides a special parameter that gives the number of elements in an array:

```
${#varname[*]}
```

or

```
${#varname[@]};
```

Either expression gives the same result:

```
$ print ${#fruits[*]}
4
$ print ${#fruits[@]}
4
$
```

Using the number-of-elements parameter, you can rewrite the loop to work for any number of elements:

```
$ integer ctr=0
$ while ((ctr < ${#fruits[*]}))
> do
> print element $ctr contains "´${fruits[ctr]}´"
> let ctr=ctr+1
> done
element 0 contains ´ORANGE´
element 1 contains ´ROME APPLE´
element 2 contains ´GRAPE´
element 3 contains ´PAPAYA´
$
```

ksh

You can also use the number-of-elements parameter to add another element to the end of an array, like this:

```
$ fruits[${#fruits[*]}]=pear
$ print ${fruits[*]}
ORANGE ROME APPLE GRAPE PAPAYA PEAR
$
```

An Example Using Variable Arrays

The following shell script scans all the files in the current directory and maintains a count of each unique file name suffix found; that is, it counts all the files whose names end in .c, for example. You can use the shell script to find out which set of suffixes are in use in a particular directory. The shell script uses two arrays: one to keep track of the suffixes that have been found, and another to count the number of files found with each suffix.

Listing 12.3 presents the text of the shell script.

Listing 12.3. The `suffixes` shell script.

```
# suffixes - print usage of filename suffixes

typeset -i count[50] last i

for FILE in *
do
    s=$(expr "$FILE" : '.*\.\([^.][^.]*\)$')
    i=0
    while ((i<last))
    do
        if [ "$s" = "${suffix[i]}" ]
        then
            let count[i]=count[i]+1
            continue 2
        fi
        i=i+1
    done
    # Suffix not found - add to list
    suffix[last]="$s"
    count[last]=1
    last=last+1
done

# print out the suffix list
i=0
while ((i<last))
do
```

```
        print "suffix '${suffix[i]}' occurs ${count[i]} times"
        let i=i+1
done
```

The following shows a sample output from the `suffixes` shell script:

```
suffix 'c' occurs 16 times
suffix 'h' occurs 13 times
suffix '' occurs 18 times
suffix 'xpm' occurs 4 times
suffix 'a' occurs 1 times
suffix 'out' occurs 1 times
```

The `typeset` statement declares some integer variables the program will use: `count` to hold frequency counts for each suffix, `last` to record the number of different suffixes found, and `i` as a loop control variable.

The main body of the program is executed for each file in the current directory by the `for` statement.

The first assignment in the loop uses the UNIX `expr` command to find the suffix of the file name. The suffix is returned without the leading period (`.`). If the file name has no suffix, the variable s will be set to the null string. The `expr` command uses a special notation called *regular expressions* to describe the portion to be cut from a string. This book has not discussed regular expressions, but regular expressions are necessary to the proper use of many UNIX commands. To find out more about regular expressions, consult a more advanced book such as *UNIX Programmer's Reference* by John Valley (Que, 1991; ISBN 0-88022-536-X).

The `while` loop searches the variable array named `suffix` for the presence of an element whose value matches the current suffix. To do the search, the code must examine each of the array elements in turn, using the integer variable `i` to step through the index numbers. If an element of the `suffix` array matches the string value of s, then the same index value `i` is used to update the corresponding counter in the `count` array.

If the suffix s is not found, then it's a new suffix and has to be added to the list of suffixes kept in the `suffix` array. The statement `suffix[last]="$s"` stores the new string in the next available element of the array. The statement `count[last]=1` initializes the count for that suffix to 1 because one file with that suffix has just been found.

Finally, the command `last=last+1` updates the count of array elements in use.

12

| ksh |

When the `while` loop completes, the array variable `suffix` contains all the unique suffixes as its elements, and the array variable `count` contains the number of times each suffix was found in a file name. The final short `while` loop steps through the two variable arrays to print a report of the suffixes that were found.

This program would be much more difficult to write without array variables. The problem is that you have no idea how many different suffixes will be found while scanning the directory, so you can't use hard-coded variable names such as `suffix1` and `suffix2` to keep the list of suffixes in. If you try to use a string to hold the suffix list and counts (for example, `suffix= "c h y xpm"` and `count="8 15 7 12"`), you will find it difficult to search the suffix list, and difficult to increment the counts.

Summary

| ksh |

In this final chapter you've encountered some very powerful facilities of the Korn shell: job management, coprocessing, the `select` statement, and array variables.

Job management—consisting of the `jobs`, `bg`, and `fg` commands, and the new built-in command `kill`—provides a new level of control over foreground and background command execution. The STOP key (you assign a particular key to the STOP function with the `stty` command) enables you to temporarily halt the execution of any program, even a full-screen editor like `vi`. Once the execution is stopped, you can execute other commands, move the stopped command into background execution with the `bg` command, or move the stopped command into foreground execution with the `fg` command. The job management facility gives you improved control over your terminal, letting you decide what to do at any moment.

The coprocessing feature lets you redirect both the standard input and standard output of a command to your shell script. With both sides of a command's I/O stream redirected, the command is completely under your control. If the command is an editor such as `ed`, you can write an editing command to its standard input, and then read the result from the editor's standard output. When you use coprocessing, you effectively substitute your program for the terminal; you decide what input the coprocessing command receives, and you read its output.

The whole purpose of the `select` statement is to simplify the process of communicating with the user in a menu style. The syntax of `select` is similar to that of the `for` command: it has a control variable and an `if` clause followed by a list of words.

The body of the `select` statement consists of `do` and `done`, between which you provide any commands you want but usually a `case` statement. The `select` statement repeats the list of commands between `do` and `done` over and over until the `break` command is executed.

The `select` statement automatically formats your choices into a menu display, prompts the user for a reply, sets the control variable to the choice the user selected, and then executes your statements between `do` and `done`.

Array variables, the final topic of this chapter, provide a feature available in most programming languages but long missing from the shell. Simply put, an array variable is like a row of boxes, each labeled with a number from 0 to 511 (or more), into each of which you can store a distinct string value. You can assign a value to one of the boxes by using a subscripted assign statement; for example, `message[5]="File not found"` assigns the text string `File not found` to the sixth value of the message array. To retrieve a value from one of the boxes, use an expression like `${message[5]}`; its value is the string in the sixth box.

12

With the addition of these facilities and many others discussed earlier in this book, the Korn shell takes its place among the family of programming languages as a full-featured tool.

Part

Quick Reference

Shell Syntax

he syntax of the Bourne and Korn shell languages is complex and subtle. This appendix describes the syntax of the language as accurately and completely as possible without overwhelming you with nit-picking details. For example, newline characters are permitted wherever the semicolon (;) is permitted, and in many other places as well; the syntax description here does not describe the usage rules for newline characters at all because you probably will develop a feel for it as your familiarity with the shell grows.

This section only describes syntax—the meaning and usage of the shell language is described fully in the main chapters of this book. If you need to know how to use a statement, command, or syntactical element, please refer to the chapter that deals with that particular subject.

Syntax descriptions use the following notation conventions:

Convention	*Meaning*
monospaced	A typeface (called *monospace*) similar to that of a typewriter emphasizes words and special characters that must be typed literally. Do not make any substitutions for text written this way.

continues

Convention	Meaning
italics	Syntactic variables are written in italics. You must substitute a value for the word or words in italics when you enter the command.
[...]	Text enclosed in square brackets is optional. The brackets themselves should not be entered. Brackets that you are intended to type are written in monospace: [ ]. Syntactic brackets are written like this: [].
...	An ellipsis (...) means that you may repeat the immediately preceding element as many times as you want. If a separator is needed between repetitions, it will be shown immediately before the ellipsis, like this: *filename*,... (meaning "enter any number of file names separated by commas").

A

Statement Groups

---

job

list newline
list ;
background-command
coprocess

---

list

statement
job
job ... *statement*

---

background command

statement &

```
coprocess

statement ¦&
```

```
statement

simple-command
compound-statement [ io-redirection ... ]
```

Compound Statements

```
if Statement

if list ; then list ; [ else-clause ] fi
```

```
else-clause

[ elif list ; then list ; ] ... else list ;
```

```
case Statement

case word in case-item ... esac
```

```
case-item

[ ( ] pattern [ ¦ pattern ] ... ) list ;;
```

for Statement

for *name* [in *word* ...] ; do *list* ; done

while Statement

while *list* ; do *list* ; done
until *list* ; do *list* ; done

select Statement

select *name* [in *word* ...] ; do *list* ; done

Conditional Statement

statement && *statement*
statement ¦¦ *statement*

Pipe

statement ¦ *statement*

Expression Statement

((*expression*))

Test Statement

[[*test-expression*]]

A

Brace Group

{ *list* ; }

Subshell

(*list* ;)

Function Definition

name () *brace-group*
function *name brace-group*

Simple Command

[*name*=[*word*] ...] [*token* ...]

A

Arithmetic Expression

expression

term
(*expression*)
unary-op expression
expression binary-op expression

term

integer-variable-name
[*radix* #] *constant*

---

radix

Decimal number from 2 to 36 (defaults to base 10)

---

constant

A string of digits and letters

---

unary-op

-	Sign inversion
!	Logical negation (not)
~	Bitwise 1's complement

---

binary-op (Priority)

*	1	Multiplication
/	1	Integer division
%	1	Remainder
+	2	Addition
-	2	Subtraction
<<	3	Left shift
>>	3	Right shift
<	4	Less than
<=	4	Less than or equal to
>	4	Greater than
>=	4	Greater than or equal to
==	5	Equal to
!=	5	Not equal to
&	6	Bitwise and
^	7	Bitwise exclusive or
¦	8	Bitwise or
&&	9	Logical and
¦¦	10	Logical or
=	11	Assignment
op=	11	Same as *expr* = *expr op expr*

A

```
op=

*=  /=  %=  +=  -=  <<=  >>=  &=  ^=  ¦=
```

Test Expression

```
test-expression

test
test-expression && test
test-expression ¦¦ test
```

test (Specify Any *word* **for** `file`**)**

-r `file`	`file` is readable
-w `file`	`file` is writable
-x `file`	`file` has execute permission
-f `file`	`file` is a regular file
-d `file`	`file` is a directory
-c `file`	`file` is a character-special file
-b `file`	`file` is a block-special file
-p `file`	`file` is a named pipe
-u `file`	`file` has set-uid permission
-g `file`	`file` has set-gid permission
-k `file`	`file` has sticky bit set
-s `file`	`file` size is greater than zero
-L `file`	`file` is a symbolic link
-O `file`	`file` owner is effective-user-ID
-G `file`	`file` group is effective-group-ID
-S `file`	`file` is a socket
-t [`fd`]	`file` descriptor `fd` is a terminal
-o `name`	Option `name` is set
-z `file`	String `word` is zero length
-n `file`	String `word` is not zero length

Operators That Match a Word to a Wild-Card Pattern

word = *pattern*   String *word* matches *pattern*
word != *pattern*   String *word* does not match *pattern*

Operators That Compare the Sort Order of Two Strings

s1 < *s2*   Word *s1* is less than *s2*
s1 > *s2*   Word *s1* is greater than *s2*

Operators That Compare the Timestamps of Two Files

word -nt *word*   Newer than
word -ot *word*   Older than

Operator That Checks for Links

word -ef *word*   Is the same file as

Operators That Compare the Values of Arithmetic Expressions

e1 -eq *e2*   Equal to
e1 -ne *e2*   Not equal to
e1 -lt *e2*   Less than
e1 -le *e2*   Less than or equal
e1 -gt *e2*   Greater than
e1 -ge *e2*   Greater than or equal

Tokens

---

name

letter [*letter* or *digit*] ...

---

token

word
io-redirection

A

word

string...

---

string

regular-char ...
double-quoted-string
single-quoted-string
back-quoted-string
variable

---

double-quoted-string

" [\c or *not-dq* or *variable*] ... "

---

single-quoted-string

´ [any character but ´] ... ´

---

back-quoted-string

` [ \c or *not-bq* or *variable* ] ... `

---

not-dq

Any ASCII character except "

---

not-bq

` Any ASCII character except `

---

regular-char

Any nonspecial character

Patterns

---

pattern

pattern-char...

---

range

c	Matches any character except newline
c1-c2	Matches all characters from *c1* to *c2*

```
pattern-char
```

`regular-char`	Matches itself
`[ [range]... ]`	Matches any listed character
`[ [!] [range]... ]`	Matches any unlisted character
`?`	Matches any character
`*`	Matches any length string
`?(pattern[¦pattern]...)`	Matches any *pattern*
`*(pattern[¦pattern]...)`	Matches zero or more occurrences
`+(pattern[¦pattern]...)`	Matches one or more occurrences
`!(pattern[¦pattern]...)`	Matches anything except any *pattern*

Variable Reference

A

```
variable
```

`$@`	Command arguments
`$*`	Command arguments
`$#`	Number of arguments
`$-`	Option flags
`$?`	Last exit value
`$$`	Current process-ID
`$!`	Process-ID of last background job
`$digit`	*n*th command argument
`$name`	Value of variable *name*
`${name}`	Value of variable *name*
`${name[:]-word}`	*word* if null or not set
`${name[:]+word}`	*word* unless null or not set
`${name[:]=word}`	Assign *word* if null or not set
`${name[:]?word}`	Print *word* and exit if not set
`${name#pattern}`	Remove small left pattern
`${name##pattern}`	Remove large left pattern
`${name%pattern}`	Remove small right pattern
`${name%%pattern}`	Remove large right pattern
`${#name}`	String length of value
`${#name[*]}`	Number of elements in array
`${#name[@]}`	Number of elements in array

I/O Redirection

---

io-redirection

[*digit*] *file-redirect word*	Redirect I/O to or from file *word*
[*digit*] *fd-redirect fd*	Redirect I/O to or from file descriptor *fd*
[*digit*] <&-	Close input
[*digit*] >&-	Close output
here-document	Read from an inline file

A

---

file-redirect

<	Assign input from
>	Assign output to
>>	Append output to
>¦	Assign output and ignore *noclobber*
<>	Assign input and output

---

fd-redirect

<&	Read from open file descriptor
>&	Write to open file descriptor

---

here-document

<<[-] *word*	Read up to *word*

B

Syntax of Built-In Commands

This appendix lists the built-in commands available with the Bourne and Korn shells. Those commands provided only by the Korn shell are highlighted with the KSH icon, in the style used throughout this book.

```
: [ arg ... ]
```

```
. filename
```

```
alias [ -x ] [ name[=value] ] ...
alias -t [ name ... ]
```

```
bg [ job ]
```

```
break [ n ]
```

```
cd [ dirname ]
```

```
cd -
cd old new
```

```
continue [ n ]
```

```
echo [ arg ... ]
```

```
eval arg ...
```

B

```
exec command
```

```
exit [ n ]
```

```
export name ...
```

```
fc [ -e editor ] [ -nlr ] first last
```

```
fc -e - [ old=new ] [ command ]
```

```
fg [ job ]
```

```
getopts options name [ arg ... ]
```

```
hash [ -r ] name ...
```

```
jobs [ -lp ] job
```

```
jobs [-lnp] [job...]
```

```
kill [ -sig ] job ...
```

```
let expr ...
```

```
newgrp [ - ] [ group ]
```

```
print [ -Rnprsu[n] ] [ arg ... ]
```

```
pwd
```

B

```
read [ name ... ]
```

```
read [ -prsu[n] ] [ name?prompt ] [ name ... ]
```

```
readonly [ name ... ]
```

```
return [ n ]
```

```
set [ ±aefhkntuvx ] [ arg ... ]
```

B

```
set [ ±aefhkmnpstuvx ][ ±o option ]...[ ±A name][arg...]
```

```
shift [ n ]
```

```
test expr
[ expr ]
```

```
times
```

```
trap [ command ] [ signal ... ]
```

```
type name
```

ksh
```
typeset ±f[tux] [ name ... ]
typeset [ -FLRZeilprtux[n] ] [ name=value ... ]
```

```
ulimit [ -[HS][a] ]
ulimit [ -[HS]cdfnstv ] [ limit ]
```

```
umask [ nnn ]
```

ksh
```
unalias name ...
```

B

```
unset name ...
```

ksh
```
unset [ -f ] name ...
```

```
wait [ n ]
```

ksh
```
whence [ -v ] name
```

Shell Environment

his appendix includes descriptions of the interfaces to the shell besides its command language:
shell invocation options and predefined variables.

Shell Invocation Options

Option	Usage
-c *string*	Execute commands in *string*, then exit
-i	Interactive shell
-p	Permit real and effective IDs to differ
-r	Restricted shell
-s	Read commands from standard input

Set Command Options

Option	Usage
-a	Export a variable when set
-e	Exit immediately on a nonzero command exit status
-f	Disable file name generation
-h	Remember functions when read
-k	Place all keyword arguments in the environment
-n	Read commands but do not execute them (*no execute*)
-t	Exit after reading and executing one command
-u	Treat a reference to an unset variable as an error
-v	Print shell input as it is read (*verbose*)
-x	Print commands before executing them (*trace*)

Named Options (-o Flags)

Option	Usage
allexport	Same as -a
bgnice	Run background jobs at reduced priority
emacs	Enable emacs command editing mode
errexit	Same as -e
gmacs	Enable gmacs command editing mode
ignoreeof	Ignore keyboard end-of-file
keyword	Same as -k
markdirs	Append / to generated directory names
monitor	Same as -m
noclobber	Prevent output redirection to an existing file
noexec	Same as -n
noglob	Same as -f
nolog	Do not save functions in history file
nounset	Same as -u
privileged	Same as -p

C

Option	Usage
trackall	Same as -h
verbose	Same as -v
vi	Enable vi command editing mode
viraw	Process each character as it is typed
xtrace	Same as -x

Predefined Variables

Name	Set by	Usage	Value Format
_	Shell	Last command executed	Path
CDPATH	User	Directory search path	[dir][:[dir]]...
COLUMNS	User	Screen width	Integer
EDITOR	User	Preferred editor	Command
ERRNO	Shell	Status of last system call	Integer
ENV	User	Command profile script	Path
FCEDIT	Shell/User	Preferred command editor	Command
FPATH	User	Function search path	[dir][:[dir]]...
IFS	Shell/User	Field separator characters	String
HISTFILE	User	Command history file	Path
HISTSIZE	User	Minimum history lines	Integer
HOME	System	User's home directory	Path
LINENO	Shell	Current line in script	Integer
LINES	User	Num of lines for select	Integer
LOGNAME	System	User login name	String
MAIL	System/User	File to check for mail	Path
MAILCHECK	System/User	Mail check frequency	Integer
MAILPATH	User	List of mailboxes	file[:file]...
OLDPWD	Shell	Previous working directory	Path
OPTARG	Shell	Command parsing	String

continues

Name	Set by	Usage	Value Format
OPTIND	Shell	Command parsing	Integer
PATH	System/User	Command search path	[*dir*][:[*dir*]]...
PPID	Shell	Parent process-ID	Integer
PS1	Shell/User	Primary prompt string	String
PS2	Shell/User	Secondary prompt string	String
PS3	Shell/User	Prompt for select	String
PS4	Shell/User	Debug tracing prefix	String
PWD	Shell	Current directory path	Path
RANDOM	Shell	Random number	Integer
REPLY	Shell	User's reply to select	String
SECONDS	Shell	Time since shell invoked	Integer
SHELL	System/User	User's preferred shell	Path
TMOUT	Shell/User	Maximum idle time (seconds)	Integer
VISUAL	User	Edit command	Command

Shell Built-In Variables

Name	Usage
$?	Last command exit value
$#	Number of shell arguments
$$	Current process-ID
$0	Invocation name of shell
$1 - $9	Shell arguments 1 to 9
$*	All shell arguments ("$1" "$2"...)
$@	All shell arguments ("$1" "$2"...)

UNIX Commands

his appendix presents a brief description of almost every UNIX command. In times past, the need for a written command summary was small because every UNIX system included a set of on-line manual pages. Since System V Release 3.2, however, there has been a growing tendency to omit the on-line manual pages. You should find these pages to be a handy reference when you know the command but can't remember its format or the meaning of an option.

For more reference information about a UNIX command, consult *The UNIX V System 4 User's Reference Manual* (Prentice-Hall, 1986; ISBN 0-13-931510-1) or the documentation accompanying your UNIX system.

D

ar   Archive Maintenance Tool

```
ar [ -V ] [ - ]key [ posname ] afile [ name ... ]
```

-V	Print version number
key	Archive function (one of the following):
	d[s][v] Delete *name* ... members

r[u][v][c][s][abi]	Replace *name* with like-named files
q[v][c][s]	Quick append of *name* files
t[v][s]	List archive table of contents
p[s]	Print named members (default is all)
m[v][s][abi]	Move *names* to archive end or to *posname*
x[v][s]	Extract named files (default is all)

posname   Member name (valid only with a/b/i)

afile   Archive file name

name   Member file names to be added, deleted, and so on

The optional suffixes to *key* have the following meanings:

a   Move/insert members *after* posname

b   Move/insert members *before* posname

c   Suppress archive created message

i   Same as b

s   Force regeneration of symbol table

u   Replace only if file is newer than member

v   Verbose (with t, print file details)

---

at   Schedule Execution of Commands at a Later Time

```
at [ -f script ] [ -m ] time [ date ] [ + num increment ]

at -l [job ... ]

at -r job ...
```

-f   From *script* read the commands to be executed

-l   List specified (default is all) jobs scheduled

-m   Mail notice of job completion

-r   Remove the specified jobs

time   One of *h*[:]*m*[am ¦ pm][zulu], noon, midnight, now

date   One of *Month day*[,*year*], today, tomorrow

increment   One of minutes, hours, days, weeks, months, years

atq

List Jobs Submitted with at **or** batch

```
atq [ -c ] [ -n ] [ username ... ]
```

-c   List jobs in order of creation
-n   Print just the total number of queued jobs
username List only the named users' jobs (privileged)

---

atrm

Remove Jobs Submitted by at **or** batch

```
atrm [ -afi ] arg ...
```

-a   Remove all jobs
-f   Suppress error messages
-i   Inquire for each job whether it should be removed
arg   User name or job number

---

awk

Data Processing Language

D

```
awk [ -Fc ] [ -f prog ] [ 'string' ] [ args... ] [ file...]
```

-Fc   Input fields are separated by the character *c*
-f *prog* Read the awk program text from file *prog*
string' Read the awk program text from *string*
args   Define awk variables in the form name=value
file   Read data from *file* (use - to read standard input)

banner   **Print Large Block Letters**

```
banner word ...
```

word   Print the list of words in large letters

basename   **Return File Name Portion of a Path Name**

```
basename path [ suffix ]
```

path   Any absolute or relative path name
suffix   String to be stripped from the end of the file name

batch   **Submit a Job for Immediate Execution**

```
batch
```

D

bc   **Calculator and Math Programming Language**

```
bc [ -c ] [ -l ] [ file ... ]
```

-c   Compile only; send dc commands to standard output
-l   First file is an arbitrary-precision math library

bdiff

diff **Front End for Big Files**

```
bdiff file1 file2 [ n ] [ -s ]
```

file1 File to use as baseline
file2 File to use as target
n Number of lines to pass to diff in one batch (3500)
-s *Silent*; suppress error messages

bfs

Big File Scanner

```
bfs [ - ] file
```

- Suppress printing of file sizes

cal

Print Calendar

```
cal [ [ month ] year ]
```

D

month A number from 1 to 12
year A 1- to 4-digit year (83 means 83 A.D.)

calendar

Daily To Do List

```
calendar [ - ]
```

- Execute for every user with a file `calendar` in his or her login directory; with no argument, executes only for the current user

cancel

Cancel a Print Request

```
cancel [ requests ¦ printers ]

cancel -u login-list [ printers ]
```

requests	Cancel the print jobs by `lp` request-ID
printers	Cancel the currently printing job on the named printers
-u	Cancel all print requests originated by the user names in *logins-list*; if *printers* is specified, cancel jobs only for the named printers

D

cat

Copy Named Files to Standard Output

```
cat [ -s ] [ -u ] [ -v[te] ] [ file ... ]
```

-s	Suppress error messages about missing files
-u	Unbuffered output
-v	Display unprintable characters in a visual format
-t	Print tabs as `^I` and form feeds as `^L`
-e	Display each newline character as $

chgrp   Change Group Ownership of a File

```
chgrp [ -R ] [ -h ] group file ...
```

- `-R`   Recursively descend all directories and symbolic links, changing the group-ID of all directories and files encountered
- `-h`   Change a symbolic link instead of the file to which the link points
- `group` Group name or numeric group-ID
- `file`   Path name of a file or directory

chmod   Change File Access Permissions

```
chmod [ -R ] octal file ...
chmod [ -R ] [who]op[perms] file ...
```

- `-R`   Recursively descend through directories and symbolic links, applying the change to all files and directories
- `octal` Permission bits to be set as an octal number, or one of the following special numbers:

  4000   Set-uid permission
  20#0   Set group-ID on execution if number is odd. Set mandatory file locking if number is even
  1000   Sticky bit

- `who`   The set of permission bits to set (any combination of the following):

  u (*user*) file owner permissions
  g (*group*) file group permissions
  o (*other*) other users' permissions
  a (*all*) all—same as `ugo`

  If omitted, defaults to a (all)

D

op   Operator (any one of the following):

+ Add the *perms* permissions

- Remove the *perms* permissions

= Set to *perms*

perms   Permission bits (any combination of the following):

r Read permission

w Write permission

x Execute permission

l Mandatory locking

s Set ID on execution

t Sticky bit

u Use file owner permissions

g Use group owner permissions

o Use others permissions

file   List of files and directories to be changed

---

chown   **Change File Owner**

```
chown [ -R ] [ -h ] user file ...
```

-R   Recursively descend through directories and symbolic links, applying the change to all files and directories

-h   Change a symbolic link instead of the file it points to

user   User name or numeric user-ID to assign as file owner

file   List of files or directories to be changed

D

---

clear   **Clear the Terminal Screen**

```
clear [ term ]
```

term   Use terminal type *term* (a terminfo terminal name)

cmp   Compare Two Files for Equality

```
cmp [ -l ] [ -s ] file1 file2
```

-l   Print offset and values of differing bytes

-s   Suppress error messages

file1   File name or - to read from standard input

col   Filter Unprintable Line Motions

```
col [ -bfpx ]
```

-b   Filter out backspacing and overprinting

-f   Retain forward half-line motions

-p   Pass escape sequences through to the output file

-x   Suppress conversion of white space to tab characters

comm   Show Lines Common to Two Files

D

```
comm [ -123 ] file1 file2
```

-1   Print lines only in *file1*

-2   Print lines only in *file2*

-3   Print lines that appear in both files

compress   **Compress Files to Reduce Their Size**

```
compress [ -cfv ] [ -b bits ] [ file ... ]
```

-c	Write to standard output
-f	Force compression
-v	(Verbose) print percentage reduction ratios
-b	Limit substring code to *bits* length (9 through 16)
file	Files to be compressed; if omitted, read standard input

cp   **Copy Files**

```
cp [ -ipr ] file ... target
```

-i	Confirm before replacing an existing file/directory
-p	Preserve file modification times and permissions
-r	Recursively copy directory trees
file	File or directory to be copied; if *target* is a file, only one *file* argument is allowed
target	If a file name, the name of the file copy; if a directory, the directory where the copied files are to be stored with their original names

D

cpio

Copy File Archives

```
cpio -i[bBcdfkmrsStuvV6] [-C size] [-E file] [-H hdr]
    [-I file [ -M message ] ] [-R ID] [pattern ...]

cpio -o[aABcLvV] [-C size] [-H hdr] [-O file [-M message]]

cpio -p[adlLmuvV] [-R ID] directory
```

- a　　Reset access times
- A　　Append files to an archive (-O option required)
- b　　Swap bytes
- B　　Block records to 5,120 bytes
- c　　Use ASCII header information for portability
- C　　Use record blocks of *size* bytes
- d　　Create directories as needed
- E　　Read the list of file names from *file*
- f　　Copy all files *except* those matching *pattern*
- H　　Use one of the following *hdr* formats (uppercase also is recognized):

　　crc　　ASCII header with expanded device numbers and an additional per-file checksum
　　ustar　　IEEE/P1003 Data Interchange Standard
　　tar　　tar header and file format
　　odc　　ASCII header with small device numbers

- I　　Read input from *file*
- k　　Skip bad file headers and I/O errors if possible
- l　　Link files if possible instead of copying them
- L　　Follow symbolic links (default is not to follow)
- m　　Restore file modification times
- M　　Define the *message* to prompt for media switching
- O　　Write output to *file*
- r　　Interactively rename files
- R　　Assign file owner and group to that of user *ID*
- s　　Swap bytes within each halfword of two bytes

D

-s   Swap halfwords within each word of four bytes

-t   Print a table of contents without copying

-u   Copy unconditionally (default is to copy only if the modification time of the input file is newer than the existing output file)

-v   (Verbose) List files copied; with -t, print full details

-V   Print only a . for each file copied to show the progress of program execution

-6   Use UNIX Sixth Edition archive format

---

crontab   **Manage** crontab **Files**

```
crontab [ file ]

crontab [ -elr ] [ user ]
```

-e   Edit the system copy of the current user's crontab file using the editor named by the *EDITOR* shell variable

-l   List the named or current user's crontab file

-r   Remove the named or current user's crontab file

file   Install *file* in the system area; if omitted, read standard input

user   Work with *user*'s crontab file (superuser only)

D

crypt   **Encrypt/Decrypt Filter**

```
crypt [ password ]

crypt [ -k ]
```

-k   Use the value of *CRYPTKEY* as the encryption key

password   An arbitrary string used as the encryption key

csh

C Shell

```
csh [ -bcefinstvVxX ] [ arg ... ]
```

-b Break option processing; subsequent arguments will not be considered options even if they start with -

-c Execute the next *arg* as a command, then exit

-e Exit immediately on a nonzero command exit value

-f Fast start: skip .cshrc and .login file processing

-i Interactive shell

-n Parse but do not execute commands

-s Read commands from standard input

-t Read and execute one command line

-v (Verbose) Print commands as they are executed

-V Same as -v but takes effect before reading .cshrc

-x Print commands after substitution but before execution

-X Same as -x but takes effect before reading .cshrc

arg Initial arguments; if neither -c nor -s is specified, the first *arg* is taken as the name of a shell script

csplit

Context-Sensitive File Splitter

D

```
csplit [ -s ] [ -k ] [ -f prefix ] file arg ...
```

-s Suppress printing of character counts

-k Keep all generated files if csplit fails

-f Prefix all generated file names with *prefix*

file Read from *file*; use - to read from standard input

arg	A series of search strings identifying break points:

	/rexp/	Break before regular expression *rexp*
	%rexp%	Break before *rexp* and discard the section
	num	Break before line number *num*
{count}	Repeat the previous *arg count* times	

ct   **Dial a Terminal and Initiate Login Sequence**

```
ct [ -h ] [ -sspeed ] [ -v ] [ -wn ] [ -xn ] telno ...
```

-h	Suppress attempts to hang up the line before dialing
-s	Use line speed of *speed* bits per second (1200)
-v	Write progess reports to standard error
-w	Wait *n* minutes for a free line
-x	Write debug messages at level *n* (1 through 9)
telno	Telephone numbers to be tried; digits are 0 through 9 - = * #

ctags   **Create a Tags File for Use with Vi**

```
ctags [ -aBFtuvwx ] [ -f tagsfile ] file ...
```

-a	Append output
-B	Use backward search patterns (?...?)
-F	Use forward search patterns (/.../)
-t	Create tag entries for typedef names
-u	Update entries for each named file
-v	List entries on standard output
-w	Suppress warning messages
-x	Print a list of the object entries

D

-f   Write tag entries into *file* (default is tags)

file   Files to be searched for tag items

---

cu   **Call Another UNIX System**

```
cu [ -ctype ] [ -lline ] [ -sspeed ] [ -bn ] [ -e ] [ -h ]
   [ -n ] [ -o ] [ -t ] [ -d ] destination
```

-c   Use only lines of type *type* listed in the Devices file

-l   Use special file *line* to establish the connection

-s   Use line speed *speed*

-b   Use *n* bits per character (7 or 8)

-e   Even parity

-h   Half-duplex

-n   Prompt user for the telephone number

-o   Odd parity

-t   Destination terminal is in auto-answer mode

-d   Print debugging information

dest   A UUCP system name, a telephone number, or omitted

---

cut   **Select Columns or Fields from Input Lines**

D

```
cut -ccols [ file ... ]

cut -ffields [ -dc ] [ -s ] [ file ... ]
```

-c   Select columns; for *cols* list one or more column ranges
      separated by commas: -12,15-18,25-

-f   Select fields; for *fields* list one or more field ranges separated
      by commas: 1-5,7,10

-d   Field delimiter character is *c*

-s   Skip lines having no delimiter character

file   Input files; use - to read standard input

date   **Print or Set the Current Date and Time**

```
date [-u] [+format]

date [-a [-] nnn.nnn ] [-u] [ [mmdd]HHMM ¦ mmddHHMMyy]
```

-a   Adjust the time later (earlier) by *nnn.nnn* seconds

-u   Specify Greenwich Mean Time (GMT)

mm   Month number

dd   Day of the month

HH   Hour using a 24-hour clock

MM   Minute

yy   Year in full (*1981*) or as the last two digits

+format   Print date and time according to a format specification

dc   **Desk Calculator**

```
dc [ file ]
```

file   Optional file containing dc commands

dd   **File Copy**

```
dd option ...
```

if=*file*	Input file
of=*file*	Output file
ibs=*n*	Input block size
obs=*n*	Output block size
bs=*n*	Block size for input and output (overrides ibs, obs)
cbs=*n*	Conversion buffer size
files=*n*	Concatenate *n* input files (magnetic tape)
skip=*n*	Skip *n* input blocks before copying
iseek=*n*	Seek to input block *n* (disk only)
oseek=*n*	Seek to output block *n* before copying (disk only)
seek=*n*	Same as oseek
count=*n*	Copy *n* input blocks and stop
conv=*id*	One or more conversion options separated with commas:

ebcdic	Convert EBCDIC to ASCII
ibm	Alternate form of EBCDIC to ASCII
block	Convert lines to fixed-length records
unblock	Convert fixed-length records to ASCII lines
lcase	Force letters to lowercase
ucase	Force letters to uppercase
swab	Swap pairs of bytes
noerror	Ignore errors
sync	Pad input blocks to input block size

deroff   Remove nroff **Commands from a Text File**

D

```
deroff [ -m[m¦s¦l] ] [ -w ] [ file ... ]
```

-m	Interpret macros in the m*x* package style
-w	Print each word of the input on a separate line
-mm	Interpret macros in the mm package style
-ms	Interpret macros in the ms package style
-ml	Interpret macros in the ml package style

df
Report Disk Free Space

```
df [ -F FSType ] [ -begklntV ] [ s5-opts ] [ -o fs-opts ]
    [ directory ¦ special ¦ resource ] ...
```

-F	File system type for unmounted file systems
-b	Print only the free space in kilobytes
-e	Print only the number of free i-nodes
-g	Print the entire statvfs structure
-k	Print allocation in kilobytes
-l	Report only locally mounted file systems
-n	Print the FSType of mounted file systems
-t	Print usage with totals for all or named file systems
-v	Include percent of blocks used in report
-V	Verify the command line
-o	FSType-specific options
s5-opts	System V specific options

diff
Print Differences between Two Files

```
diff [ -bitw ] [ -c¦e¦f¦h¦n ] file1 file2

diff [ -bitw ] [ -C number ] file1 file2

diff [ -bitw ] [ -D string ] file1 file2

diff [ -bitw ] [ -c¦e¦f¦h¦n ] [ -l ] [ -r ] [ -s ]
     [ -S name ] dir1 dir2
```

-b	Ignore excess blanks in the two files
-i	Ignore case
-t	Expand tab characters in output lines

D

-w   Ignore white space

-c   Print three context lines around each difference

-e   Describe differences using Ed commands

-f   Same as -e but in the opposite order

-h   Halfhearted but fast

-n   Similar to -e but reversed and with line counts

-C   Print *number* context lines around each difference

-D   Make a file that can generate either *file1* or *file2* using the C
      preprocessor and option -D*string*

-l   Print a long format report

-r   Recursively descend through directories

-s   Report identical files

-S   Start a directory scan at file name *name*

diff3   Three-Way diff

```
diff3 [ -exEX3 ] file1 file2 file3
```

-e   Produce an Ed-compatible script to incorporate all differences into
      file1

-x   Same as -e but include only common lines

-3   Same as -e but include only changes in *file3*

-E   Same as -e but mark lines that are the same in both *file2* and
      file3

-X   Same as -x but mark lines that are the same

dircmp   Directory Comparison

```
dircmp [ -d ] [ -s ] [ -wn ] dir1 dir2
```

D

-d   Print a `diff` listing for files with the same name

-s   Ignore identical files

-w   Set the output line width to *n* columns

---

dirname   **Print Directory Portion of a Path Name**

```
dirname string
```

string   Relative or absolute path name

---

disable   **Disable Line Printers**

```
disable [ -c ] [ -r reason ] [ -W ] printer ...
```

-c   Cancel any files currently being printed

-r   Assign an explanatory text to the disabled printer

-W   Wait for an active printer job to complete

printer   One or more printer names as known to the LP subsystem

D

---

du   **Summarize Disk Usage**

```
du [ -ars ] [ name ... ]
```

-a   Print a report for each file found

-r   Print error messages (default is to ignore errors)

-s   Print only the total for each specified *name*

name   File and directory names to be summarized

---

echo   **Print Command Arguments**

```
echo [ -n ] [ arg ... ]
```

-n   Do not append a newline (csh and BSD compatibility)

---

ed   **Text Editor**

```
ed [ -s ] [ -p string ] [ -x ] [ -C ] [ file ]
```

-s   (Silent) Suppress character counts and the ! prompt

-p   Prompt for input with *string*

-x   (Encryption) Input file may be plain text or encrypted

-C   (Encryption) Input file must be in encrypted form

---

edit   **Variant of ex for Casual Users**

D

```
edit [ -r ] [ -x ] [ -C ] file ...
```

-r   Recover *file* after a system crash

-x   (Encryption) Input file may be plain or encrypted

-C   (Encryption) Input file must be in encrypted form

egrep   **File Search Using Full Regular Expressions**

```
egrep [ -bcihlnv ] [ -e string ] [ -f script ] regexp
     [ file ... ]
```

-b	Print the block number of the datablock containing each matched line
-c	Print only a count of the matching lines
-i	Ignore case distinctions
-h	Do not prefix output lines with the file name
-l	Print only the names of files containing matches
-n	Print the line number of each matched line
-v	Print all lines except those containing a match
-e	Treat the next argument as a search string
-f	Read a list of search expressions from *script*
regexp	Search pattern as a full regular expression

enable   **Enable Line Printer**

```
enable printer ...
```

printer   One or more printer names as known to the LP subsystem

env   **Set Environment for Command**

```
env [ - ] [ name=value ... ] [ command [ arg ... ] ]
```

-	Ignore the current environment
name=value	Add the *name=value* pair to the new command environment
command	Command to be executed; if omitted, print the resulting environment strings

ex   **Text Editor**

```
ex [-CLRsvx] [-c command] [-r file] [-t tag] file ...
```

-C   (Encryption) Input files must be in encrypted form

-L   List files for which recovery is possible

-R   Read-only; edited files may not be rewritten

-s   Noninteractive mode

-v   Visual mode; invoke the Vi editor

-x   (Encryption) Input files may be plain or encrypted

-c   Execute *command* as the first edit command

-r   Recover the named *file* after a system crash

-t   Look up *tag* and edit the file that contains it

expr   **Evaluate an Expression**

D

```
expr arg ...
```

arg   A list of arguments forming these expression types:

expr \¦ *expr*

expr \& *expr*

expr { =, \>, \>=, \<, \<=, != } *expr*

expr { +, -, *, /, % } *expr*

expr : *expr*

exstr   **Extract Strings from Text Files**

```
exstr file ...

exstr -e file ...

exstr -r [ -d ] file ...
```

-e   Extract strings

-r   Replace strings with calls to gettxt

-d   Use the extracted string as default text

file   One or more C-language source files

face   **Invoke the Framed Access Command Environment**

```
face [-i init] [-c command] [-a alias] [ file ... ]
```

-i   File name of the initialization file

-c   File name of the commands file

-a   File name of the aliases file

file   A Menu.*xxx*, Form.*xxx*, or Text.*xxx* file name

factor   **Print the Prime Factors of a Number**

```
factor [ number ]
```

number   Integer to be factored (default is to prompt for it)

false

Return Error Exit Status

```
false
```

fgrep

Search for Fixed Character Strings

```
fgrep [-bchilnvx] [-e string] [-f script] strings [file ...]
```

-b	Print block number containing each matched line
-c	Print only a count of the matching lines
-h	Do not prefix output lines with the file name
-i	Ignore case distinctions
-l	Print only the names of files containing matches
-n	Print the line number of each matched line
-v	Print all lines except those containing a match
-e	Treat the next argument as a search string
-f	Read a list of strings from *script*
strings	One or more strings separated by newline characters

D

file

Determine the Type of a File

```
file [ -h ] [ -m mfile ] [ -f ffile ] [ file ... ]
file -c [ -m mfile ]
```

-c	Check the magic file for format errors
-h	Do not follow symbolic links

-m   Use magic file *mfile* instead of /etc/magic

-f   Read a list of file names from *ffile*

find   **Find Files**

```
find path ... expr
```

path   One or more path names to be searched

expr   A combination of the following tests:

-name *pattern*	All file names matching *pattern*
-perm [-]*octal*	All files with *octal* permissions
-size *n*[c]	All files of size *n* (characters)
-atime *n*	Last access time *n* days
-mtime *n*	Last modification time *n* days
-ctime *n*	Last status change time *n* days
-exec *command*	Execute *command* (always true)
-ok *command*	*command* returns 0
-print	Print found file names
-newer *file*	All files newer than *file*
-depth	Depth-first recursive search
-mount	Search only mounted filesystems
-local	Ignore remote paths
-type *c*	All files of type [bcdlpf]
-follow	Follow symbolic links
-links *n*	All files with *n* links
-user *user*	All files owned by *user*
-nouser	All files without a valid user-ID
-group *group*	All files owned by group *group*
-nogroup	All files without a valid group
-fstype *type*	All files on filesystem type *type*
-inum *n*	Files with i-node number *n*
-prune	No recursive search below *pattern*
(*expr*)	Combined options
! *expr*	True if *expr* is false
-o *expr*	Logical *or* of conditions

D

finger

Identify Local and Remote Users

```
finger [ -bfhilmpqsw ] username ...

finger [ -l ] username@hostname ...
```

-b   Do not print user's home directory and shell

-f   Do not print the listing header

-h   Do not print the .project file

-i   Print information only for idle terminals

-l   Long output format

-m   Match arguments on full user name

-p   Do not print the .plan file

-q   Quick output format

-s   Short output format

-w   Do not print full names in short format output

fmli

Invoke FMLI

```
fmli [-a afile] [-c cfile] [-i ifile] file ...
```

-a   Specify the name of an aliases file

-c   Specify the name of a command override file

-i   Specify the name of a FMLI initialization file

file   One or more file names of the form Menu.*xxx*, Form.*xxx*, or
        Text.*xxx*

D

fmt

Simple Text Formatters

```
fmt [ -cs ] [ -w width ] [ file ... ]
```

-c   Crown margin mode

-s   Split lines only

-w   Set line width to *width* columns

fmtmsg

Format and Print an Error Message

```
fmtmsg [-c class] [-u subclass] [-l label] [-s severity]
       [-t tag] [-a action] text
```

-c   Message type: hard, soft, or firm

-u   Message subclass: appl, util, opsys, recov, nrecov, print, or console

-l   Message source

-s   Message severity: halt, error, warn, info

-t   Message identifier code

-a   Message action

text   Single string argument giving the text of the message

fold

Fold Long Lines

```
fold [ -w width ¦ -width ] [ file ... ]
```

-w   Maximum line length in characters

ftp

File Transfer Program

```
ftp [ -dgintv ] [ hostname ]
```

-d   Enable debugging

-g   Disable file name expansion

-i   Suppress interactive prompting for file transfers

-n   No auto-login on connection

-t   Enable packet tracing

-v   Display responses from the remote server

gcore

Get Core Images of Running Processes

```
gcore [ -o filename ] process-ID ...
```

-o   Use *filename* instead of core in output file names

gencat

Generate a Formatted Message Catalog

D

```
gencat [ -m ] catalog file ...
```

-m   Build a single *catalog* compatible with earlier versions of gencat

catalog   File name of the output message database

file   One or more message file names

getopt

Parse Command-Line Options

```
getopt optstring [ arg ... ]
```

optstring	Options string consisting of keyletters that are valid options in the command line; a keyletter followed by : must have an option value
arg	Command arguments to be parsed

getoptcvt

Convert Shell Script to Use getopts

```
/usr/lib/getoptcvt [ -b ] file
```

-b	Support both getopt and getopts
file	File name of shell script to be converted

gettxt

Retrieve Message Text

```
gettxt msgfile:msgnum [ default ]
```

msgfile	Name of the messages catalog file
msgnum	Message identifier
default	Default message text if cataloged message not found

D

grep   **Search a File for a String Pattern**

```
grep [ -bcihlnsv ] expr [ file ... ]
```

-b	Print block number containing each matched line
-c	Print only a count of the matching lines
-h	Do not prefix output lines with the file name
-i	Ignore case distinctions
-l	Print only the names of files containing matches
-n	Print the line number of each matched line
-s	Suppress error messages about unreadable files
-v	Print all lines except those containing a match
expr	Regular expression search pattern

group   **Print Group Membership**

```
groups [ user ]
```

user   Print group memberships of *user*; if omitted, print memberships of current user

D

hashcheck   **Compare Two Spelling Lists**

```
/usr/lib/spell/hashcheck spelling_list
```

spelling_list   An existing hashed, compressed spelling list

hashmake

Make Hash Codes for spellin

```
/usr/lib/spell/hashmake
```

head

Display First Lines of a File

```
head [ -n ] [ UIfile ... ]
```

n   Number of lines in each file to print (default is 10 lines)

iconv

Code Set Conversion

```
iconv -f UIfromcode -t UItocode [ file ]
```

-f   Code set of input file (one of the following):
  - 8859   US ASCII
  - 656de   German
  - 646da   Danish
  - 646en   English ASCII
  - 646fr   French
  - 646it   Italian
  - 646sv   Swedish

-t   Code set of converted output file

D

id   **Print User Name and Group**

```
id [ -a ]
```

-a   Report all groups including the current user

ipcrm   **Remove an IPC Resource**

```
ipcrm [ -qms id ¦ -QMS key ] ...
```

-q   Remove message queue identified by *msqid*
-m   Remove shared memory segment identified by *shmid*
-s   Remove semaphore set identified by *semid*
-Q   Remove message queue identified by *msgkey*
-M   Remove shared memory segment identified by *shmkey*
-S   Remove semaphore set identified by *semkey*

ipcs   **List Active IPC Resources**

D

```
ipcs [ -qms ¦ -bcopta ] [ -C corefile ] [ -N namelist ] [ -X ]
```

-q   List all active message queues
-m   List all active shared-memory segments
-s   List all active semaphore sets
-b   Print maximum sizes of each resource type
-c   Print creator's login name and group name

-o   Print outstanding usage

-p   Print using processes information

-t   Print time information

-a   Print all optional information

-C   Use file `corefile` instead of `/dev/kmem`

-N   Use `namelist` instead of `/stand/unix`

-X   Print XENIX resource information

ismpx   **Return Layers State of Terminal**

```
ismpx [ -s ]
```

-s   Suppress output but set exit value to 0 if the current terminal is
       controlled by `layers`

join   **Form the Database Union of Two Files**

```
join [-an] [-e s] [-jn m] [-o list] [-tc] file1 file2
```

-a   Include unpairable lines in output

-e   Replace empty output fields with string *s*

-j   Join on the *m*th field of file *n*

-o   Include fields in output: `file.field` ...

-t   Input fields are separated by character *c*

jterm

Reset the Layer of a Windowing Terminal Attached to a Standard Error

```
jterm
```

jwin

Print Size of Layer

```
jwin
```

kill

Signal a Process

```
kill [ -sig ] pgid ...
kill -sig -pgid
kill -l
```

-sig   Specify signal to be sent (default is 15 Terminate)

pid   Specify process-ID of the processes to receive the signal

-pgid   Send the specified signal to all procession process group pgid

-l   List the supported symbolic names corresponding to each valid signal number

D

ksh   **Korn Shell**

```
ksh [ ±aefhikmnprstuvx ] [ ±o option ] ... [ -c string ]
    [ arg ] ...
```

- -a   Export all changed variables
- -c   Execute the next argument as a command, then exit
- -e   Exit immediately on a nonzero command exit value
- -f   Suppress file name generation
- -h   Define all commands as tracked aliases
- -i   Force interactive execution
- -k   Export *name=value* arguments anywhere on the command
- -m   Run background jobs as a separate process group
- -n   Syntax check input but do not execute commands
- -o   Set named options (see table in Appendix C called "Named Options")
- -p   Set protected mode
- -r   Run as a restricted shell
- -s   Read shell input from standard input
- -t   Exit after reading and executing one command
- -u   Treat unset variables as errors
- -v   Print all shell input as it is read
- -x   Print commands after substitution but before execution

D

last   **Indicate Last Few Terminal Logins**

```
last [ -n number ¦ -number ] [ -f filename ] [ name ¦ tty ]
```

-n	Print only *number* entries
-number	Same as -n
-f	Use *filename* instead of /var/adm/wtmp
name	Print last few logins by user *name*
tty	Print last few logins on special file *tty*

layers   **Initiate Layered Windows on a Terminal**

```
layers [-s] [-t] [-D] [-m max-pkt] [-d] [-p] [-h modlist]
    [-f file] [layerpgm]
```

-s	Report protocol statistics on exit from layers
-t	Enable packet tracing
-D	Enable debugging output to standard error
-m	Set maximum packet size (32 to 252 bytes)
-d	Print firmware patch sizes
-p	Print firmware patch downloading statistics
-h	Push a comma-separated list of STREAMS drivers
-f	Start layers using initialization script *file*
layerpgm	Firmware patch file name

D

line   Copy One Line from Standard Input to Standard Output

```
line
```

listusers   List User Password Information

```
listusers [ -g groups ] [ -l logins ]
```

-g   List all users belonging to *groups*, a comma-separated list of group names

-l   List user information for each user in *logins*, a comma-separated list of user names

ln   Create Hard or Symbolic File Links

```
ln [ -f ] [ -n ] [ -s ] file1 [ file2 ... ] target
```

-f   Attempt to create the link regardless of permissions; do not report errors

-n   Do not overwrite an existing file

-s   Create a symbolic rather than a hard link

filen   One or more existing files

target   If only *file1* is specified, *target* may be a directory name or a new file name alias of *file1*; if two more file names are given, *target* must be a directory; new links are created in the *target* directory with the same file name as the source files

login

Sign on

```
login [ -d device ] [ name [ environ ... ] ]
```

-d   Execute login on terminal name *device*

name   User name to log in under

environ   Positional or keyword arguments to be added to the environment of the initial shell

logname

Get Login Name

```
logname
```

lp

Send Files to the LP Print Service

```
lp [-c] [-d dest] [-f form] [-d any]] [-H hdlg] [-m] [-n copies]
    [-o option] ... [-P pages] [-q prty] [-s]
    [-S charset] ¦ [-S pwheel]
    [-t title] [-T content [-r]]
    [-w] [-y modes]
    [ file ... ]
```

-c   Copy files (default is to link the user's files)

-d   Send files to printer name or class name *dest*

-f   Print files on form-name *form*. Also specifies -d any if the file can be printed at any destination

D

-H	Specify one of the following handling restrictions:

hold	Don't print until notified
resume	Release a held print request
immediate	Print the files next

-m	Send mail after the files have been printed
-n	Print *copies* copies of each file
-o	Specify a printer-dependent option; for *num* specify an integer number of units or a fractional number of inches (*m*[.*n*]i) or centimeters (*m*[.*n*]c):
nobanner	Do not print a banner page
nofilebreak	Do not skip a page between files
length=*num*	Use page length *num*
width=*num*	Use page width of *num*
lpi=*num*	Use line pitch of *num* lines per inch
stty='*list*'	Set up *list* stty options before printing
-P	Print only the specified list of page ranges
-q	Assign files to print priority *prty* (0 through 39)
-s	Suppress informational messages
-S	Print using specified character set or print wheel
-t	Print *title* on the banner page
-T	Print to a printer supporting *content* type
-r	Reject a content (-T) request if no printer supports it
-w	Write a message when the files have been printed
-y	Print using printing modes in *modes* (locally defined)

lpstat

Display Information about Printers

```
lpstat [ options ]
```

-a [*list*]	Report whether destinations are accepting requests; for *list* specify printer names and/or classes
-c [*list*]	List all class names and member printers; for *list* specify one or more class names
-d	Report the default destination

-f [*list*]	Verify that the *list* of form names (default is all) are acceptable to the LP service; also specify -1 together with this option
[*list*]	Report status of output requests; for *list* specify one or more printer names, class names, and/or request-IDs
-p [*list*]	Report the status of the printers named in *list*
-D	Report printer description (option -p required)
-r	Report whether the LP scheduler is running or not
-R	Report the relative position of job in the printer queue
-s	Display a status summary
-S [*list*] [-1]	Verify that the character sets or printer wheels named in *list* are supported by lp; use -1 to see which printers support the character sets or printer wheels
-t	Display all LP service status information
-u [*login-list*]	Display the status of output requests for the user names in *login-list*
-v [*list*]	Report the device pathnames of the specified printers

ls

List Files

D

```
ls [ -abcdfgilmnopqrstuxCFLR1 ] [ path ... ]
```

-a	List *all* file names (even those beginning with .)
-b	Display unprintable characters as \nnn codes
-c	Sort and print time of last file status change
-d	List the *directory* rather than its contents
-f	Forcibly process the named files as directories
-g	Drop the owner column from the long listing format
-i	Add the *i-node* number to the long listing format
-1	*Long* listing format

-m	Stream format (`name, name, name, ...`)
-n	Display owner and group *numbers* rather than names
-o	Drop the group column from the long listing format
-p	Print / after the name of a directory (*path* option)
-q	Show unprintable characters in file names as ?
-r	*Reverse* the sort order of the listing
-s	Add the *size* in blocks in front of each line
-t	Sort the listing by date and time rather than by name
-u	Sort and print using time of last access
-x	Arrange output in columns across the page
-C	Arrange output in columns down the page
-F	Append *flags* to the file name: / (directory), * (executable), @ (symbolic link)
-L	List the target of a symbolic link
-R	*Recursively* list all subdirectories of a directory
-1	Print one file per line of output

mail   **Read or Send Mail**

Send mail:
```
mail [ -tw ] [ -m mtype ] recipient ...
rmail [ -tw ] [ -m mtype ] recipient ...
```
Read mail:
```
mail [ -ehpPqr ] [ -f file ]
```
Forward mail:
```
mail -F recipient
```

-m	Add the header line `Message-Type:` *mtype*
-t	Add the header line `To:` for each recipient
-w	If a recipient is a remote user, do not wait for the message to be transmitted
-e	Do not print mail; set the exit value to 0 mail is waiting, or 1 if no mail

-h	Display a window of headers instead of the last message
-p	Print all messages without prompting
-P	Print all messages with all header lines
-q	Terminate on interrupts
-r	Print messages in reversed (first-in first-out, or FIFO) order
-f	Read messages from *file* (default is mbox)
-F	Forward all incoming mail to *recipient*

mailalias   **Translate Mail Alias Names**

```
mailalias [ -s ] [ -v ] name ...
```

-s	Do not print the name being translated
-v	Write debugging information to standard output

mailx   **Interactive Message Processing**

```
mailx [ options ] [ name ... ]
```

-d	Turn on debugging output
-e	Test whether mail is waiting
-f [*file*]	Read messages from *file* rather than mbox
-F	Record an outgoing message in a file named after the first recipient *name*
-h *num*	The number of network nodes visited so far
-H	Print header summary only
-i	Ignore interrupts
-I	Print the newsgroup and article-ID lines
-n	Do not execute the .mailrc initialization script

D

-N	Do not print a header summary on start-up
-r *addr*	Use *addr* as the return address
-s *subj*	Set the subject header field to *subj*
-T *file*	Record message-ID and article-ID header lines in *file*
-u *user*	Read *user*'s mailbox
-U	Convert UUCP addresses to internet addresses
-V	Print the mailx version number

makekey

Generate Encryption Key

```
/usr/lib/makekey
```

mesg

Enable or Disable Terminal Messages

```
mesg [ -n ] [ -y ]
```

-n   Disable write commands directed to your terminal

-y   Enable write commands to your terminal

D

mkdir

Make Directories

```
mkdir [ -m mode ] [ -p ] dirname ...
```

-m   Set access permissions to *mode* (same format as chmod)

-p   Make all nonexistent parent directories

mkmsgs   **Create Message Files for** `gettxt`

```
mkmsgs [ -o ] [ -i locale ] istrings msgfile
```

`-i`	Install `msgfile` in `/usr/lib/locale/locale/LC_MESSAGES`
`-o`	Overwrite `msgfile` if it exists
`istrings`	File name of the file containing the original messages
`msgfile`	File name where `mkmsgs` output is to be written

more   **Display a Text File One Page at a Time**

```
more [ -cdflrsuw ] [ -lines ] [ +lnum ] [ +/pattern ]
     [ file ... ]
```

`-c`	Clear the screen before displaying each page
`-d`	Display error messages
`-f`	Do not fold long lines
`-l`	Ignore form feed (^L) characters in the input file
`-r`	Display control characters instead of ignoring them
`-s`	(Squeeze) Display multiple blank lines as one
`-u`	Do not generate underline escape sequences
`-w`	Wait for a keypress before quitting at end of file
`-lines`	Display `lines` lines per screen
`+lnum`	Start the display at line number `lnum`
`+/pattern`	Start the display at first line containing `pattern`

D

mv   **Move Files**

```
mv [ -f ] [ -i ] file ... target
```

-f   Ignore permissions and suppress error messages

-i   Prompt for confirmation if a file would be overwritten

target   New file name if only one *file* argument, otherwise
          directory name

nawk   **Improved Version of** awk

```
nawk [ -F re ] [ -v name=value ] [ 'prog' ¦ -f script ]
     [ file ... ]
```

-F   *re* is a regular expression specifying the characters that
          separate fields (for example [:,])

-v   Define variables before nawk starts

-f   File name of a script containing nawk commands

prog   A nawk command script

file   One or more input file names; use - to read standard input

D

newform   **Change the Format of Text Files**

```
newform [-s] [-itabspec] [-otabspec] [-bn] [-en] [-pn] [-an]
        [-f] [-cchar] [-ln] [ file ... ]
```

-s   Shear off leading characters of each line up to the first tab and append up to eight of them at the end of the line

-i   Input tab specification (see the tabs command)

-o   Output tab specification (see the tabs command)

-b   Truncate *n* characters from the front of the line if the line is longer than the maximum length (-1)

-e   Truncate characters at the end of the line

-p   Prefix *n* characters to the beginning of each line less than the effective line length (-1)

-a   Same as -p but append to the end of the line

-f   Write tab specification in front of the output file

-c   Set prefix/append character to *char* (default is a space)

-1   Set effective line length to *n* characters (default is 72)

newgrp   **Log in to a New Group**

```
newgrp [ - ] [ group ]
```

-       Execute the login profile

group   Group name to become the real and effective group-ID

news   **Print News**

D

```
news [ -a ] [ -n ] [ -s ] [ items ]
```

-a   Print all items whether new or not

-n   List the names of all news items

-s   Report the number of available news items

items   File names of news files to be printed

nice   **Run a Command at Lowered Priority**

```
nice [ -inc ] command [ arg ... ]
```

-inc	Integer amount to decrease priority (1 to 19) (default is 10)
command	Command to be executed
arg	Optional command arguments

nl   **Line Numbering Filter**

```
nl [-btype] [-ftype] [-htype] [-vstart#] [-iincr] [-p]
    [ -lnum] [ -ssep] [ -wwidth] [ -nformat ] [-ddelim]
    [ file ]
```

- -b   Body line groups to be numbered, where *type* is:

a	Number all lines
t	Number lines with printable text only
n	No line numbering
pexp	Number only lines containing the regular expression *exp*

- -f   Same as -b*type* except for footer; default *type* for page footer is n
- -h   Same as -b*type* except for header; default *type* for page header is n
- -v   Start numbering lines at *start#*
- -i   Increment line numbers by *incr*
- -p   Do not restart numbering at logical page breaks
- -l   Count *num* blank lines as one
- -s   Insert *sep* character between line number and text
- -w   Width of line number field (default is 6)

-n   Line numbering format:

    ln   Left-justified without leading zeroes

    rn   Right-justified without leading zeroes

    rz   Right-justified, zero fill

-d   Change the delimiter between logical page sections from the default of \: to *delim*

nohup   **Run a Command Protected from Hangup and Quit**

```
nohup command [ arg ... ]
```

notify   **Request Notification of New Mail**

```
notify -y [ -m mfile ]
notify [ -n ]
```

-m   File name where new mail should be saved (default is $HOME/.mailfile)

-n   Do not notify on receipt of new mail

-y   Activate notification

D

od   **Octal Dump**

```
od [ -bcDdFfOoSsvXx ] [ file ] [ [ + ] offset[.¦b] ]
```

-b   Format as bytes in octal

-c   Format as bytes in characters

-D	Format as long words in unsigned decimal
-d	Format as words in unsigned decimal
-F	Format as double long words in extended precision
-f	Format as long words in floating point
-O	Format as long words in unsigned octal
-o	Format as words in octal
-S	Format as long words in signed decimal
-s	Format as words in signed decimal
-v	(Verbose) Show all formats
-X	Format as long words in hexadecimal
-x	Format as words in hexadecimal
+	If offset is supplied but *file* is omitted; + must be entered to take the place of the file name
offset	Start at octal byte offset *offset*
offset.	Start at decimal byte offset *offset*
offsetb	Start at block *offset*

pack

Compress Files

```
pack [ - ] [ -f ] Uifile ...
```

-	Print character frequency counts at end of run
-f	Force packing even if no savings result

page

Page through a Text File

```
page [ -cdflrsuw ] [ -lines ] [ +lnum ] [ +/pattern ]
     [ file ... ]
```

-c	Clear the screen before displaying each page (default)
-d	Display error messages

-f	Do not fold long lines
-l	Ignore form feed (^L) characters in the input file
-r	Display control characters instead of ignoring them
-s	(Squeeze) Display multiple blank lines as one
-u	Do not generate underline escape sequences
-w	Wait for a keypress before quitting at end of file
-lines	Display *lines* lines per screen
+lnum	Start the display at line number *lnum*
+/pattern	Start the display at first line containing *pattern*

pcat
Print Compressed Files

```
pcat file ...
```

file   One or more file names of tye form *xxx*.Z; the suffix .Z may be omitted, in which case it will be assumed

passwd
Change Login Password

```
passwd [ name ]
passwd [ -l¦d ] [ -f ] [ -n min ] [ -x max ] [ -w warn ] name
passwd -s [ -a ]
passwd -s [ name ]
```

name	Change password information for user *name*
-l	Lock password entry
-d	Delete password for *name*
-f	Force user to change password at next login

D

-n   Minimum days between password changes

-x   Maximum days between password changes

-w   Number of days before expiration to warn user

-s   Show password attributes for *name* or current user

-a   All users

paste   **Merge Lines Together**

```
paste [ -s ] [ -dlist ] file1 file2 ...
```

-s   Merge adjacent lines of the same file

-d   Use characters in *list* to concatenate lines

file   Input file names; use - to read standard input

pg   **File Browsing Filter**

```
pg  [ -lines ] [ -p string ] [ -cefnrs ] [ +lnum ]
    [ +/pattern ] [ file ... ]
```

-lines   Number of screen lines to use

-p   Prompt string; use %d for current page number

-c   Clear the screen before each page

-e   Do not pause at the end of each file

-f   Do not split lines

-n   Accept commands without waiting for newline

-r   Disallow escaping to the shell (restricted mode)

-s   Display messages and prompts in standout mode

+lnum	Start at line number *lnum*
+/pattern	Start at the first line containing *pattern*
file	Input files (default is standard input)

pr

Format Files for Printing

```
pr [ options ] [ file ... ]
```

+num	Begin printing with page number *num*
-cols	Print input lines in *cols*-column style (default is 1)
-a	Print columns across the page instead of down
-m	Print files in up to eight columns across the page
-d	Double-space the output lines
-eck	Expand tabs to character positions $k+1$, $2k+1$, and so on (default is every eight columns); use optional *c* as the tab character
-ick	Convert white space to tabs, with tabs at $k+1$, $2k+1$, and so on; use optional *c* as the tab character
-nck	Number each line with a *k*-digit line number; append *c* (if specified) to the number for spacing
-ww	Use line width *w* for multicolumn output
-on	Offset each line by *n* character positions
-ln	Set page length to *n* lines (default is 66)
-h header	Print string *header* at the top of each page
-p	Pause before printing each page
-f	Separate pages with form feed rather than blank lines
-r	Suppress messages about files that can't be opened
-t	Do not print page headings and footing lines
-ssep	Separate columns with *sep* rather than spaces
-F	Fold input lines to fit the column or page width

D

printf   **Print Formatted Output**

```
printf format [ arg ... ]
```

format   Model output text; supported substitutions are the following:

         %s   insert next *arg* in model text

         %%   insert a literal % in model text

arg   Zero or more strings to be substituted into *format*

priocntl   **Process Scheduler Control**

```
priocntl -l

priocntl -d [-i idtype] [idlist]

priocntl -s [-c class] [options] [-i idtype] [idlist]

priocntl -c [-c class] [options] command [ arg ... ]
```

-l   List currently configured classes

-d   Display scheduling parameters

-s   Set scheduling parameters

-i   Specify process identifiers of the following type:

         pid   *idlist* specifies process-IDs

         ppid   *idlist* specifies parent process-IDs

         pgid   *idlist* specifies process-group IDs

         sid   *idlist* specifies session IDs

         class   *idlist* specifies a class name

         uid   *idlist* specifies user-IDs

         gid   *idlist* specifies group-IDs

         all   No *idlist* is needed

-c   Specify class to be set: RT or TS

options Real-time class-specific options are the following:

-p *pri*   Real-time process priority

-t *q* [-r *res*]   Time quantum (and resolution)

Time-sharing class-specific options are the following:

-m *tsuprilim*   User process priority limit

-p *tsupri*   User process priority

-e Execute *command* in the specified class and with the specified class-specific option settings

ps   **Report Process Status**

```
ps [ -edalfcj ] [ -r sysname ] [ -t termlist ] [ -u uidlist ]
   [ -p proclist ] [ -g grplist ] [ -s sidlist ]
```

-e List all processes (default is just your processes)

-d List all processes except session leaders

-a List all processes associated with a terminal

-l Long listing format (more info than -f)

-f Full listing format

-c Show scheduler properties

-j Show session-ID and process-group ID

-r Remote system name to be interrogated

-t* List only processes using the specified terminal; for *termlist* give full terminal names or tty suffixes

-u* List only processes owned by the specified users; for *uidlist* give user names or IDs

-p* List only process-IDs given in *proclist*

-g* List only processes in the process groups in *grplist*

-s* List only session leaders in *sidlist*

* To give multiple items in a list, separate the items with commas or enclose a blank-separated list in quotes

D

pwd

Print Working Directory

```
pwd
```

rcp

Remote File Copy

```
rcp [ -p ] file1 file2
rcp [ -pr ] file ... directory
```

-p Preserve modification and access times, and permissions
-r Recursively copy all subdirectories and files

relogin

Rename Login Entry of Current Layer

```
/usr/lib/layersis/relogin [ -s ] [ line ]
```

D

-s   Suppress error messages
line Terminal name identifying the utmp entry to change

rlogin

Remote Login

```
rlogin [ -L ] [ -8 ] [ -e c ] [ -l username ] hostname
```

-L	Allow the session to run in litout mode
-8	8-bit characters (default is 7-bit)
-e	Use escape character c to disconnect the line
-l	Log in using remote user name *username*
hostname	Remote system name

rm

Remove Files

```
rm [ -rfi ] file ...
```

-r   Recursively remove subdirectories and files of each directory *file* specified

-f   (Force) All error messages and warnings are suppressed

-i   Inquire whether each directory and file should be deleted with a prompt; respond y or n as appropriate

D

rmdir

Remove Empty Directories

```
rmdir [ -p ] [ -s ] dirname ...
```

-p   Remove all parent directories that become empty

-s   Suppress error messages caused by -p

rsh   **Remote Shell**

```
rsh [ -n ] [ -l username ] hostname command
rsh hostname [ -n ] [ -l username ] command
hostname [ -n ] [ -l username ] command
```

-l   Log in as user *username* (default is your login name)

-n   Redirect rsh input from /dev/null

ruptime   **Show Status of Machines on the Local Network**

```
ruptime [ -alrtu ]
```

-a   Count users idle for more than one hour

-l   Sort by load average

-r   Reverse the output sort order

-t   Sort by up time

-u   Sort by number of users

rwho   **List Users Logged in on Local Network**

```
rwho [ -a ]
```

-a   List users idle for more than one hour

sag   **System Activity Graph**

```
sag [ -s time ] [ -e time ] [ -i sec ] [ -f file ] [ -T term ]
    [ -x spec ] [ -y spec ]
```

-s Select data later than *time* (*hh*:[*mm*]) (default is 08:00)

-e Select data up to *time* (*hh*:[*mm*]) (default is 18:00)

-i Select data at *sec* second intervals

-f Extract data from *file* (default is /usr/adm/sa/sa*dd*)

-T Filter output for terminal type *term*

-x Header for x axis: "*name*[*op name*]...[*lo hi*]"

-y Header for y axis (same format as -x)

sar   **System Activity Reporter**

```
sar [ -ubdycwaqvmpgrkxDSAC ] [ -o file ] t [ n ]

sar [ -ubdycwaqvmpgrkxDSAC ] [ -s time ] [ -e time ]
    [ -i sec ] [ -f file ]
```

-u Report CPU utilization (default)

-b Report buffer activity

-d Report activity for each block device

-y Report TTY device activity

-c Report system calls

-w Report system swapping and switching activity

-a Report file access system routines

-q Report average queue length

-v Report status of process, i-node, file tables

-m Report message and semaphore activities

-p Report paging activities

D

-g   Report more paging activities

-r   Report unused memory pages and disk blocks

-k   Report kernel memory allocation activities

-x   Report RFS operations

-D   Report RFS activity

-S   Report server and request queue status

-A   Report all data

-C   Report RFS data caching overhead

-o   Save samples in `file`

-s   Start time of the report

-e   End time of the report

-i   Select report records at `sec` second intervals

-f   Extract data from previously recorded file `file`

t   Sampling interval in seconds

n   Number of sampling intervals to collect

---

script   **Record Terminal Traffic**

```
script [ -a ] [ filename ]
```

-a   Append to log file

filename   Override the default log file name `typescript`

---

sdiff   **Print File Differences Side-by-Side**

```
sdiff [ -w n ] [ -l ] [ -s ] [ -o output ] file1 file2
```

-w   Output line width (default is 130)

-l   Print only the left side of identical lines

-s   Suppress identical lines

-o   Build a user-controlled merge into file *output*

---

sed   **Stream Editor**

```
sed [ -n ] [ -e script ] ... [ -f sfile ] [ file ... ]
sed [ -n ] script [ file ... ]
```

-n   Suppress automatic printing of result lines

-e   Use *script* as the edit script

-f   Read the edit script from *sfile*

---

sh, jsh   **Bourne Shell**

```
sh [ -acefhiknprstuvx ] [ arg ... ]
jsh [ -acefhiknprstuvx ] [ arg ... ]
```

-a   Export all variables created or modified

-c   Read and execute the next string argument, then exit

-e   Exit immediately on a nonzero command exit status

-f   Disable file name generation

-h   Locate and remember functions as they are defined

-i   Interactive shell

-k   Add all keyword arguments to the command environment

-n   Read commands but do not execute them

-p   Do not set the effective user- and group-IDs to the real user- and group-IDs

-r   Restricted shell

D

-s   Read commands from standard input

-t   Exit after reading and executing one command

-u   Treat a reference to an unset variable as an error

-v   (Verbose) Print all shell input

-x   (Trace) Print each command before executing it

shl   Shell Layer Manager

```
shl
```

The `shl` commands are the following:

Zcreate [*name*]	Create a layer called *name*
block *name* ...	Block the output of each named layer
delete *name* ...	Delete the named layers
help	Print syntax of the `shl` commands
layers [-l] [*name* ...]	List layer names and process groups
resume [*name*]	Make *name* the current layer
toggle	Resume the previous layer
unblock *name* ...	Unblock the named layers
quit	Exit from `shl`
name	Make *name* the current layer

D

sleep   Suspend Execution

```
sleep secs
```

secs   The number of integer seconds to sleep

sort

Sort and/or Merge Files

```
sort [ -cmu ] [ -o output ] [ -ykmem ] [ -zrecsz ] [ -dfiMnr ]
     [ -b ] [ -tx ] [ +pos1 [-pos2] ] ... [ file ... ]
```

-c	Test whether the input file is already sorted
-m	Merge the named presorted files
-u	Discard duplicate records
-o	Write the sorted output to file *output*
-y	Start the sort with *kmem* kilobytes of memory
-z	Longest line in the input file(s)
-d	Use dictionary order (only letters, digits, blanks)
-f	Fold lowercase letters into uppercase
-i	Ignore nonprintable characters
-M	Compare as months
-n	Compare the sort keys as numeric values
-r	Reverse the sort order
-b	Ignore leading blanks in a field
-t	Use *x* as the field separator character
+pos1	Starting position of field
-pos2	Ending position of field

spell

Find Spelling Errors

D

```
spell [ -v ] [ -b ] [ -x ] [ -l ] [ +dict ] [ file ... ]
```

-v	Print all words not literally in the spelling list
-b	Use British spelling
-x	Display every plausible stem
-l	Follow included files
+dict	Add words in *dict* to the spelling dictionary

spellin

Create or Extend a Spelling List

```
/usr/lib/spell/spellin n
```

n   The number of hash codes on standard input

split

Split a File into Several Files

```
split [ -n ] [ file [ name ] ]
```

-n   Segment size in lines (default is 1000)
file   Input file; use - to read standard input
name   Prefix for output file names (default is x)

srchtxt

Display or Search Message Data Bases

```
srchtxt [ -s ] [ -l locale ] [ -m msgfile,... ] [ text ]
```

-s   Suppress message sequence numbers
-l   Select message database for language *locale*
-m   Specify message files by path name
text   Display only messages matching regular expression *text*

strchg   **Change a Stream Configuration**

```
strchg -h module1[,module2 ...]
strchg -p [ -a ¦ -u module ]
strchg -f file
```

-h   Push modules onto the standard input STREAMS device
-p   Pop modules off the stream (default is top module)
-a   Pop all modules off the stream
-u   Pop all modules overlaying the named module
-f   Read stream configuration from *file*

strconf   **Query a Stream Configuration**

```
strconf [ -t ¦ -m module ]
```

-t   Identify only the top module
-m   Indicate whether *module* is present on the stream

D

strings   **Find Printable Strings in a Binary File**

```
strings [ -a ] [ -o ] [ -n number ¦ -number ] file ...
```

-a   Look everywhere (default is initialized data)
-o   Print the offset of each string found
-n   Use *number* as minimum string length (default is 4)

stty   **Set Terminal Options**

```
stty [ -a ] [ -g ] [ options ]
```

-a   Display all terminal settings
-g   Report settings in a form usable on the stty command
options   One or more option keywords separated by white space

su   **Change to Another User**

```
su [ - ] [ name [ arg ... ] ]
```

-           Execute the login profile for user *name*
name   User login name
arg   Additional arguments for the login shell

sum   **Compute Checksum and Block Count**

```
sum [ -r ] file
```

-r   Use an alternate checksum algorithm

sync

Flush Disk Buffers

```
sync
```

tabs

Set Terminal Tabs

```
tabs [ tabspec ] [ -Ttype ] [ +mn ]
```

tabspec   Set tabs to canned (-code), repeating (-n), or arbitrary
(n1,n2,...) positions, or read the tabspec from a file
(--file); canned tabspec codes are:

-a	1,10,16,36,72	IBM 370 Assembler
-a2	1,10,16,40,72	IBM 370 Assembler
-c	1,8,12,16,20,55	COBOL
-c2	1,6,10,14,49	COBOL compact
-c3	1,6,10,14,18,...	COBOL recommended
-f	1,7,11,15,19,23	FORTRAN
-p	1,5,9,13,17,21,...	PL/I
-s	1,10,55	SNOBOL
-u	1,12,20,44	UNIVAC 1100 Assembler

-T   Terminal type (default is value of TERM variable)

+mn   Adjust the left margin right n columns

D

tail

Print the Last Part of a File

```
tail [ ±number[lbcf] ] [ file ]

tail [ ±number[lbcr] ] [ file ]
```

talk   **Converse with Another User**

```
talk user [ ttyname ]
```

user	Login name of the other user
ttname	Terminal name if *user* is logged in multiple times

tar   **Tape File Archiver**

```
tar -c[vwfbL[#s]] [ device ] [ block ] files ...

tar -r[vwfbL[#s]]  [ device ] [ block ] files ...

tar -t[vfL[#s]] [ device ][ files ... ]

tar -u[vwfbL[#s]]  [ device ] [ block ] files ...

tar -x[lmovwfL[#s]] [ device ] [ files ... ]
```

-c	Create a new tape
-r	Replace named *files* on the tape
-t	Print a table of contents of the tape archive
-u	Update tape archive files
-x	Extract named *files* from the tape archive

Modifiers:

#s	Read or write tape drive # at speed *s* (1 low, m medium, h high); for example, 5h to read /dev/mt/5h
v	(Verbose) List each file processed
w	User confirmation for each action
f	Use *device* for reading and writing
b	Use *block* as the blocking factor
l	Report an error when unable to resolve all links
m	Do not restore file modification times

    o   Set file owner and user to current user's IDs

    L   Follow symbolic links

tee   **Pipe Fitting**

```
tee [ -i ] [ -a ] [ file ... ]
```

  -i   Ignore interrupts

  -a   Append output

  file Files in which to replicate the standard input

telnet   **User Interface to a Remote System**

```
telnet [ host [ port ] ]
```

  host Host name or Internet address

  port Port name (default is to use the default port)

test   **Condition Evaluation**

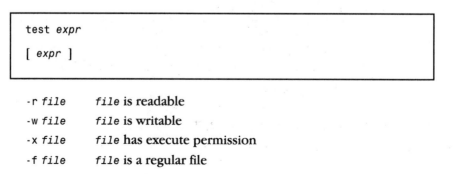

```
test expr

[ expr ]
```

  -r *file*   *file* is readable

  -w *file*   *file* is writable

  -x *file*   *file* has execute permission

  -f *file*   *file* is a regular file

-d *file*	*file* is a directory
-h *file*	*file* is a symbolic link
-c *file*	*file* is a character-special file
-b *file*	*file* is a block-special file
-p *file*	*file* is a named pipe
-u *file*	*file* has the set-user-ID bit set
-g *file*	*file* has the set-group-ID bit set
-k *file*	*file* has the sticky bit set
-s *file*	*file* has a size greater than zero
-t [*fd*]	File descriptor *fd* (default is 1) is a terminal
-z *s1*	String *s1* is zero length
-n *s1*	String *s1* has nonzero length
s1 = *s2*	String *s1* and *s2* are equal
s1 != *s2*	String *s1* and *s2* are unequal
s1	String *s1* is not null
n1 -eq *n2*	Integer *n1* is equal to *n2*
n1 -ne *n2*	Integer *n1* is not equal to *n2*
n1 -lt *n2*	Integer *n1* is less than *n2*
n1 -le *n2*	Integer *n1* is less than or equal to *n2*
n1 -gt *n2*	Integer *n1* is greater than *n2*
n1 -ge *n2*	Integer *n1* is greater than or equal to *n2*

Operators for combining tests:

!	Unary negation
-a	Binary *and*
-o	Binary *or*
(*expr*)	Grouping parentheses

D

tftp

Trivial File Transfer Program

```
tftp [ host ]
```

timex   Time a Command

```
timex [ -p [ -fhkmrt ] ] [ -o ] [ -s ] command
```

-p   List process accounting records

-f   Print fork/exec flag and exit status

-h   Print fraction of total available system time used

-k   Show total kcore-minutes

-m   Show mean core size

-r   Show CPU factor

-t   Show separate system and user CPU times

-o   Show total blocks and characters transferred

-s   Show total system activity

touch   Set File Access and Modification Times

```
touch [ -amc ] [ mmddhhmm[yy] ] file ...
```

-a   Set only the time of last access

-m   Set only the time of last modification

-c   Do not create the file

D

tput

Query Terminfo Database

```
tput [ -Ttype ] capname [ parm ... ]

tput [ -Ttype ] [ init ¦ reset ¦ longname ]

tput -S
```

-S	Read multiple capabilities from standard input
-T	Use terminal type *type* instead of *TERM* value
capname	A terminfo capability name
parm	Parameters to be plugged into the function string
init	Initialize the terminal
reset	Output the terminal's reset strings rs1, rs2, rs3, rf
longname	Print the long name of the terminal

tr

Translation Filter

```
tr [ -cds ] [ string1 [ string2 ] ]
```

-c	Complement the characters in *string1*
-d	Delete all input characters in *string1*
-s	Delete repetitions of characters in *string2*
string1	Characters to look for in the input
string2	Corresponding output for each character in *string1*

true

Return Normal Exit Status

```
true
```

truss

Trace System Calls and Signals

```
truss [ -pfcaei ] [ -[tvx] [!] syscall,... ]
     [ -s [!] signal,... ] [ -m [!] fault,... ]
     [ -[rw] [!] fd,... ] [ -o outfile ] command
```

-p Interpret *command* as a list of process-IDs

-f Follow all forked children and record their signals, faults, and system calls

-c Just count traces system calls, faults, and signals

-a Show argument strings passed on each exec

-e Show environment strings passed on each exec

-i Don't display sleeping interruptible system calls

-t List the system calls to trace or (!) exclude

-v Display structures passed to the named system calls

-x Display system call arguments in raw form

-s List of signals to trace or (!) exclude

-m List of machine faults to trace or (!) exclude

-r Show I/O buffer on each read to the named file descriptors

-w Show I/O buffer on each write to the named file descriptors

-o File name in which to store the trace output

D

tty

Print the Terminal Name

```
tty [ -l ] [ -s ]
```

-l Print the synchronous line number

-s (Silent) Exit values are:

    0 Standard input is a terminal

    1 Standard input is not a terminal

    2 Invalid options

uname   **Print Name of UNIX System**

```
uname [ -amnprsv ]
uname [ -S system ]
```

- -a   Print all information
- -m   Print the machine name
- -n   Print the node name (this is the default option)
- -p   Print the processor type
- -r   Print the operating system release
- -s   Print the operating system name
- -v   Print the operating system version
- -S   Set the node name to *system*

uncompress   **Uncompress Files**

```
uncompress [ -cv ] [ file ... ]
```

- -c   Write to standard output
- -v   Verbose
- *file*   Files to be uncompressed; if omitted, read from standard input

D

uniq   **Remove Duplicate Lines from a File**

```
uniq [ -udc [ +n ] [ -n ] ] [ input [ output ] ]
```

-u   Output only unique lines
-d   Output one copy of just the repeated lines
-c   Print unique lines with a repeat count
+n   Ignore the first *n* characters of each line
-n   Ignore the first *n* fields of each line

units   **Conversion Program**

```
units
```

unpack   **Unpack Packed Files**

```
unpack file ...
```

D

uucp

UNIX-to-UNIX File Copy

```
uucp [ -cCdfjmr ] [ -ggrade ] [ -nuser ] [ -sfile ]
     [ -xdebug ] file ... target
```

-c   Do *not* copy files (default is to copy files)

-C   Force copy of files to spool directory

-d   Make all necessary directories (default)

-f   Do not make intermediate directories

-j   Display the uucp job identification number

-m   Send mail to the requestor when the copy is done

-r   Only queue the job; do not start file transfer

-g   Use the specified service grade

-n   Notify the remote *user*

-s   Log transfer status in *file*

-x   Debug information level (1 to 9)

uudecode

Decode a File

```
uudecode [ file ]
```

file   File name to process

uuencode

Encode a Binary File

```
uuencode [ file ] label
```

file   File name to process (default is standard input)
label   Binary file name for uudecode

uuglist

List Service Grades

```
uuglist [ -u ]
```

-u   List only the service grades valid for the current user

uulog

Display Selected Lines of the UUCP Log File

```
uulog [ -x ] [ -number ] [ -ssys ] [ -fsystem ] system
```

-x   Look in the uuxqt log file for system
-number   Run a tail command of number lines
-s   Print transfers involving sys
-f   Run a tail -f command for system's file transfer log

D

uuname

List Remote System Names

```
uuname [ -cl ]
```

-c   List system names known to cu

-l   List the local system name

uupick

Retrieve Files from uucp

```
uupick [ -s system ]
```

-s   Retrieve only files sent from *system*

uustat

uucp **Status Inquiry**

```
uustat [ -q ¦ -m ¦ -p ]
uustat -kjobid [ -n ]
uustat -rjobid [ -n ]
uustat [ -a ] [ -ssystem [ -j ] ] [ -uuser ] [ -Sqric ]
uustat -tsystem [ -dnumber ] [ -c ]
```

-q   List jobs queued by machine

-m   Report the accessibility of all machines

-p   List all processes owning one or more uucp locks

-k   Kill the job numbered *jobid*

D

-r　　Touch the files associated with *jobid*

-n　　Suppress standard output messages

-a　　List all jobs in the queue

-s　　Report only jobs for remote system *system*

-j　　List the total number of jobs displayed

-u　　Report only jobs submitted by *user*

-S　　Report the job status for q (queued jobs), r (running jobs, i (interrupted jobs), and c (completed jobs)

-t　　Report average transfer rate for *system*

-d　　Override the 60-minute default for calculations

-c　　Report average queue time

uuto　　　Send Files to a Remote System

```
uuto [ -pm ] files ... target
```

-p　　Copy files

-m　　Send mail to the sender when the copy completes

uux　　UNIX-to-UNIX System Command Execution

D

```
uux [ - ] [ -bcCjnprz ] [ -aname ] [ -ggrade ] [ -sfile ]
    [ -xdebug ] command
```

-　　Pass the standard input file to *command*

-b　　Return whatever standard input was provided to the uux command if the exit status is nonzero

-c　　Do not copy local files

-C　　Force the copy of local files

- j   Print the uucp job identification

- n   Do not notify the user if the command fails

- p   Same as -; the standard input to the uux command is made the standard input to *command*

- r   Do not start the file transfer, just queue the job

- z   Send success notification to the user

- a   Use *name* as the user job identification

- g   Use service grade *grade*

- s   Report file transfer status in *file*

- x   Enable debugging reports up to level *debug* (1 to 9)

---

vacation   **Automatically Respond to Incoming Mail**

```
vacation [ -d ][ -l logfile ] [ -m mailfile ] [ -M msgfile ]
    [ -F failsafe ]
```

- d   Append the day's date to the log file

- l   Log of users who have already seen the canned message

- m   Alternate mailbox to save new messages

- M   File to send back as the canned response

- F   Forward mail to user *failsafe* if a canned response cannot be sent back to the originator

D

vi

Visual Display Editor

```
vi [ -t tag ] [ -r rfile ] [ -l ] [ -L ] [ -wn ] [ -R ] [ -x ]
   [ -C ] [ -c cmd ] file ...

view ...

vedit ...
```

-t   Edit the file containing *tag*

-r   Recover file *rfile* after a system crash

-l   Use LISP compatibility mode

-L   List all recoverable files

-w   Set the default window size to *n*

-R   Read-only mode; files can't be saved or written

-x   (Encryption) The input file may be plain or encrypted

-C   (Encryption) The input file must be in encrypted form

-c   Execute *cmd* on start-up

The view command is the same as vi except that it automatically sets read-only mode.

The vedit command is the same as vi except that it starts up with the showmode and novice flags set.

WC

Word Count

```
wc [ -lwc ] [ file ... ]
```

-l   Print only a line count

-w   Print only a word count

-c   Print only a character count

who

Who Is Using the System

```
who [ -uTlHqpdbrtas ] [ file ]

who -qn num [ file ]

who am i

who am I
```

- -u   List all users currently logged in
- -T   Standard report plus mesg state
- -l   List lines waiting for login
- -H   Print column headings
- -q   List user names and the number of users logged in
- -p   List active processes spawned by *init*
- -d   List expired processes that were not respawned
- -b   Show the time and date of the last system boot
- -r   Show the current run level
- -t   Show when the last change to the system clock was made
- -a   All options
- -s   Standard report (this is the default)
- -n   List *num* user names per line

D

whois

Internet User Name Directory Service

```
whois [ -h host ] identifier
```

- -h   Search only user names for *host*

write

Write to Another User

```
write user [ line ]
```

user User login name

line Terminal name if user is logged in more than once

xargs

Construct and Execute Commands

```
xargs [ -llinct ] [ -istr ] [ -nargct ] [ -t ] [ -p ] [ -x ]
      [ -ssize ] [ -eeof ] [ command [ arg ... ] ]
```

-l Process *linct* nonempty lines from standard input

-i Replace every occurrence of *str* with the next input word (default *str* is {})

-n Limit generated command arguments to *argct*

-t Print each generated command before executing it

-p Prompt the user before executing a generated command

-x Terminate if a generated command exceeds *size* chars

-s Maximum size of a generated command (limit 470)

-e Stop processing standard input when *eof* is read

D

zcat

Print Compressed Files

```
zcat [ file ... ]
```

file Files to be uncompressed; if omitted, read from standard input

D

Index

Symbols

Q-R

W-Z

Audio

Audio $39.95	
esign and Installation $59.95	
oubleshooting and Repair . .$24.95	
und Engineers:	
dio Cyclopedia, 2nd Ed. . .$99.95	
Build Loudspeaker	
Enclosures $39.95	
rofessional	
echniques $29.95	
l $24.95	
ig Techniques, 3rd Ed. $29.95	
s and Principles $19.95	
tal Audio, 2nd Ed. $29.95	
Handbook $49.95	
gineering, 2nd Ed. $49.95	

ctricity/Electronics

kbook $24.95	
and DC Circuits $29.95	
k, 2nd Ed. $24.95	
. . . .$19.95	
evised 2nd Ed. $49.95	
Revised 2nd Ed. $49.95	
ematics, 4th Ed. $19.95	
kbook, 3rd Ed. $24.95	
ok, 2nd Ed. $24.95	
n $24.95	
Motors $29.95	
. . . .$24.95	
igital Troubleshooting, 3rd Ed.$24.95	
olid State Electronics, 5th Ed. $24.95	

Games

SimEarth $19.95	
. . . .$16.95	

rdware/Technical

dem Communications $16.95	
1	
with the Jamsa Disk Utilities $39.95	
ed Troubleshooting & Repair $24.95	
mputer Troubleshooting	
. . . .$24.95	
roubleshooting & Repair . .$24.95	
ber Optics $24.95	

IBM: Business

to PC Tools 7 . . . .$ 9.95	
to Q&A 4 . . . .$ 9.95	
crosoft Works for the PC . . .$16.95	
rton Utilities 6 . . . .$16.95	
Tools 7 . . . .$16.95	
sonal Computing, 2nd Ed. . .$16.95	

IBM: Database

to Harvard Graphics 2.3 . . . $9.95	
toCAD $34.95	
Programmer's	
uide $24.95	
on 1.1 for the First-Time User $24.95	
base Primer Featuring dBASE IV	
. . . .$24.95	
adox 3.5 . . . .$16.95	
verPoint for Windows $16.95	
s 2.3 In Business $29.95	

phics/Desktop Publishing

e to Lotus 1-2-3 . . . .$ 9.95	
rvard Graphics $24.95	
rvard Graphics 2.3 . . . . .$16.95	
Paintbrush $16.95	
S: First Publisher $16.95	

IBM: Spreadsheets/Financial

Best Book of Lotus 1-2-3 Release 3.1 . . . . $27.95	
First Book of Excel 3 for Windows $16.95	
First Book of Lotus 1-2-3 Release 2.3 . . . . $16.95	
First Book of Quattro Pro 3 . . . . $16.95	
First Book of Quicken In Business $16.95	
Lotus 1-2-3 Release 2.3 In Business $29.95	
Lotus 1-2-3: Step-by-Step $24.95	
Quattro Pro In Business $29.95	

IBM: Word Processing

Best Book of Microsoft Word 5 . . . . . . $24.95	
Best Book of Microsoft Word for Windows . $24.95	
Best Book of WordPerfect 5.1 . . . . $26.95	
First Book of Microsoft Word 5.5 . . . . . $16.95	
First Book of WordPerfect 5.1 . . . . $16.95	
WordPerfect 5.1: Step-by-Step $24.95	

Macintosh/Apple

First Book of Excel 3 for the Mac $16.95	
First Book of the Mac $16.95	

Operating Systems/Networking

10 Minute Guide to Windows 3 . . . . $ 9.95	
Best Book of DESQview $24.95	
Best Book of Microsoft Windows 3 . . . . . $24.95	
Best Book of MS-DOS 5 . . . . $24.95	
Business Guide to Local Area Networks . . . $24.95	
DOS Batch File Power	
with the Jamsa Disk Utilities $39.95	
Exploring the UNIX System, 2nd Ed. $29.95	
First Book of DeskMate $16.95	
First Book of Microsoft Windows 3 . . . . . $16.95	
First Book of MS-DOS 5 . . . . $16.95	
First Book of UNIX $16.95	
Interfacing to the IBM Personal Computer,	
2nd Ed. $24.95	
The Waite Group's Discovering MS-DOS,	
2nd Edition $19.95	
The Waite Group's MS-DOS Bible, 4th Ed. . $29.95	
The Waite Group's MS-DOS Developer's Guide,	
2nd Ed. $29.95	
The Waite Group's Tricks of the UNIX Masters $29.95	
The Waite Group's Understanding MS-DOS,	
2nd Ed. $19.95	
The Waite Group's UNIX Primer Plus, 2nd Ed. $29.95	
The Waite Group's UNIX System V Bible . $29.95	
Understanding Local Area Networks, 2nd Ed. $24.95	
UNIX Applications Programming:	
Mastering the Shell $29.95	
UNIX Networking $29.95	
UNIX Shell Programming, Revised Ed. . . . $29.95	
UNIX: Step-by-Step $29.95	
UNIX System Administration $29.95	
UNIX System Security $34.95	
UNIX Text Processing $29.95	

Professional/Reference

Data Communications, Networks, and Systems $39.95	
Handbook of Electronics Tables and Formulas,	
6th Ed. $24.95	
ISDN, DECnet, and SNA Communications . $49.95	
Modern Dictionary of Electronics, 6th Ed. . $39.95	
Reference Data for Engineers: Radio, Electronics,	
Computer, and Communications, 7th Ed. $99.95	

Programming

Advanced C: Tips and Techniques $29.95	
C Programmer's Guide to NetBIOS $29.95	
C Programmer's Guide	
to Serial Communications $29.95	
Commodore 64 Programmer's	
Reference Guide $24.95	

Developing Windows Applications	
with Microsoft SDK $29.95	
DOS Batch File Power $39.95	
Graphical User Interfaces with Turbo C++ . .$29.95	
Learning C++ $39.95	
Mastering Turbo Assembler $29.95	
Mastering Turbo Pascal, 4th Ed. $29.95	
Microsoft Macro Assembly Language	
Programming $29.95	
Microsoft QuickBASIC	
Programmer's Reference $29.95	
Programming in ANSI C $29.95	
Programming in C, Revised Ed. $29.95	
The Waite Group's BASIC Programming	
Primer, 2nd Ed. $24.95	
The Waite Group's C Programming	
Using Turbo C++ $29.95	
The Waite Group's C: Step-by-Step $29.95	
The Waite Group's GW-BASIC Primer Plus .$24.95	
The Waite Group's Microsoft C Bible, 2nd Ed. $29.95	
The Waite Group's Microsoft C Programming	
for the PC, 2nd Ed. $29.95	
The Waite Group's New C Primer Plus . . .$29.95	
The Waite Group's Turbo Assembler Bible . .$29.95	
The Waite Group's Turbo C Bible $29.95	
The Waite Group's Turbo C Programming	
for the PC, Revised Ed. $29.95	
The Waite Group's Turbo C++Bible $29.95	
X Window System Programming $29.95	

Radio/Video

Camcorder Survival Guide . . . . $ 14.95	
Radio Handbook, 23rd Ed. $39.95	
Radio Operator's License Q&A Manual,	
11th Ed. $24.95	
Understanding Fiber Optics $24.95	
Understanding Telephone Electronics, 3rd Ed. $24.95	
VCR Troubleshooting & Repair Guide $19.95	
Video Scrambling & Descrambling	
for Satellite & Cable TV $24.95	

For More Information,
See Your Local Retailer
Or Call Toll Free

1-800-428-5331

All prices are subject to change without notice.
Non-U.S. prices may be higher. Printed in the U.S.A.

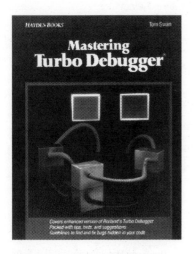
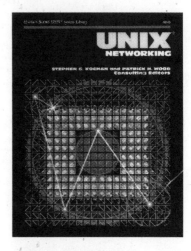

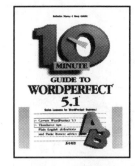

Sams' First Books Get You Started Fast!

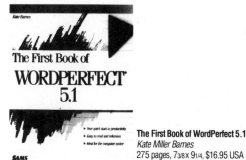